WISH YOU WERE HERE

SHERIDAN JOBBINS

AFFiRM press

Published by Affirm Press in 2017
28 Thistlethwaite Street, South Melbourne, VIC 3205
www.affirmpress.com.au

10 9 8 7 6 5 4 3 2 1

National Library of Australia Cataloguing-in-Publication entry available for this
title at www.nla.gov.au.
Title: Wish You Were Here / Sheridan Jobbins, author.
ISBN: 9781925475609 (paperback)

Cover and internal design by Christa Moffitt, Christabella Designs
Typeset in Minion 12/18 pt by J&M Typesetting
Author photograph by Korby Banner
Proudly printed in Australia by Griffin Press

For my husband, like, der

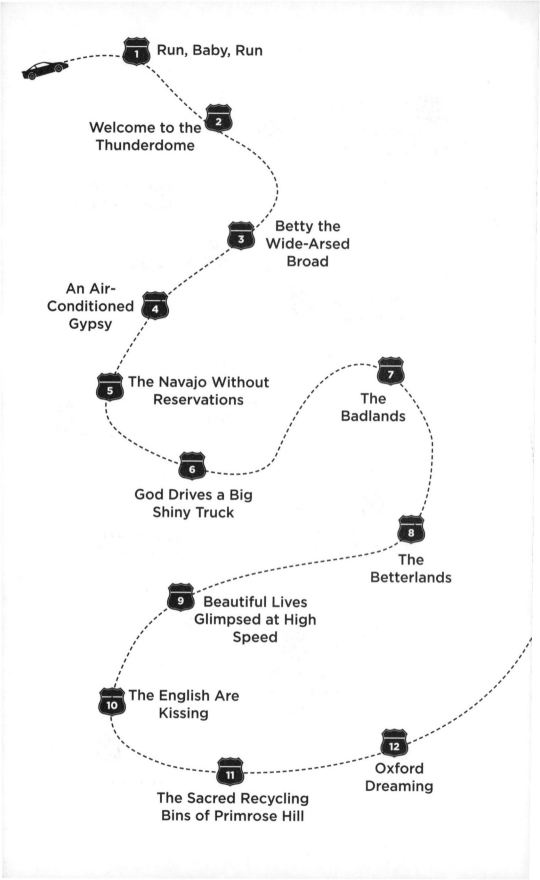

1 Run, Baby, Run

2 Welcome to the Thunderdome

3 Betty the Wide-Arsed Broad

4 An Air-Conditioned Gypsy

5 The Navajo Without Reservations

6 God Drives a Big Shiny Truck

7 The Badlands

8 The Betterlands

9 Beautiful Lives Glimpsed at High Speed

10 The English Are Kissing

11 The Sacred Recycling Bins of Primrose Hill

12 Oxford Dreaming

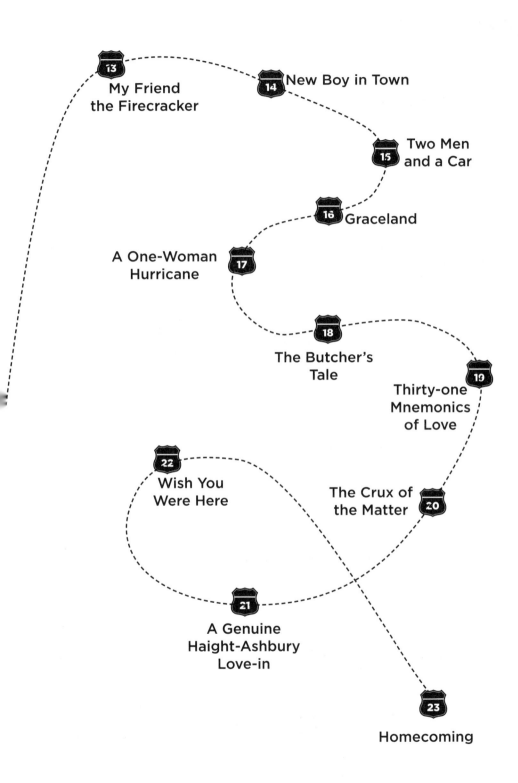

RUN, BABY, RUN

There are few moments in life you can point to and say, *That's it. That's when everything changed forever.* Some are unmissable – this person is born, that one dies, two cars collide. But others are subtle, sly even. A breeze shifts and you lift your eyes to discover you're sailing in a new and exciting direction.

I was in London on a dreamy summer's evening visiting a friend who was hosting an end-of-exams drinks party in her university's ancient walled garden. It was so far from the classic student piss-ups in Australia, I jokingly dubbed it the Philosopher's Ball. Under a darkening sky criss-crossed by apricot vapour trails, studious young things gathered together into human bouquets discussing – I don't know, philosophy, probably. I don't know because I'm a film maker by trade, a professional bullshitter and these people were uncharted territory to me.

My friend handed me a drink and sat me between two young men before disappearing into the crowd. My new companions were intent on their conversation, so I could stare at them shamelessly while pretending to be interested in what they were saying. As they spoke, an occasional word or phrase snuck into my cranium and bounced around. *Sheep. Barn. Gettier. Knowledge.*

The most handsome of the two men turned to reveal deep brown eyes with an enormous welt blossoming above them. 'What do you think?' he asked, oblivious to the fact he looked like a magnificent deer, struck in the headlights by a piece of 4B2.

I thought he had a lovely face and searched it for clues to the right answer. 'Sheep and barns,' I said, taking a stab at what I'd heard, 'I guess there's a limit to what you can know.'

He laughed, and time slowed like it does when the adrenaline is pumping. Blood rose to my cheeks. My fingers tingled. Every detail – the shifting breeze in his hair, the sparkle of light behind him, the smell of grass giving up its moisture – they were all preserved in the amber of first contact.

And that was my moment.

The handsome man laughed like I was beautiful and for the first time in a long time my life zigged when it could have zagged.

'Is that an Australian accent?' he asked. 'Are you visiting, or do you live here in London?'

'Technically, I'm driving across America.'

'Then technically you're lost'

'I am, but don't worry, it's my default setting.'

He smiled again, 'You're a long way from home. What brings you here?'

'My life is in flux.'

I would have liked to tell him more, pour my life story into his gaze, but it was complicated and I didn't know where to start. Eventually British reserve got the better of him, so when I didn't add more, he smiled and resumed talking with his friend.

Fate planted her flag and moved on.

So why was I on the move? Lost on life's highway.

The source of all this complication, the 'flux capacitor' in my life, was a soon to be ex-husband. Mine. Or rather, *was* mine. I returned home from a business trip to discover the man I was married to had changed. It wasn't a vague thing – there was a stranger in my bed.

When pressed to define his problem, he relented, saying he couldn't stand the thought of sleeping with only one woman for the rest of his life – and that was that. A bubble of black despair. A cancerous belch of true emotion. Our lives changed forever.

Months later, while stewing over this in the middle of the night, I could see it would have been better to take this way too lightly – ride his tsunami of pain saying, 'I know, I know, isn't it awful?' But in the moment of impact my emotions were raw and I couldn't do that. Instead, I descended through the three stages of betrayal:

Forensic: Sifting through our lives for incriminating evidence, I found a single strand of yellow hair, a new shirt and a phone bill with lots of calls to an unusual number.

Judicial: I confronted him with the hair, the shirt and the bill. He wanted to deny it, but his body betrayed him. He went white with horror.

Postal: Using a fork, I shredded the shirt, which had been a gift to him from the blonde. I stabbed it in the pocket, in the back, in the chest, in the stomach. I dragged the fork through the white loose weave (a lovely Egyptian cotton) until the tines twisted, the head bent back and there was nothing left but a sad, tattered flag of defeat.

He moved out.

They say it takes half the length of a relationship to get over it. I don't know if that's true, but I definitely spent the same amount of time in agony that I spent in ecstasy.

Burn in. Burn out.

$\longleftrightarrow$

My soon-to-be-was husband and I met eleven years earlier when I was working on a kids' TV show. It was one of those MTV-type things where everyone was under thirty and over-sexed. To say it was a 'hotbed of talent' would be to go two words too far.

At the time, I was the worst researcher the show ever hired. I had no experience, no aptitude and no stamina. What I did have, and I hesitate to call them qualifications, were big tits and a ballsy approach. I think that confused the producers, because they promoted me to an on-camera position.

The first time I saw *him* was on television. I was watching our show go to air when onto the screen came this beautiful man being funny. Slapstick. He fell over and I fell for him. The French call this a *coup de foudre* – struck by lightning. I fell in love with a complete stranger on TV.

I looked up the program rundown to find out who he was, but all it said was 'vox pop'. My friend Michele, one of the film editors, explained that 'vox pop' means 'voice of the people'.

'So do we know who the people are?' I asked.

'No, they're mostly randoms off the street. Why?'

The thought, *I've missed my destiny*, went through me so violently it actually came out my mouth, but instead of offering consolation, Michele laughed at me.

Turned out I hadn't missed a thing. Sometimes when stuck for people to interview, the crew roped in friends and family. The funny man was Michele's flatmate, and she offered to introduce us.

It is a truth universally acknowledged, that an Australian in possession of good character, must be in want of a nickname. This man was in possession of a particularly good character. He was patient, funny, gracious – so noble, in fact, I nicknamed him 'The

Pig Dog Bastard' in the hope others might imagine him to be a little tougher than he seemed. I even had the name embroidered onto a cap for him, but the first day he wore it to work, everyone laughed so hard the only name that stuck was 'Pig' – because he was such a Babe.

By the time I left the show we'd become the perfect piggy couple. He was Pig and I was Piggy and we were nice to each other, even when no one was looking. He was my best friend, my heartland, my home, and I had no immunity against him leaving.

Eleven years later, while he was trying to find himself in Thailand, I was fumbling around our kitchen cupboards trying to find some Horlicks – at four in the morning. You know that story about some butterfly flapping its wings in Tokyo making a banker weep in New York? My crisis started like that.

The Horlicks was in an overhead kitchen cupboard – one of those four-door jobbies that's undivided out the back – so when my blind hand reached in, it pushed some tea bags to one side, which pushed a can of peaches, which nudged a pack of muesli, which pressed a wine glass against a cupboard door, opening it. Out onto the sink leaped the wine glass …

… snapping the stem in two

I stood there blinking in disbelief. How, while being *so* reasonable, could I end up with such a disastrous result?

It was all connected. Even the particular glass – a wedding gift from Sparkles, my first boyfriend ever. I picked up the two pieces and considered if they could somehow be fused back together.

Who was I kidding? The glass was ruined. We were ruined. It had been a beautiful thing, but now it was ruined. With first the right and then the left hand, I threw the pieces to the ground where they smashed to smithereens.

Hmm. That felt good.

In the kitchen was a whole drawer dedicated to broken crockery – shards of love waiting for Araldite.

Not anymore.

The first thing I saw was a birthday present from Pig, a willow-patterned Burleigh Ware cup that had lost its handle. It fitted so neatly into my hand.

I pitched it into the floor where it created a most satisfying shatter.

Oh yeah – this is doing it for me.

I pulled the drawer out and one by one methodically smashed the lot. Even now I can feel the shiver of pleasure that rose from deep within my guts. Opening cupboard after cupboard, you could hear cups and saucers quake as I stormed through my own Kristallnacht. Anything chipped, crazed, ugly or his. *Smash. Smash. Smash.*

An adorable Carlton Ware cottage milk jug we bought in Murchison on our honeymoon – now crazed, like us. *Smash.*

A Wedgwood breakfast teacup, a tender something from my matron of honour, its pretty Picardy pink flowers chipped from washing it in the sink with other cups. *Smash.*

A large white Shelley plate, an anniversary present from Aunty Patty in two perfect pieces.

No regrets.

By the time I'd cleaned out the cupboards I was exhausted, and piled back into bed for the best sleep I'd had in months.

Je ne regrette rien.

The next day was sunny and soundless as though a strong wind had blown all the noise away. I padded into the kitchen. You should've seen how much bone china was smashed on the kitchen floor. There were even shards in the bathroom. That's like, ten metres away, around a corner. I actually laughed when I found a piece of yellow

Johnson Brothers (Made in England) embedded in the opposite wall. It took all morning to clean up, and, with a deep spiritual calm, I stepped onto the landing holding a garbage bag full of remnants …

… and into my neighbour, who seemed to be waiting for me.

'So, how are things?' he asked with unusual tenderness.

'Good,' I said, squinting sincerely. 'Really good.'

'You're getting along alright by yourself in there?'

'Yeah. No. Good. I think I'm doing alright.'

'Okay. Well, take it easy then.'

What was I thinking? I lived in a block of flats and I'd broken every plate, mug and cup in the apartment at four in the morning.

My life had completely stalled. And through the emptiness of this moment floated the word 'America'. It was as far away from Australia and my current life as I could imagine.

America.

I had wanted to run away from home when I was little, only my childish brain couldn't work out how to convince my mother (the love of my life) to come with me. America was where we would have gone. It was the land of sitcoms with happy endings and weekly comedy shows. It was Disneyland, the Muppets, and sandwiches made with that most mysterious combination: peanut butter and jelly.

Growing up in Australia, everything seemed to focus outward. I could recite the American Declaration of Independence by heart. I loved Lucy. I knew the excitement of prom night and Halloween even though they weren't celebrated in my country.

As the youngest of five kids my world was about long fights and short showers. I never saw that on TV. All I saw there was America – the real world. If I could just get there, everything would be all right. Like the memory of an old friend, that idea washed through me, *Run away to America.*

I felt the dull weight of the garbage bag of broken lady crockery in my hand. Pig and I had been trying to conceive using IVF, which had proved as fruitless as my other ventures. I worked in a production company developing television shows for executives who didn't buy them. I was in my mid-thirties and I wanted more.

There are some things you can do which strike a chord with everyone. Buying a flash American tank of a car and driving across the United States is one. The only person who couldn't see the romantic majesty of this gesture was my mother, Joy.

'Darling, if you insist on letting this problem devolve into full-blown crisis, can't you at least do it closer to home where I can keep an eye on you?'

Mum and I are good friends. I love her (according to my birth certificate I'm contractually obliged to) but, more importantly, I like her. She's courageous and generous. She used to be in Marketing and can put a positive spin on almost anything – but running away from your problems isn't one of them.

When she started out in business in the 1950s, there was such a shortage of female leadership that her role models were limited to Lucille Ball and the Queen of England. Accordingly, she is both imperious *and* hilarious, with the sort of love of language that can only come from swallowing a dictionary.

'This mad peregrination – you simply haven't thought it through. Where will you go? What will you use for money? Scotch may be the same in every language, but a woman can't live on whiskey alone.'

Mum knew a lot about money and whiskey. Dad died a decade earlier after a long and tempestuous relationship with them both. My father, Harry, a brilliant advertising copywriter, won the Johnny

Walker account in the late 1970s. Their marriage and fortunes went downhill from there, but Mum worked hard to keep the family afloat.

When I was nine years old she devised and produced a television program called *Cooking with Sheri*. It was screened nationally during the first wave of celebrity chefs. I had the dubious distinction of holding the Guinness World Record for the youngest host of their own TV show.

Being on telly made for a chaotic but highly entertaining childhood. What I lost in school holidays (spent filming the five-minute episodes with my granddad, Poppy) was more than made up for in the pleasure of playing grownups. I grew up thinking that work and life were the same thing. The experience taught me that to be happy you need to do something you love with people you like. Or, to quote my mother, 'Bite off more than you can chew, then chew like buggery.'

It's generally good advice, but hard work wasn't going to save my marriage. The way I saw it, Pig left and I was taking his cue to do the same. If Mum wanted to convince me of the folly of my plan to run away and drive across America, she'd need to helicopter in the cavalry.

She went one better and called Sue.

Sue came to Sydney from Wales as a 'Ten Pound Pom'. She was younger than Mum, but not young enough to be her daughter. I was younger than Sue, but also not young enough to be her child. The same was true of Sue's sons and me. Between us we formed an intergenerational chain of friendship that spanned four decades.

'So what's this about going to America and killing yourself in a car?' Sue asked over Mum's signature pea and lettuce soup. (I knew I was in trouble when Mum broke out the Royal Worcester *and* ironed her good linen for lunch.)

'Well, the plans are pretty ad hoc,' I told her. It was an exaggeration – there were no plans. 'There's family in LA so I'll stay with them.

I've got a school friend outside of New York – she'll put me up for a few days in Connecticut. Then I might visit Michele from the kids' show. She's studying philosophy in London. Qantas is doing this great deal where you get two cities in America and a free trip to Europe.'

'See,' said Mum, 'that's not a plan. It's barely an itinerary.'

'Where does the car come in?' asked Sue.

'I'll drive from LA to New York. Americans love cars. I bet I can buy a good one for under five grand.'

'Five *thousand* dollars,' said Mum. 'Where are you going to get that sort of money?'

'I figured I could sell the car at the end …'

'The world doesn't work like that.' Mum was getting agitated, because Sue seemed to be crunching numbers on the back of an envelope and not contributing to the argument. 'You can't swan off to the Grand Canyon and then – what? *Drive* to New York? That's thousands of miles of deserts, and … I don't even know what's in the middle of America. What if you break down? What'll you do then?'

'Meet people?'

'What sort of people?' she continued. 'What if you break down in Washington or New Orleans or the Alamo? Who will you meet there?'

'Harry Connick Jr? He's from New Orleans, isn't he?'

Mum looked at me and then to her friend for support. 'Sue!' she said. 'Say something.'

'Fuck it, I'm in.'

We both looked at Sue in surprise. *You what?* In choosing her friend to be the weapon of choice in this fight, Mum had forgotten one small thing – Sue can't say no to adventure. It doesn't matter how small. If you want a cohort in calamity, say skinny dipping or a midnight picnic, Sue's the one you call.

'Sorry, Joy,' (she apologised for the swearing, not changing camps) 'we're too old to be frightened and too young to die.' She turned to me, 'I'll lend you the five grand.'

I think I squealed. I certainly hugged her. 'I'm going to America!'

'And I'll *give* you half if you let me drive back with you.'

'You're going too?' Mum's voice rose like nails on a blackboard. 'What about the restaurant?'

'I love the restaurant, but do I own it or does it own me? If Sheridan can pick me up in New York, I'll drive back with her.'

Mum was waving her soup ladle in an attempt to stir up some counter-argument. Droplets of pea soup and flecks of lettuce were splattering everywhere. She seemed to have run out of ideas.

'Whaddya say?' I asked Mum. 'Why don't you do the first leg with me? Las Vegas? The Grand Canyon? You can say hello to Pipi and Charlotte.' Pipi was my girlfriend from high school. Her flagrantly youthful mother, Charlotte, was the same age as my eldest brother. Mum had always viewed Pipi and Charlotte as sisters.

'Don't be absurd,' Mum said petulantly. 'Someone in this family has to keep working.'

She thought about it for a moment before sighing in defeat, dropping the ladle back into the tureen, 'Well, if you insist on playing Thelma and Louise, you're not allowed to carry a gun.'

I cashed in my meagre savings, took leave from the film production company where I worked, and before you could say 'Phuket' I was in Los Angeles with a bloody big ocean between me and my problems.

WELCOME TO THE THUNDERDOME

Maybe I was misguided in trying to find myself in the City of Lost Souls. Americans like to tell you that Los Angeles is not like the rest of America. What they fail to appreciate is how little it is like anywhere else in the world.

The city is huge, monstrous, half the population of Australia living on a dot, and everyone's here for glory. Wealth, beauty, brains: they're all available for a price. Sure, that price seems to be your soul, but since it's the richest city in America, you'll probably get good money for it.

Out on the street I found a roaring trade in cynicism and sexual frustration. Although maybe that was just me. I was having difficulty recalibrating my self-image – distorted by gazing too long into someone else's eyes.

Some of the landmarks on my ongoing journey back to selfhood had been thrilling – like returning home to find my house in exactly the same condition as I left it. Others were depressing – like returning home to find my house in exactly the same condition as I left it.

Taking off my wedding ring, taking off my engagement ring, filing his photos – they were all pitiful. A few things were so sentimentally tender that neither of us could bear to do anything with them. Our childhood teddies, for instance, were still clutching each other in a cupboard back at home.

As I was leaving Australia, customs officials gave me an exit visa with a choice of boxes to tick: Never Married, Now Married, Divorced, Widowed, Separated But Not Divorced and De Facto. I cried right there in Immigration. Life was travelling down this predictable checklist to death, and all the good options were behind me. Now I'd need new check boxes with things like Dumped, Unlovable or, maybe if I was lucky, Lone Wolf.

They stamped my visa and let me loose into the world, even though I perjured myself by not selecting the box that said Separated But Not Divorced.

On arrival in the States I discovered another casually unpleasant thing about breaking up a marriage: what do you do with, what do you call, all those stray bits of family you've come to love as a brother/sister/mother/father-in-law?

I chose LA because I had family there – my sister's ex-husband, Marc. While some people lose friends when they split up, our family seems to gather more. I blame Mum. Her natural inclination is to include everyone, even old boyfriends' new girlfriends. Seriously. At a dinner Mum hosted before Marc returned to America, everyone was invited – including a girlfriend with whom he'd recently broken up. Halfway through the meal, the girlfriend pushed back from the table in tears saying, 'I can stand being an ex, but not the ex of an ex.'

So Marc was part of our family, and I for one was grateful that he saw it that way too. However, the one problem was that I no longer had a name for our relationship: friend-in-law? Brother-out-law? Father-of-the-nephew?

I was having the same problem with Pig's parents. They had a unique place in my life and contrary to popular stand-up comedy I loved them. For more than a decade our hopes and expectations had been inextricably married. Now we were dancing around the possibility of all that being sundered.

In some respects it may have been worse for them. They were from another generation, one which had weathered a World War, the Great Depression and a sexual revolution. After forty years together they knew the value of commitment.

Marc, my brother-out-law, lived near the 101 with my nephew, Oscar. He invited me to come and stay with them in the shadow of the famous rickety Hollywood sign. It was a great location, central to everything and easy to navigate home, because you can see that sign from everywhere.

Marc had recently started dating Stacy, a teacher at Oscar's school. Their lives were fuelled by the first flames of love. (Or is it flamed by first fuel?) Either way it was hot – and sobering to me since they were starting a journey I was finishing. Their lives weren't yet weighted down by the baggage we all gather. They were still travelling light enough to overcome their differences.

Marc was a screenwriter who worked from home. He'd knock on my door around midday and suggest we go for lunch. The first place we went to was the Biltmore. Officially, the Millennium Biltmore Hotel.

'Awesome,' I said on entering the elegant Beaux Art lobby with its old world nymphs and vaulted grandeur. 'It's my mother made of marble and mortar.'

The hotel had been host to the film industry since she opened her doors in 1923. It's where the Academy Awards were created, and where they hosted the first eight ceremonies. It was here that Bette Davis named the smooth-fronted statue Oscar after one of her (apparently dickless) ex-husbands. *I see you, babe.*

We opened our menus and discussed what I wanted from LA.

'Well, you could bury me here,' I said under the vined chandelier, beside the sweeping staircase. 'I've died and gone to Hollywood.'

Marc suggested some other Beaux Art people palaces, like the Central Library and Union Station, but the idea of touring the city made me feel flat.

'I'm not a tourist, am I?' I asked.

'I don't know what you are.' Marc grew up in Texas, a lifetime in Australia hadn't scrubbed away any of his direct manner. 'What do you think you want?'

'A pastrami on rye?'

'I mean from life,' said Marc. 'Besides, this isn't the place for a deli sandwich. I brought you here because they make a passable cup of tea. If you want sandwiches –'

'Bagels and lox? Matzo ball soup …'

That's how I discovered Marc was a connoisseur of the Authentic American Diner. From then on, every lunch was spent on a taste tour of LA. First we tried the New York-style delis: Lenny's down on Westwood, then Canter's and Schwartz's on Fairfax. Subsequently we went to Art's, Factor's and Greenblatt's – all open late with bottomless cups of coffee. Afterwards, we'd browse the bookshops or the 'purveyors of fine vinyl' that always seemed to be next door.

The deli sandwiches were delicious and the soup was plentiful. There was more cured animal flesh than in a vet's diary. The cakes riffed on an Eastern European theme – almond crescents dusted in sugar, swirling gugelhupf, sticky donuts. Sometimes Marc's screenwriter friends joined us and the conversation, on cushy banquettes at laminated tables, was as funny as anything on *Seinfeld*.

'Is this what postmodern children do?' I said, biting into a juicy gherkin. 'Curl up in the lap of popular culture with a pickle?'

Later we branched out to the family restaurants which thrived during the depression. Barney's Beanery on Santa Monica, cram-packed with beatnik curios. (Rumour is, Quentin Tarantino wrote *Pulp Fiction* there.) And The Apple Pan, the family-run business on West Pico Boulevard where nothing ever changes.

There were even a couple of nutty throwbacks to the Gold Rush, places like Bigfoot Lodge near Silver Lake and Clifton's Brookdale Cafeteria in downtown LA. They both housed turn of the century frontier designs with stuffed bears and wooden Indians. These places were already nostalgic a hundred years ago when they first opened their doors.

I discovered the Hollywood Hills Coffee Shop all by myself. It wasn't much of an achievement, mind you, since it was in the block where we lived. The sign outside said *Last cappuccino before the 101*, which was funny since it was on an entrance ramp to the freeway, in a part of town where you can't spit without hitting some place selling coffee.

When I first went for breakfast, a vintage Porche 356 was parked outside. Inside, the only customer looked like Brad Pitt. *Does Brad Pitt drive a speedster? Does Brad Pitt have breakfast?*

I was eating (delicious) hash browns with eggs over-easy while reading a story in the *Los Angeles Times* about a woman who'd been rushed to hospital, unconscious. When staff took her blood, vapours from it knocked them out as well. The blood had *crystallised*. I gasped. Three nurses were in a critical condition and the hospital had to be evacuated.

'Are you reading about the alien sighting down at Riverside General?' It was Brad, or at least his doppelganger.

'Is it for real? It sounds like a 50s schlock horror film.'

Blue-eyed Brad was super handsome and chatty. He speculated about whether the woman had attempted suicide by eating weed killer or drinking antifreeze.

'Or maybe she's from one of those religious groups,' I suggested.

'You know, the ones who die trying to hitch a ride from a flying saucer.'

He thought earnestly for a moment, nodding his head. 'Now there's a thought.'

I've noticed that people from LA don't actually laugh. They sort of nod their heads thoughtfully and say, 'That's funny.' It occurred to me (out loud) that their disposition must be inherently earnest if they need to flag a joke. 'Australians do it the other way,' I said. 'We take the piss all the time, then have to flag it when we're serious.'

'Ha,' he said, nodding. 'Now *that is* funny.' Sweet. The handsome American was making a joke. 'I saw you walk in,' he continued. 'Those glasses suit you.'

'My glasses?' I was surprised. 'What are you, an optician?'

'An optometrist. My compliment was professional as well as personal,' he said picking up his coffee, then flicking me a glance. 'But I think you'll find the correct response is, "Thank you." It takes a lot of courage for a man to talk to a beautiful woman.'

I blushed. Actual red cheeks. Not only for the compliment, which was gratefully received, but because I was embarrassed to be caught using poor form.

'Thank you,' I said with a smile, and changed the subject by telling him how much I liked the coffee shops in LA.

'They call the style "Googie",' he said, 'after a place down on Sunset. People use other names for it though – Populuxe, Doo Wop, Streamline Moderne – but if you love it, it's Googie.'

Brad took out a pen and doodled shapes on a napkin. Googie architecture started along Route 66 but took off in LA, where a post-war boom and the rise of car culture led restaurant owners to choose bold shopfronts and plentiful parking to attract customers. 'The design is all about jets. The Space Age. The Atom. It's wide-eyed technological optimism. The vision of a light-filled future.'

'That's what I want. A light-filled future.' He was describing the America I'd always imagined. 'Where do I find more?'

I never saw Brad or his fancy Porsche again, but he left me the generous legacy of a list of Googie diners. Starting that lunchtime, Marc and I expanded our daily dose of delis to include every Googie cafe we could find.

It was a grand adventure. Let me pour light onto the pot of glitz at the end of this rainbow. We started with Pann's, Jan's and then Astro. Once you know what you're looking for they're absolutely everywhere. Buildings with dramatic angles and swathes of glass and rough-hewn sandstone feature walls. The plentiful neon motifs are of stars, boomerangs, atoms and 'soft' parallelograms that look like they were built by George Jetson.

Here at last was the Great American Optimism of the Can-Do Land. Bob's Big Boy on Riverside Drive, Norms on La Cienega, and Corky's in Sherman Oaks, where Billy Joel was a piano man in the 1970s.

These were the nostalgic diners we've come to associate not just with *Seinfeld* but *Mad Men*, *Happy Days*, *I Love Lucy* and *American Graffiti*, as well as every atomic Starline drive-in, bowling alley and carwash at home.

And it was such a relief to be eating again. When Pig left, he'd taken my appetite with him. I called it the Dumpee Diet. My weight dropped a stone and while I looked Hollywood-ready, I didn't have enough ballast to keep me sane.

Hypoglycaemia is a normal part of digestion. When you burn all your calories from breakfast, your pancreas releases extra adrenaline to extract fat and process it into sugar. Your brain and kidneys use 90 percent of the glucose so the adrenaline also gives your head a spike to warn it that reserves are dropping.

Anyone who's done a fast knows this can feel nice, a little burst of energy and euphoria, but if you don't have much fat to burn or you have an over-enthusiastic pancreas – or a whole lot of adrenaline pumping because your pig dog bastard husband had his mid-life crisis early – well, things can get strident. Before you know it, hunger has turned you into a rampaging Valkyrie in screeching search of your next sandwich.

And by 'you' I mean 'me'.

There. I said it. I'm a skinny white bitch who has to eat regularly or my brain hurts like it's being attacked by bees.

For me, diners were the soothing manifestation of the away to which I'd run. The nurturing, living incarnation of television culture. But I was perplexed to discover that as an Australian I needed a native to guide me through this foreign world.

Generally speaking it would be easier if Americans didn't speak English, because then we wouldn't expect to understand them. George Bernard Shaw said it witty-like, describing the British and Americans as 'two people divided by a common language'. For example 'lemonade' is made with lemons or it's a 'soda' called 7 Up. Entrees are 'appetisers', and mains are 'entrees'. Tea is served cold with a lemon – although they'll bring you milk if you ask them, only they'll call it 'cream'. Either way, milk in tepid tea is disgusting. 'Chips' are Mexican and made of corn. Biscuits are 'cookies' and scones are 'biscuits'. Steak is 'broiled' not grilled, but chicken is sometimes 'boiled'. Sweets are 'candies' and never dessert, which may be called 'pie'. You wash up before a meal in a 'vanity' not a sink. You tip 15 per cent if you hate the service and 25 per cent if you don't.

We see Americans in the movies, hear them in music, they come into our homes on television. They speak English and we think we know them. We don't. And this doesn't become clear until we meet them en masse on home turf.

One day I was walking south (as they say) on Hollywood Boulevard, a sweaty melting pot of flashing lights and humanity.

On the roof of a post office, a deranged man was swearing his head off at everyone below. If he'd been closer I might have offered him a banana – because nothing is better for a head-thumping sugar low. As it was, I considered whether he might be carrying a gun.

Australia's no honey pot when it comes to freedom of speech, but for the most part when the lunatics take to the parapets they're only armed with BO and invective. Here, every threat is potentially backed by a bullet. Thirty-five people were shot and killed in one weekend as a heat wave swept the country. It usually takes Australians a year to do that.

No one died that day, but I know Americans feel the fear too. They must. Whenever I told an American about my Big Adventure, about buying a car and driving around their country, they'd gape in horror. 'Aren't you afraid you'll be murdered?'

'No,' I'd reply, 'I'm driving at high speed on the wrong side of the road. I'm frightened I'll die in a car accident.'

After a fortnight playing bachelor girl in LA I was ready to forgive Pig and take him back. That my forgiveness wasn't sought was a minor hitch I was fully prepared to work around. All I required was for him to ring me and tell me the whole thing was a terrible mistake.

I had no intention of taking him back immediately. In this reunion fantasy I tortured him for at least a week, humiliating his every attempt to re-woo me before finally relenting and driving off with him into the sunset.

Wasn't going to happen.

Days turned into weeks, and with every twist of the clock it became harder to imagine my stubborn-as-hell was-husband finding any acceptable scenario in which to apologise. More infuriating, he was even resisting my attempts to seem forgiving. There was nothing for it. This weird new life was here for the long haul and I better make the best of it.

Among the gifts I was given before leaving Sydney was this piece of hippy wisdom: 'The universe rewards action.' It's fun to let it roll around your mind, look at it the other way too – 'Nothing comes of nothing', 'You always fail if you never try' – but there's something particularly satisfying about being challenged to action. If it's true, if the universe really does reward action, then I planned to be the most decorated participant in life's theatre of conflict. I made it my personal mission to test the theory and say 'Yes' to everything.

My first action (the first to be rewarded) was to move my body.

Since Pig left, I'd been doing a lot more exercise. Some of it was a thinly veiled, Freudian attempt to express sexual energy. Some of it was to spend adrenaline and rage. A small portion was a desire to feel better about myself, while the rest was about getting out, having fun and meeting people.

I've always liked yoga, but that was part of my old life. I wanted something new, something that would benefit from my pent-up frustrations and throw sweaty men in my path. At home my brother introduced me to touch football – a less strenuous form of rugby. Here in LA that void was filled by a game called 'Ultimate'. (It should have been be called 'Frisbee', but that was trademarked. They considered calling it 'basketball played with a spherical flying plastic disc' but that was deemed unwieldy.) I loved both these games. Physical contact requiring neither prophylactic nor commitment.

As is my wont (or will, as the case may be) I've formed a theory about this. When men are lonely, confused or in need of physical exercise, they tend towards games: soccer, football, tennis and squash, then head out to the pub for a drink. Women go for more individual activities: yoga, swimming or aerobics, maybe with a hot drink in a cafe afterwards. It's probably got something to do with society's over-emphasis on women's self-image and men's competitive spirit. Either way, I figure if you're looking for new friends, then a yoga retreat should put you in the path of available women, while footy and a quick game of pool might help you find men. This won't necessarily lead to your life partner, but may provide an answer to the cry of, 'Where are all the single men?' You're all out there – on different flight paths with different landing patterns.

That said, neither Ultimate nor touch accounted for my two romantic near misses in LA. That dubious honour rested with my sister, Saturday. (Yeah, yeah, that's her name.) She'd recently spent three months visiting Oscar in LA and gave me the phone numbers of some new friends to hook up with.

Not like that. When I was last on the market, 'hook up' meant 'come up to my place for a cup of coffee'. Or – wait?

Coming out of a long-term relationship was like waking up from cryogenic freezing. The world had moved on. The pill had been the defining accessory of my dating years. To my newly awakened, blinking eyes, condoms looked like the symbol of being responsibly single, but God, where to start? How do you even know what size to buy? Do they come in skin tone? Whose skin? How often do you see a black bandaid?

I decided to try the 'drug store' in Westwood, the university district of LA, figuring they'd be cool about it. There I found an extensive condom collection smack bang (excuse me) in the middle of the feminine hygiene section.

Cool, I'm thirty-five. I'm allowed to buy condoms.

Before I could choose though, there was this (*whisper it*) *man* buying them. Only, not so much buying, as mulling over his choices. Minutes he took, looking first at one packet then another. Picking up a third. Comparing the contents. How hard is this going to be when even a guy can't choose? Maybe he was making an aesthetic choice – drapes and carpets, or some such.

His ritual made it clear there's no casual way to buy a condom. You can mull all you want, but sooner or later you simply have to brazen it out. 'So,' I asked, with my best children's-TV-hostess smile, 'What do you look for in a condom?'

There was a brief and frankly satisfying flash of panic (even cute young men don't like being sprung in the party shop). After I'd been assessed as mostly harmless, he turned out to be German, disarmingly unselfconscious and impressively well-informed about the merits of different condoms. So here's what he said, German market research at its best: Some condoms are made from sheepskin. Sheepskin ones have natural pores that keep out sperm but are unreliable for viruses. Most other condoms are made of latex, which can cause allergic reactions. (Try saying this out loud: prophylactic anaphylaxis.) When the packet says *Extra Sensitive* it means they're low allergen, rather than extra thin. One size fits all but, when I noted my tutor was holding a packet marked 'extra wide', he grinned sheepishly, which was also appropriate.

The latex Kimono brand I bought had three in a packet – I didn't want to seem greedy. I opened the box when I got home and dissected one to see what it was like. Mucky. I posted another to Pig with a note saying if he ever wanted to come home he'd better practise safe sex. I concede that was stalkerish, but I've never pretended I wasn't behaving like a crazy lady. The third condom I put in my wallet.

From the start I had an ambivalent relationship with my condom. It wasn't so much a practical purchase as a symbolic one. Part of me wanted to make the most of my time as a single woman, but after eleven years of marriage, I wasn't even sure what I found attractive anymore. For instance, I have never kissed a woman. If everything is up for grabs, why not my sexual orientation?

Yeah, no. Not going to happen.

You know how the Religious Right bang on about homosexuality being a choice? We're going to have to name them the Religious Wrong. I was curious and courageous, but it wasn't enough for me to 'choose' to change. My orientation is straight, and my respect for those who acknowledge their fluid sexuality is high. It takes a lot of courage to buck the system, and I imagine more than a little heartache, so, yeah, all my dates in LA were male.

First there was Bob, who gallantly agreed to help me buy a knee brace so I could play Ultimate. Our afternoon together was a delightful twist on the scene in *Pretty Woman* where Julia Roberts tries on dresses for Richard Gere. In our scenario, Bob was seated in a low-slung chair in the Beverly Hills Sports Supply shop, his hands clasped thoughtfully under his chin in voyeuristic contemplation, as I modelled first the blue, then the skin-toned and finally (to his approval) the menacing black brace with full steel knee support.

Bob was a nice bloke – bright, well read and recently separated from his wife. In the way Americans have, he delivered his romantic history like a resume. His wife had become confused, lied about another man, mucked him around, made him feel like a cuckold, then left. As a writer, he'd been the main caregiver to their teenage daughter. He now felt he was having the wife's experience of being thrown over for someone less homebound.

I was empathetic to start with, but as he unfolded the complications of his breakup I began to back off. He had a bitter edge that was repellent. We weren't talking about the same situation at all, only the same bewilderment.

Pig and I didn't break up because we were unsuited. If anything, we'd lost ourselves in each other. I must have been getting somewhere, because for the first time I could see that we'd been so close that parts of each of us were dying, like the outer leaves on a pot-bound plant.

The epiphany of Bob's grief was this: 'You have to prune to bloom.'

The world was holding up a mirror, showing me what attachment and bitterness looked like – and it wasn't pretty. I stood outside of who I had become in my marriage and was struck by a most prosaic piece of Tao: *My husband may have left, but he didn't take me with him.* Each of us is at the centre of a unique event in the universe, and whatever our external relations to people and things, the absolute fact remains that no one else can live our inner life for us.

More than anything, I wanted to rise above the sadness of our separation and find the pure love that I had for my husband. The love that is outside of judgment. The love that is outside need, outside sex with other people. A love that is equal only to the love I have for myself.

So of course I would have to discover that as well.

The weird part was, I could feel all of this as clearly as I write it here, but then I would ring Pig to tell him, and all that would bubble out was hurt, anger and longing. I would berate him expensively on international phone calls until he sounded as weak as I felt.

Plainly I had to stop phoning him.

And then there was Justin. Ah, Justin.

Justin was funny, stylish and wickedly intelligent. He had a real job as the manager of a wine importing business, which revealed his one fatal flaw: Justin liked to drink … a lot.

I didn't notice this at first since we met at a wine tasting. It was a rowdy and funny night. By the time we left, Justin had my phone number and I had a pleasant feeling that the whole experience had been flattering and exotic.

Justin rang the next night to arrange The Date. My first inkling that he was more than a social drinker came was when he asked whether he should bring one or two bottles of wine for dinner. Since it would only be the two of us, I thought one would be fine but he brought two anyway.

We went to a fancy restaurant. I knew it was fancy because Drew Barrymore was sitting behind me. The wine was delicious – grown in Albania. Justin told me that to import Albanian wine you needed a good knowledge of not only grape and climate but also civil unrest, since intermittent bombing could force a harvest to be late, early or decimated. Delicious. I had one glass. The owner had a glass. Justin drank the rest.

I started to get nervous. My father was a brilliant alcoholic. I had grown up amid the violent mood swings and effusive apologies. No amount of razzle nor dazzle would lure me into that dragon's lair.

After dinner we went out for a drink.

Later, we went back to his place for a nightcap and he showed me some poetry he'd written – three sonnets that had taken as many years to write. When he talked about his writing he was shy, modest.

If you think about it, writing poetry, much less confessing to it on a first date, is pretty brave. Art for me is foreplay. Some women find wealth and power a turn on, for others it's physical beauty. Art and smarts spin my wheels. You might be a mild-mannered wine salesman by day, but if you're Jack Kerouac or Hunter S. Thompson when the sun goes down – I'm gone too.

Justin's entry for the Library of Congress poetry prize was called 'Ode to an Unrequited Vagina'. God knows what the Library of Congress made of it, but I thought it was bloody brilliant – ugly like a south-side laneway, righteous in its honesty. Justin was definitely gifted with the right crazed, glazed verbal clay for me, but my brain was stuck on this drinking business.

I have no illusions – it's impossible to change another person. That I could even criticise his drinking was ironic because, frankly, I was critically flawed myself. I may have been presenting as sane, but I was psychotic with grief. I was so thunderstruck by the collapse of my marriage that what little personality I had left was stripped back to a computer-style binary code: One for Yes. Zero for No. More complicated questions like 'Who am I?' and 'What do I want?' remained unanswered. All I heard was the clack of my consciousness leaving my darkened brain and shutting the door.

Yet every situation, every choice, came back to these two questions: 'Who am I?' and 'What do I want?' Is it only me? How can a person not know who they are? How could I criticise anyone when we're all jelly from the same sad mould? My whole situation was like that pantomime shtick, where the good guy is looking for the villain but can't find him because he's attached to his back. Every time I turned around, no one was there. I was the hero, villain and chorus of children shouting, 'She's behind you.'

And into this chaotic melee were whirlpools of even uglier neuroses. *I must be completely unloveable because my husband dumped me. Who'd want an emotional cripple like me? I'll end up with an alcoholic, because girls marry their fathers.*

A couple of days after The Date, Justin and I went out for breakfast. 'I have a drinking problem,' I said. He looked at me with the narrowed eyes of a man who's heard what I was about to say before. 'I come from a long line of alcoholics and I'm no good around drinkers.'

Our next two dates were blow-by-blow descriptions of exactly how much he *hadn't* drunk. Our third date was a party at his ex-wife's place.

'It's not good if an Australian tells you that you drink too much, is it?' he asked as he got into my hire car. Given that we have the second-highest per capita alcohol consumption (and alcoholism) in the world, no, it's not good.

The party was a disaster. Justin got so drunk I didn't know where to look. I got that tired feeling of having to cope when Dad got bellicose at Sunday lunch, and that dead sensation of pretending it was okay.

It was not okay. I left.

Justin came with me.

I wanted to go to the Griffith Observatory to see Foucault's pendulum.

Justin wanted to come too.

I stopped at home to pick up a jumper.

Justin jumped in the swimming pool – naked.

My personal hell was freezing over as I offered him a towel. I got in the car. We went to the observatory.

He turned the radio up.

I turned it down.

He shouted to no one.

I shouted at him.

Finally, on the spot where Sal Mineo got shot in *Rebel Without a Cause*, I said, in my smallest voice, 'I don't want to take this any further.'

I felt so powerful.

I didn't feel guilty.

I didn't feel a need to please.

I didn't feel I had to give in.

I didn't feel I'd been cruel or hurtful. I had been the dumpee and now I was the dumper. And with it came a little rush of testosterone. *Man, that feels good.*

Bloody hell. Maybe I had learned something after all. Maybe I had learned a little self-worth and a couple of limits. That moment was definitely a reward for knowing, on some minor but fundamental level, who I was and what I wanted.

BETTY THE WIDE-ARSED BROAD

Doesn't this sound easy? 'I'll buy a car and drive across America.'

It's not. It's hard.

I may have complicated things a bit by wanting one of two specific vehicles: either a five-litre V8 Mustang (preferably in *Thelma & Louise* turquoise) or a 1970s Merc – which in Australian means a Mercedes, but in American means a Mercury. (Asking for an 'old Merc' in L.A. was akin to asking an Australian for a 1970s Hyundai, if such a thing even exists.)

This misunderstanding meant that for the first few weeks every used car dealer enthusiastically showed me a disturbing array of Camrys, Mitsubishis and really old Hondas. It seemed like I was being cast as a mid-range, middle-class, middle-of-the-road white woman – which may have been close to the truth but, damn it, it's rude to point. I wanted to exude the aura of a spiritual warrior, not some wishy-washy whoopsie who didn't know who she was.

Pragmatically, all I needed was a car that would be able to do the 10,000-mile round trip (you do the sums, but it's more in kilometres) and I wanted it to cost less than $5000 *Australian*, which at the time came to a paltry US $3600.

Wasn't going to happen. The closest thing in a Mustang cost US

$10,000 before tax, insurance or security, and I didn't see a Mercedes anywhere near that. I confess – I prayed.

Every day I imagined the perfect car (still a vintage Mercedes with low miles) and then I let it go, saying, 'Whatever is perfect for me, in a perfect and balanced way, let it happen now, with thanks.' I said that a lot while patrolling the used car yards of Santa Monica and Venice Beach, but still the universe vomited up Camrys, Mitsubishis and Hondas. Plainly I was a long way from my warrior soul, and this journey hadn't started a minute too soon.

The last car yard on Santa Monica Boulevard was called Sheridan Toyota. If it hadn't been for the fact that it was literally shouting my name with a big flashing sign saying, '*Sheridan, Sheridan, Sheridan*,' I might not have stopped.

My salesman was Rudi from Nairobi. He was a skilled flirt with a diabolical sense of the ridiculous. He showed me a red 1989 Chevy Camaro, a car favoured in certain quarters for gangland massacres.

I laughed so hard when I saw it that Rudi kinda got embarrassed and asked what I was laughing at. I was speechless at its absurdity. This huge coupe thought it was a Corvette but was little more than a hoon-mobile in a country that doesn't have a word for hoon, but should.

'No, really, what are you laughing at?'

All I could squeeze out, along with the tears, was, 'The car.'

Rudi didn't get the joke but he did think he could get the sale, and that's what he was there for, so we went for a test drive.

The car was powerful. Only six cylinders, but still way bigger than the four I drove at home. Rudi was also quick to point out that it only had 19,000 miles on the odometer, which is unheard of in LA. 'So what are you saying?' I asked flatly. 'That it's only been used by a little old lady for drive-by shootings?' This was possibly so close to the truth that Rudi didn't reply.

Not wanting to seem hasty, I went home to sleep on it. Only I never made it home. About three blocks up the Boulevard I could still hear those 19,000 miles calling me. I rang Rudi and told him I wanted the car – nothing has made me laugh so much in years.

At 8am the next morning Rudi took me to meet some Irish mechanics who inspected the vehicle and declared it to be in good condition. They pointed out that there was no space for the '1' on the odometer. The car had probably done 119,000 miles – or more.

So. The old girl's been around the block a few times.

Rudi took me back to the office to start The Negotiations. Fortunately, I'd seen *Glengarry Glen Ross* so I was sort of ready, although nothing can really prepare you for eight (count them, eight) hours of haggling with a bunch of American used car salesmen.

Rudi was The Opener – he wouldn't be the one who closed the deal. There'd be a couple of rounds of 'good cop/bad cop' before I'd meet that guy.

Next was Nick The Negotiator. I opened the bargaining by slapping US $3000 in cash on the table and telling him it was all I had. They wanted $6800 for it, but I was offering cash.

He took the money, then returned it, saying, 'No.' Then he let me leave.

According to my research, that meant I'd gone too low. I left, but then returned with a counter offer, 'I guess I could find a bit of extra money in my Visa card. I expect you'll want to handle the insurance.'

Again, he took my money away. Again, he said no to the price, but this time he didn't give it back to me. The game was afoot.

By lunchtime, I was so baffled by the sums he was writing on little pieces of paper that I went to get something to eat – and Nick came with me. Over lunch, he told me that he was recently separated. Nick wanted love, but then, Nick was a used car salesman, so I figured what he really wanted was to sell the car. He didn't leave me alone. He even followed me to the ladies' toilet and I had to glare at him sternly to dissuade him from entering the cubicle.

By 5pm, I had met every salesman on the lot. We'd haggled over the insurance, the mileage, the little things that were broken on the car, the fact that it only had six cylinders, not eight.

I'd rung Marc for advice.

I'd rung the mechanics for advice.

I'd rung AAA (the American Automobile Association) and been told that the wholesale price for the car was US $3800 before insurance, tax or a security system.

The final base-price we settled on was $3600. With taxes, insurance and a security system it came to AUD $5500. That's when the contracts started – more paperwork than Pig and I signed when we bought our apartment. More pages than a film production investment agreement on a four country co-production. And at the bottom of all these mulched trees it said in large red letters, *There is no cooling off period in California.* That was scary. The price was still below wholesale, but more than I had in my budget.

I said, 'No', and that's when they took me to meet Dave.

Dave owned the franchise. David was The Closer. I felt like I'd been sent to the headmistress's office. He had a compelling argument. 'Do you want to go through all this again? Do you really want to go through the newspapers and have no redress if it breaks down? Do you really want to handle all the paperwork alone? Everyone has said it's a good car,' he said. 'You should be pleased with yourself about the deal.'

I explained to him that I'd borrowed the money from friends at home and needed to be able to get it back at the end of the trip.

Finally he got the original owner on the phone. It was the Latino who'd served me lunch. Señor Hortas told me he loved the car but traded it in for a pickup truck so he could make extra money on weekends.

I made Dave write all that down and sign it, but still I was nervous. 'If it's such a good deal, why won't you let me leave the lot?'

'Look, lady,' he said, leaning forward, his arms stretched out across the table in supplication, 'it's Friday. It's five o'clock. I have a quota to meet. If I don't meet the quota, I lose the franchise. Buy. The. Damn. Car.'

I stared at him for a moment. I bought the damn car.

Oscar, aged six and a half, was completely pixilated by my purchase. When I picked him up from school he slapped his hands to his face and screamed, 'She's beautiful!'

I drove it nervously to the petrol station where a Latino employee wiped it down with a rag. 'She's a beautiful car.'

None of that made me happy. In fact, it depressed me. It had been such a long day, maybe tiptoeing across America in an inconspicuous Honda wasn't such a bad idea.

The car and I didn't get off to a good start. Her major shortcomings were a soft underbelly and poor shock absorbers. Like a prolapsed cat she dragged low to the ground. This caused me to beach the damn thing on a cement retaining wall outside the Department of Motor Vehicles registry office, much to the delight of about twenty applauding learner drivers.

Another problem – she was loud. Not her engine, her personality. Sometimes when I was feeling small I'd tell the car to shut up, which wasn't particularly remarkable in West Hollywood where everyone on the street was shouting at something or other. And another thing, she farted in low gears. Not every time, but at the worst times. It was embarrassing. Like after we'd stopped at the lights. I'd pop her into first, and *brrrp*, a little windy puff before she leaped forward with a mighty roar. Which also made me leery of her power, and leery was quickly turning to fear – so I made up a story to soften her image.

Firstly, the car was female – that went without saying. She was a wild Latina in a sexy red dress. She'd spent the past five years with a totally besotted male and felt betrayed by her sale to me, a pussy-footing white woman. She was grieving the loss of her love and needed compassion in her crisis. We weren't car and driver, we were compadres in a world of pain. I'd show her a good time. She'd show me how to have it.

To celebrate this narrative, I named her Betty. Sometimes she got Big Bet, occasionally Betty the Bitch, but mostly she was Betty the Wide-Arsed Broad,

Our peace was finally made when I got her out onto the LA freeways. This was where she was indomitable. Betty was absolutely magnificent when she was running between 80 and 100 mph on an open road. Yes siree, Betty was one fast lady – and I never met a man who didn't fall in love with her.

AN AIR-CONDITIONED GYPSY

After a month in LA I was beginning to think I'd never escape. There's something surprisingly seductive about that city. It's probably the only place on earth where you can be flattered to death.

I was finally shoe-horned out when Marc threw me a going away party. A funny notion, given I was already 'living the dream', but what could I do? If friends and family were farewelling me, I'd better get going. Any demons about this trip would simply have to come along.

In preparation for my departure, I did the responsible adult things and bought a Chevy repair manual, petrol can, fire extinguisher and a spare fan belt – purchases so unlikely that I need to break out some extra-special punctuation to acknowledge them!?!?

I also bought a *Leatherman*. Every girl needs a Leatherman. It's like a Swiss Army knife for cars, and includes the cutest pliers, Phillips head screw drivers and thingies for your tappets. I only used the pliers to fish teabags out of my thermos but I loved my Leatherman – he was my talisman against crisis.

At Marc's suggestion I joined the AAA. Apart from promising nationwide roadside assistance they also provided trip planning, including the recommendation to buy a navigation device. This presented me with a conundrum. I made my living through screens and wanted this to be a journey into the real world. I wasn't taking any cameras or electronic devices, and so chose an old-fashioned paper map – the Rand McNally road atlas – their deluxe edition, which clipped into a natty faux-leather folder.

Packing Betty's small boot required applied geometry and sheer bloody mindedness. I had to squash in travel clothes, city clothes, bathroom products and way too many books – mainly spiritual stuff for a delusional voyage of self-discovery: *The Upanishads*, *The Odyssey* and that all-time bestseller, *The Bible*. My delusion wasn't about the choice of books per se – that owed more to an overweening existential crisis. The madness was thinking I'd have time to read them.

You see, I did the math. (I presume Americans don't pluralise mathematics because they only plan to do it once.) I wanted to travel Route 66, the great Mother Road. A quick check revealed that America's first highway was 2500 miles long. If I drove for five hours a day at 100 miles an hour, I calculated that I could be with my friend Pipi in Connecticut in five days. Make it a week for dawdling, finding accommodation, and *bingo*! I'd have plenty of time to read all those books in the shade of those mighty rivers: Colorado, Missouri and Mississippi.

Congratulations at home if you've noticed my three (3) fundamental errors. Yes, I confused miles for kilometres. No, you can't drive that fast in America. And get yourself a beer and piece of chocolate cake if you know that Route 66 finishes in Chicago. Worse, Route 66 was decommissioned in 1985 and a quarter of the road doesn't even exist anymore.

The joy of that revelation was still in front of me. For now, brimming with optimism, all I needed to get going on my six-week road odyssey was to sit for my Californian driver's licence. It wasn't essential, but an ambiguity between the car insurance and my travel insurance would be cleared up if I had a local permit.

Getting one required a social security number, which turned out to be weirdly easy. The US Social Security Administration gave me a green card in two days. *A miracle!* Until I saw they'd stamped the words *Alien Non-Working* across it. Obviously they could see through my flesh-coloured skinsuit and into my reptilian soul. This fancy little piece of paper was an identity card printed on green paper. I couldn't use it for anything more exciting than getting my driver's licence and opening a bank account.

With my identity card in hand, I then sat for the written test. Cool. I studied and only got one question wrong: Where is it legal to carry an open container of alcohol?

(a) In the driver's hand.

(b) On the back seat.

(c) In the trunk of your car.

(d) In the living quarters of a mobile home.

Well, (a) is silly, (b) is tricky, (c) messy, (d) makes sense – like, in the refrigerator in the living quarters of a mobile home, so you could have drinkies after a hard day touring America.

Wrong. It's only legal to carry an open container of booze in the trunk of your car. Why on earth would you do that? It would spill everywhere. Anyway, no biggie, one wrong was a pass, so now I could do the driving test.

Three hours. The queue to do the test was three hours long, and that was *with* an appointment. Furthermore, I had to bring a Californian-licensed driver with me in case of failure. Marc (gorgeous, long-suffering Marc) came, and was incredibly gracious about it.

We waited, we read, we got coffee, we got pissed off at the petty tyrant running up and down the queue telling everyone to move up.

Finally it was my turn. Before we could go anywhere I had to prove that I had brake lights, indicators and a horn. Horn. *HORN*.

I had no horn.

They wouldn't let me do the test. I was furious. That arsehole marshalling the queue could have told me about the stupid horn and in three hours I could have got it bloody fixed. *Arghh.*

I drove home in an absolute fury. Marc told me it was the first time I'd driven the car properly since I bought it.

I wasn't going to sit in that queue again. Ambiguity or not, I had been thrown a leaving party and that was that. I stormed out of town promising to ring Marc every three days in case the bogeyman got me.

As I drove out of LA the tension peeled away. It was even better than I had imagined. Cross my heart and hope to die, there's nothing as satisfying as living a fantasy. I'd wanted to run away from home since I was a kid and, finally, there I was. A runaway at thirty-five.

Crossing the border from California into Arizona, I started to yip and holler and slap the side of the car. This is who I was, an air-conditioned gypsy, a free spirit on my way to the wild frontier.

I played *all* my CDs instantly.

I *Ran, Baby, Ran* with Sheryl Crow.

I drove.

I thought, *Shit, this looks like Australia.*

I flamenco guitared with Ali Farka Touré.

I played the soundtrack to *The Last Temptation of Christ*, which has to be the sexiest piece of music ever written. Betty could feel it too as she rose and fell on her appalling shock absorbers to the sound of the drums.

No one else was on the road. Not a soul. And it was hot. Desert hot. The horizon was wide and the trees were weird. The sky was high and benign. Soft ambers and deep blues. I was wearing my red spotty dress. I like the red spotty dress. I'm wearing it now.

The sensuality that underlaid this moment was deep and eternal. The utter physicality of beauty. It was Spiritual. Transcendent. Erotic. The reds floated orange into turquoise. A body breeze through the window was a thousand curious fingers caressing my being.

The expectations of this journey are all caught in that moment, and suspended as an outstanding life-memory. It lies in the same mental file as a honeymoon swim at Marble Bar in Western Australia; the pale mauve light of Fiesole outside Florence; a cloud rolling in over Mount Penang; rounding a distant path in the Himalayas to Pavarotti singing 'Nessun Dorma'; and my first perfect love throwing rice over me on a wedding anniversary because I told him I feared the absence of it at our wedding had caused my infertility.

But they're only memories. This was the perfect now. In this moment I am perfect. I am free to be whoever I want, and all I want to be is a woman in a red spotty dress, speeding into her future in a shiny red car.

Out in the wild, the romance of paper maps came into its own. I snapped open the *Rand McNally* and it shimmered with the promise of treasure. Captain of my own ship. I loved the legend, with its tiny pictures of campsites and green dots of scenic beauty. I traced the roads with my finger, enjoying all that possibility, following the switchbacks and straights, triangulating letters and numbers, looking for adventure.

The story this map told me was that I should zigzag cross-country northeast to the I-40, where a lengthy fragment of old Route 66 would take me towards Kingman and then south to Prescott, where

I'd pre-booked a night's accommodation. I clicked the road atlas shut, hoisted sail, and set forth with a fair tail wind.

Two hours later and I still hadn't reached my destination. I had crossed over from euphoria into a thumping sugar low when I rounded a corner, missed the sign that said Oatman, and discovered in the middle of the road an enormous piebald donkey. A goddamned burro – the ass – standing on a Route 66 shield that was painted onto the tarmac.

Betty squealed to a halt in a flurry of dust. Her headlights lit the obdurate beast perfectly, the full nuance of its glaring contempt captured in every tick and click of the cooling motor.

I leaned down over the steering wheel so I could see the building where I had stopped. The Oatman Hotel. *Hmm.* If I abandoned my pre-paid accommodation, maybe I could stay here for the night? Sleep in a rumble tumble saloon left over from a Clint Eastwood movie. Sounded good.

Inside, the folksy bar was plastered floor to ceiling with thousands of one dollar bills. The forty-something waitress, Julia, greeted me warmly as she set my table. 'You're in luck, I was about to close for the night. We had a Chamber of Commerce meeting, so I don't have much to offer. How about a pulled pork sandwich and something to drink?'

Perfect.

It seems I'd stumbled into an original gold-mining town. Oatman, Julia told me, was the living spirit of Route 66. 'We've had all the luck. A Gold Rush in the 1800s. Another in 1919. A regular boom when the highway came through and bust when they re-routed to the Interstate.'

It was Julia who broke the news that Route 66 didn't go to New York. 'Don't get caught on the road number, doll,' she said. 'Route 66 is a romance. An idea concocted by two businessmen – Avery and

Woodruff wanted to join all the main streets from Chicago to LA. Ain't that some big thinking?'

'What about New York? How do you get there?'

'Take the 40, or anything like it. Just stay off the Interstate. The side roads *are* Route 66.' She went and got me something to eat.

'So what's with the wallpaper?' I asked when she returned. It was impossible to ignore the money plastered to every surface, including the ceiling.

'Tabs. Back in the early days, miners used to stick a note down for their drinking tab. Now it's become a bit of a thing.'

'So this isn't a Hollywood set?'

'Hell, no. Though Clark Gable and Carole Lombard spent their honeymoon here.'

'True story?'

'Uh huh.' She showed me their room to prove it. The 'honeymoon suite' was as unpretentious as in any pub you'd find in rural Australia. 'I think they liked it that way,' said my new friend. 'They weren't always Hollywood folk, you know.'

I decided to throw away the money I'd pre-paid for Prescott and spend the night here, but that wasn't going to happen. Julia didn't let rooms anymore, 'You might get something in Kingman,' she said, 'but by the time you found it – you may as well keep going.'

And so I did. With a belly full of pork and some 7 Up for the road, I drove into the night in anticipation of an unpretentious room on Route 66.

It was dark when I arrived at the Prescott Inn. The guide book had described it as 'an inspiration to other hoteliers owning older-style motels'.

Inspiration to what?

The owner let me in with a warm smile and showed me to my room. It looked like the cottage fairy had vomited in it.

'Oh my. Someone's been busy,' I said with a city smile. It was everything I could do not to laugh. The owner was proud as Punch. Did the whole thing herself.

After she closed the door I stood alone for a moment, trying to decide what to make of it. Never in the history of interior design had so many stuffed toys been gathered so senselessly into one tiny space. Classic aphorisms had been meticulously embroidered, framed and hung (damn it) on every inch of floral-papered wall. And it didn't stop there. The stuff that wasn't wallpaper was gingham or chintz, or a patchwork of both, with stars and stwipes on an ickle wickle Charlie Brown theme.

The things you see when you don't have a gun.

The next morning, as dawn broke over a satanic patchwork Snoopy doll, I was already on my way in search of something more enduring.

The Grand Canyon is less than a day's drive from LA, making it a popular weekend destination. My expat friends in California had fallen in love with every square inch of it. Or so it seemed. When I told them about my journey, they all gave me bulk suggestions for things to do, from hiring a plane to visiting an Indian reservation. There were faith healers, horse rides and artist colonies on their must-do lists. One very specific tip involved detouring to see a particularly scenic undulation in the road near Sedona.

The route I finally chose combined only the most emphatic suggestions. I'd travel north towards Jerome and Sedona, then detour via Camp Verde and Montezuma Castle to catch that pretty bump in the road.

Jerome was indeed a charming detour, a friendly ghost town floating a mile above the valley floor. The road switchbacked past wooden houses with aging hippies bathing in sunshine, and then twisted and turned until I found myself driving out of town again. Nothing looked open.

I drove back and parked to check my map. The morning sun was casting long shadows through the sagebrush. It was so beautiful I got out to breathe in the view. Behind me, a man was smoking on the verandah of a two-storey Victorian house that looked like it may have had a past life as a mining-town brothel.

'She's something, isn't she?' he said to me. I thought he meant the view, before he added, 'We don't see a lot of Camaros up here.'

Ah, Betty's magic wiggle. 'You don't know where I can find some breakfast, do you?' I asked, squinting up at him. 'I'm starving.'

'You're in luck. I've put the griddle on. Nothing fancy mind, just biscuits and gravy if that's okay.'

Nothing fancy? 'Yes, please,' I replied, giving Betty an affectionate pat before stepping into the hotel.

Allen, the proprietor, presented me with two 'biscuits', cut in half and covered in a (yes, delicious) eggy-meaty sauce.

'Only, that's not a biscuit,' I said. 'That's a scone.'

'So I hear. And I suppose you'd like it prepared with whipped cream and jelly?' He laughed with a pleasing, deep chuckle. 'That's so wrong.'

I pulled out my map to show him where I was going and the list of places my friends had suggested. He took my pen and circled the best bits.

'Sedona is in Red Rock State Park. It's glorious country. Chimney Rock, Devil's Bridge, Airport Mesa, Coffee Pot Rock. Once you get to Sedona there's the Tlaquepaque Arts & Crafts Village.' He pronounced it *t-lockey-pockey.* 'Then Snoopy's Belly, Cathedral Rock and Courthouse Butte ...'

I started to giggle. 'Who got the job naming these places? Cheech and Chong?'

He looked at the list. 'I don't know, but I think Charles Schultz lived around here someplace. Maybe he got Charlie Brown to do it.'

Turned out the cartoonist and creator of Snoopy had lived in Needles, a town near Oatman where I'd had dinner the night before. I wondered if I should go back to Prescott and apologise to that nice old lady for mocking her Snoopy dolls.

After breakfast Allen packed some 'biscuits' for me to take, and I drove out into the morning making a note to come back one day and stay at the Ghost City Inn.

I followed the trail he suggested and it was good, but about an hour into the drive I started to sink. Of all the places in all the world, the scenery most reminded me of the magical landscape around Marble Bar in Western Australia. The second hottest place on earth, made of jasper and quartz with mica stripes that sparkle in the sunlight. I know all that because I spent part of my honeymoon there. Working.

It was my fault. When we wed, I accidentally double booked myself out on our honeymoon. I'd signed on to film a science and technology series being shot in Australia, the US, UK and Japan. Being a freelancer I didn't have the luxury of turning it down, so Pig came along for the ride.

It turned out to be among the best work experiences, and the weirdest honeymoon ever. We went to strikes, riots and factories. I met the astronomer Fred Hoyle and was given the keys to NASA by an officer who mistook me for a secretary. There was even a surreal moment in a darkened bathroom – the ladies' room in a British laboratory – where a scientist broke Polo sweets with a nutcracker to show the spark of blue light that breaking sugar gives off. She was doing this to demonstrate how amino acids could form during a meteor shower.

The series included a visit to Marble Bar to see crater sites in the desert of Western Australia. And here I was, eleven years later, with that same desert landscape laid out before me. Alone. *Is this cosmic sarcasm?* Why had my friends pulled such a callous trick, sending me to such an evocative place? Everyone's memories are lit by the conditions under which they lived them. My friends had visited Sedona with their lovers. These were their softest, most romantic memories, and I was drowning in them.

Montezuma's Castle is an 11th-century city hewn out of rock by long-dead Pueblo Indians. I looked deep into the limestone well. A sinkhole, 470 feet wide and more than 55 feet deep. This well had watered the fields of an ancient civilisation. It had been the centre of a thriving community, the nurturing water supply to generations of families, and yet here it was, abandoned and ruined. After the initial thrill of leaving LA, and twenty-four hours in my own company, the magnitude of what had happened in my life was sinking in. Betty and I ran screaming before we both jumped in that well.

The first glimpse of the Grand Canyon nearly knocked me off the road. In the rosy glow of afternoon light it was humbling – a vast, deep and powerful tribute to the glory of chaos and decay. Finally, here was something no one can prepare you for, the physicality of its beauty has to be experienced.

It was getting late when Betty and I arrived. The possibility of finding accommodation was dwindling. We did a lap of the village before stopping outside the Bright Angel Lodge – a front-row motel with a retro log-cabin design. Blind optimism led me to reception, where I was rewarded with a cancellation vacancy. 'It's a double room with a shared bathroom. I hope that's alright.'

Alright? It was bloody marvellous. A registered national historic landmark built in the 1930s, the Bright Angel Lodge came complete with old world rustic charm and Native American motifs. It was comfortable and welcoming.

Taking a Rolling Rock beer after dinner, I went outside and sat on the rim of the Grand Canyon. It was a bright, blue-black night, lit by a gibbous moon. The silence from the gaping maw below was as deep as it was mysterious.

'Come,' said the darkness, 'float down upon me.'

Have you ever had that thought, in a tall building perhaps, with a swimming pool below? *I could jump into there from here.* It's hypnotic. Scary. I gathered myself and moved away from the edge.

If I wanted to hike the canyon the next day I'd need an early start, so I gathered some maps from reception and went to bed to count my blessings: a world of adventure, a safe car and the resources to be free.

I turned out the light and listened to the rural silence.

The rural near-silence.

What is that noise?

Lying in the dark, there was the unmistakable sound of lovers in the next room. I lay there listening to them as she started to climax.

That train never arrived.

Their lovemaking went on and on.

I was at first jealous, then curious. *Would this root never end?*

Her orgasm kept going. *Oh, now you're just showing off.*

I started to wonder if it could be something else. A tiny kitten, perhaps, stuck in the wall. The more I listened, the more it sounded like distressed mewing.

Oh my god! There's a kitten trapped in the wall.

I crawled over to listen and see if I could locate it, to help it escape. I paused for a moment, near-naked on all fours with my ear to the log cabin wall. No. It wasn't a cat. It was definitely people. I considered banging on the wall but decided against it and went back to bed. I put in ear plugs and fell asleep.

The next day broke sunny with a blue sky full of fair-weather clouds. I took some fruit from the buffet then made a cheese sandwich and stowed it in my backpack. I bought a bottle of water and, using the hotel map as a guide, stepped out into the day.

The Grand Canyon is 4380 feet (or 1335 metres) in a straight line from the top of the south rim to the bottom. It's much, *much* further to walk along its twisting path.

There was a surreal, underwater quality to the canyon. It reminded me most of the Great Barrier Reef. Scudding clouds sent shafts of light to dance among the tree tops like so much green coral. It seemed unbelievable that you couldn't take a lungful of air and push off into it.

Walking down the Bright Angel Trail, it was good to be alive. To be pounding the ochre earth one step at a time. Down, down, down. Halfway into the canyon at the Indian Gardens lookout, I refilled my water bottle and thought about how far I could keep going. Although the rim now looked to be a million miles away, the river was still a thumbnail sketched into the shadows. I could definitely make it down in a day but not all the way back up. You don't need to be Sherlock Holmes to work out if going down two or three thousand feet takes a couple of hours, going up will be much longer.

I walked the extra mile out to Plateau Point and sat. The steepest part of the hike was still ahead. A young couple came and stood in front of me to take a selfie. They didn't soak up the view, they turned their back on it, talking the whole time. She was annoyed that she'd carried a hat for him to wear but he refused to put it on. He didn't want to wear the hat because he thought it looked stupid. The scratchiness of their relationship. The time they spent berating their love. The monument to their hearts behind them, unobserved.

For all its power and stupendous grace, it seemed as though we humans could only glimpse the canyon within the tawdry experience of being human. Whether it was the macho climbers racing the clock or the daggy day trippers in their neatly ironed shorts (God, please, never let me iron my shorts) there was no escaping the invasion I was a part of.

I'm a tourist in my own life.

While eating my sandwich, I chewed over whether to walk to the bottom and hope for emergency accommodation, or go back to the top and drive somewhere else for the night. If I'd thought about it beforehand (any of it, really) I might have hitched a ride on a donkey back to the top. Instead, I repacked my water bottle and started walking back up. The decision felt good.

I'll come back with Sue, I thought, as I started the long march to the top. *I'll plan it in advance and we'll make it to the bottom.* This was a place to be shared. *Then I won't be a tourist anymore. I'll be someone living in the moment.*

I put my head down and picked up my feet.

The second half of the day hiking the Grand Canyon is notorious for accidents: blisters, sun stroke, heat exhaustion and hypothermia can all lead hikers to take what locals call, 'The Fifteen-Second Tour' – getting disoriented and falling over the edge. I suspect my fellow hikers thought I was a candidate for this as I staggered around taking photos of the dust and laughing, because …

While I was staring at the ground, repeating my mantra, *Shit, this is hard, shit, this is hard,* I saw a pattern forming in the footprints in front of me. Like a 3D image emerging from a printer, there in the dust was a perfect Wandjina – a replica of the ancient-space cadets with their helmet-heads that are painted on cave walls in the Kimberley in Western Australia. When I was growing up I had a picture book with the stories of the Aboriginal Dreamtime. I didn't understand then that they were a symbol of creation, fertility and renewal, but rediscovered them years later while filming a TV segment. And here they were again, not an hallucination, but a manifestation made real in the heels of Nike consciousness. Surely this was a sign, if ever I needed one, that I was finally on the path with heart. A goddess of renewal was showing me the way.

THE NAVAJO WITHOUT RESERVATIONS

On the way to Sedona, Betty's farty noise had become something far more serious. She stalled a couple of times in low gears in the canyon. That had been alarming, but now as we drove away down the freeway she was stalling in third gear. It was clear she was on the verge of collapse.

Reading the car manual by the side of the road revealed a possible transmission problem, or a computer error, or, erm, something wrong with the guts of the car. My final assessment was that it was Saturday afternoon in the middle of nowhere and the car and I were totally cactus. I'd finally found the American frontier when I needed it least.

Betty and I limped 85 miles into Tuba City on the Navajo reservation. The reservation was the size of Pennsylvania and included exotic scenery, from snow-covered mountains to the Painted Desert. Not that any of this registered with me as I drove through it. I was too terrified the car would conk out on the freeway.

My relief on arriving at the Chevy dealership was somewhat diminished when I discovered it was closed. It closed at 5pm on Saturdays. I arrived at 5.30.

Frustration bubbled up over fear – and by bubbled I mean flowed like lava. I found a pay phone and berated, whined, cried, and offered money to the man who answered if someone (anyone) could find a mechanic to look at my car.

Nope. They'd return at 8.30 on Monday. If I was still there, they'd look at the car then.

I went to the local supermarket, which was open til seven, and begged them for help.

Nope.

I could see I was behaving like a noisy white woman throwing her weight around, Bad Queen #9, but I couldn't stop, even as my tantrum turned people against me.

Finally, Betty and I both ran out of steam in the parking lot of an outrageously expensive motel. I booked a room and resigned myself to being.

I also took a Serepax and went to sleep.

In the morning, Tuba City was still there.

I simply couldn't get things started. Not the car. Not the town. Not my attitude. I was frustrated and furious.

Maybe I try too hard.

I tried stopping.

You try stopping. It's harder than you think.

I went to breakfast. Everyone was brusque – polite, but uninterested. If I did nothing, nothing would happen. *The universe rewards action.* If I was going to be stuck here until Monday, I'd have to *do* something. I asked the waitress if she had a friend with a car who might drive me around. I was willing to pay.

She didn't.

I asked the receptionist, the woman in the gift shop, the cleaner.

Blank wall. Not only not helpful, but kind of baffled, like I was asking to hire skis or something.

Okay, I get it. I can't gatecrash Navajo culture.

I decided to do my laundry and then wash Betty so that come Monday the mechanic would think I liked the car and take more care with her.

On Sundays the laundromat in Tuba City was a throbbing heart of community, full of women and grandfathers doing the family wash. Piles of it. Tons of it. With children chasing each other through the dust outside, and teenagers swapping gossip under a peppercorn tree by the Dairy Queen.

One woman pulled up in a truck whose front licence plate read, *America – love it or give it back.* Another said, *Get a real job – be a housewife.*

But I made them uncomfortable. Each time I walked in to check my washing the joyful sounds stopped, like we were in some female equivalent of the saloon scene in a Western.

The day still had plenty of life in it, so when everything was squeaky clean I returned to the motel and asked the receptionist again – could she think of anyone who would drive me around. 'You know, a person with a driver's licence who's not going to kill me.'

'You could ring the police, I suppose.'

Really? That's the best you can do? 'Okay. What's their number?'

She wrote it on a piece of paper. I couldn't believe I was doing this. She turned her phone around for me and I rang it. Like an idiot.

When the operator answered, I could hear the 911 line booming out over a two-way speaker. There was something bad going down – I could hear a woman calling out for help – and then there's me on the other line saying, 'Oh, this isn't a police matter, I just wondered if you can recommend anyone who might be interested in taking me sightseeing for the afternoon for, say, seventy dollars?'

Seventy dollars! I must have been out of my head. I'd started by offering the waitress thirty, but had been raising the price in five-dollar increments thinking that was the problem.

Anyway, the operator put me on hold then came back with the name of Constable Laudable Adams. He finished his shift at four, and would be delighted to show me around.

As you would expect of anyone called Laudable, he was an upstanding guy – even if GI Joe is your yardstick. He showed up punctually, still wearing his gun and police-issue shorts, and offered to show me some Anasazi ruins. So, with his six-year-old son in tow, we climbed into the Navajo Nation police car and drove off into the desert.

The word '*Anasazi*' is Navajo and means 'the Ancient Ones' or 'Ancient Foreigners' depending on who you speak to. There's no evidence that the Anasazi were Navajo, culturally they're more likely to have been related to the Hopi. They built extensive cities in canyons all around Arizona, Colorado, Utah and New Mexico, but mysteriously they all disappeared at the close of the 13th century. Hundreds of thousands of Anasazi vanished from the face of the earth without a trace. Popular theory has it that they farmed the land into oblivion then moved on. Some speculate that disease or fighting may have wiped them out, but there's little sign that they left in a hurry or amid tragedy.

The mystery is deepened by the fact that the desert has perfectly preserved the cities they built high up on the cliff faces. These are the original skyscrapers – made of wood and mud, and dug deep into sandstone cliffs – sophisticated cities with a network of retractable ladders to navigate them. The Anasazi also left many well-preserved artifacts from their distinctive black and white pottery decorated in geometric designs, to cave paintings featuring a pantheon of hallucinogenic anthropomorphic gods.

Laudable told me that the Anasazi ruins at Mesa Verde, halfway between Cortes and Telluride in Colorado, were among the most impressive. 'It's an abandoned medieval city snuggled into the side of a cliff,' he said. 'One look will tell you these were extraordinary people. Stone age New Yorkers.'

Archaeologists have spent long and healthy careers trying to unravel the mystery. 'The New Agers find it tantalising too,' said Laudable. 'They think the cities are built on ley lines and that the original inhabitants haven't gone at all, but are merely vibrating at a higher consciousness.'

I looked at this clean-cut young policeman. He didn't seem to be the sort who'd go in for anything flakey. 'What do you think?' I asked. 'Is that possible?'

He didn't take his eyes off the road, but his lips curled into a smile, 'I think maybe they're vibrating somewhere else as well. That's not a professional opinion.'

'No. Funny, but.'

After so much reticence in the town, I was surprised by how easy our conversation was. We quickly got to talking about our families (my mum, his dad) and the things we'd learned from them. I observed that because my father was dead, I found the advice he'd given me was more accessible than my mother's, which was still caught up in the stuff of daily life.

I'd been thinking about Mum a lot lately. Before I left she told me: 'Know when you're happy.' It sounds simple but it's really effective. 'Happiness can only exist in the present,' she said. 'In the past it's memory, in the future it's a dream.'

'Like now,' I told Laudable. 'I'm happy.'

It turned out that his dad had died recently. The legacy he left his son had been an impressive store of Indian knowledge – tracking, hunting and Indian history. 'I can tell a lot about a person from how they move through the world.'

When we stopped the car I leaped out and ran off saying, 'Okay, tell me about me.'

I hadn't gone more than three steps before he started talking. '125 to 135 pounds. That dress is unflattering. Injured left knee, broken right arm, right handed, with what looks like a small stone in your shoe – maybe a blister.'

I was completely blown away. I walked back to the car as he and his son got out. 'How did you know I broke my arm when I was seven?'

He took the points one by one. My weight was based on the depth of the print in the sand. The way I turned indicated right handedness. The varying length of my stride showed I had a weakness in the left knee (it was shorter than the stride of the right). The way I was rolling my foot suggested a small irritation, a blister or stone. The broken right arm was indicated by the way I lifted my arm to open the door.

This was too much fun. I wanted more.

We stood on top of a mesa (one of the great rocky outcrops that define the impressive landscape) and listened to the wind. Blowing through the piñon pines it sounded like the ocean, but through juniper it created a soothing 'pink' noise, and sagebrush amplified the wind till it sounded like the prairies were calling to us.

Laudable's son was seeing how far he could throw rocks.

'Can you hear the deer?' asked Laudable.

I strained to hear the softest clicking sound.

'That's it,' he said. 'They're scared by the rocks.' We listened to the wind and the deer. 'Dad used to say that anywhere in the world, if you listen long enough, you'll hear the sound of food.'

'I reckon if you listen long enough,' I replied, 'you'll hear the sound of little boys throwing rocks too.'

Laudable said that the Navajo way is to be still, to observe, to listen, to wait. To wit, when we were driving back to town we stopped near a Kombi Van so that Laudable could ensure everything was okay. Instead of walking up to the van (which an Aussie cop would have done) he parked behind it and waited. When I finally asked him why he didn't approach it, he asked if I had noticed the curtain twitch. I had and he added, 'So there's a person inside, are they white or an Indian?' I told him it had been too dark and too small a glimpse to know. He said the occupant was Navajo because they were so quiet. 'White people are noisy.'

Driving back we played a game: recalling what passengers in passing cars looked like. I wasn't good at it, but guessed that sooner or later he'd ask me to describe what he was wearing. I was prepared and methodically listed everything from head to foot. He was impressed. Then I produced my trick. Navajo or not, men the world over rarely notice the things closest to them. Without looking, Laudable couldn't tell me what his son was wearing.

He dropped me back at the hotel where, an hour later, the phone rang – no mean feat since no one knew where I was. It was Laudable, he wanted to come and talk to me. I felt uncomfortable about him coming to my hotel room and wondered if I'd misjudged how friendly I'd been. I was pretty embarrassed when he gave me my seventy dollars back. He said he'd had a good time, and showing me around had made him feel close to his father. He felt wrong taking the money when I was going to need it for the car.

I felt like a schmuck for doubting him.

He wanted to come inside, but I wasn't feeling like that much of a schmuck, and suggested that we go out and get something to eat with the money. Which is how I came to be eating Taco Bell in a police car, overlooking an abandoned runway and watching some guy setting off early Fourth of July fireworks.

'Aren't they pretty?' I said.

'Yeah. Illegal, but,' he replied.

Isn't it amazing how quickly the ANZAC vernacular spreads?

Monday morning in Tuba City was remarkably like Sunday, the only difference being after a lesson in the silent power of patience, waiting became a game of observing passers-by instead of watching time pass.

At 8.30 the *Closed* sign at the Chevy dealership promptly turned to *Open*.

Marvin, the mechanic, was a spectacular-looking Indian with a huge scar down his face. Like all men, he had a sweet spot for Betty, and treated her with the reverence usually reserved for a first date with a beautiful woman who shows the promise of sex.

He took her for a test drive and she sprang to life in a way she never did for me. He quickly deduced that she needed a new air intake filter, which would cost two hundred dollars (*argh*) because the part had to come from Flagstaff, which was a three-hour round trip. (*Double argh!*)

Enter Bernard, the spare parts manager I had berated down the phone on Saturday. 'I was so rude,' I said, mortified by how loud and aggressive I'd been, 'I was all over the shop like a madwoman's breakfast. I am so sorry. Will you forgive me?'

'Well that's a fine way to start the day.' He accepted my heartfelt apology by allowing me go along for the ride to Flagstaff.

Bernard was a blast. During our adventure he told some great stories. (If they turn out to be apocryphal, do me a favour and keep your myth-busters to yourself.) So: one day Bernard's elderly grandfather turned up at the dealership and said, 'Come, Bernard, we must go into the desert.' Bernard asked his grandfather what it was about, but the old man was evasive, so Bernard assumed it was Indian business.

Bernard's grandfather had been a code talker in World War II. In the Pacific, the Americans were at a loss for a code that the Japanese couldn't break. Navajo is a unique language with complicated grammar, so someone came up with the idea of turning it into an unbreakable code. Hundreds of Navajo were hired as radio operators and deployed to the Pacific, where they communicated military information over the air in a coded version of their native tongue.

This was a prized secret. To protect it, the US Army assigned a marine to each code talker. Their sole job was to shoot the radio operator if they were captured. Can you imagine what type of relationships those men had? They lived together, shared sleeping quarters and for years were inseparable – with the sole focus of one being the murder of the other if necessary.

A Navajo code talker had been at the fall of Iwo Jima, and is in the famous *Life* magazine photograph of the flag being raised. The US Army wanted to make a hero of him but he was so traumatised by the war he shunned the attention and froze to death alone on the reservation.

Bernard's boss at the dealership had also served as a code talker, as such, he was sensitive to the needs of the grandfather. Without question he gave Bernard the day off .

As the two men drove out into the desert, the old man seemed to be navigating by a third sense. 'Have you been there before?' asked Bernard, curious to know where they were going.

'No,' said the grandfather.

'Are you meeting a friend there?'

'Yes.'

'Who?'

'I don't know them yet.'

They were a long way into the desert when, magically, a house appeared on the horizon. *The* house. The grandfather rejected Bernard's offer to be part of the ceremony, and left him to wait patiently in the car.

Forty minutes later, the grandfather reappeared looking happy and relaxed. The house turned out to be a brothel. Bernard had taken a day off work to drive the old man out into the desert for a root.

Outside of Flagstaff, Bernard indicated a small red hill. The trees had been razed by a recent bushfire, which made its brilliant colour stand out among the other, pale yellow hills. To the right, the landform looked like a sleeping woman. As Bernard pointed it out, I began to see her reclining figure and soft breasts, an arm thrown over her waist with a blanket over her legs.

'Grandfather says that the red hill is her heart. If it ever makes its way over to the woman, she'll wake up. Which is pretty interesting, because that's a dormant volcano.'

I loved the idea of the woman's heart wanting to find its way home. Obviously I got the geological significance, but more than that, I felt like I was sleepwalking, my body disconnected from my heart awaiting the violent eruption that would be caused by their reunion.

'Bring on the heat, I say.'

By the return journey, Bernard was telling me about his marriage. He was separated from his wife of fifteen years. *God, who isn't in this country?* His wife, a willowy, blue-eyed blonde, became frustrated with living on the reservation, 'A community so small that you can't scratch without someone knowing you had an itch'. Their separation had been acrimonious. I guessed he was still in love with her.

We got to talking about Pig, and why he left me. 'I have no answer to that.'

'Was there someone else?'

'Probably, but I don't think that's what happened. The "other woman" seems too glib. Discontent is a powerful force in your thirties, and midlife crises swing both ways.'

'Do you believe that?'

'I believe he loved me. I just can't believe he burned our life to the ground. If there was a dead body, at least I'd know what to do with it.'

Bernard looked at me askance before slapping the steering wheel and roaring with laughter.

At the garage, Marvin had his magical way with Betty – which is to say he replaced her broken parts and I left Tuba City feeling grateful for the kindness and help the Navajo had given me. I had been shrewish and unhinged, but they saw through that and responded to me with Grace and Kindness – monuments to the human condition as peaceful and enduring as the landscape I was driving through.

Entering Monument Valley from the south in the late afternoon was a perfect time to see it in all its front-lit splendour. The landscape of *Thelma & Louise* was more of everything than I'd imagined. More impressive, more alive, and more confronting. It took about an hour to drive through the valley and out of the state.

Over the border into Colorado I passed a truck stop near Cortez with a bunch of pickup trucks outside. I did a U-turn and pinged the door on the way in. I wanted to think about Monument Valley, maybe go back and see it again. Something vague was brewing behind my eyeballs, and I needed a good cup of tea to clear my vision.

Inside were a bunch of old-time cowboys, some Navajo Indians, two tourists, and a biker who stared at me. Having filmed various stories with bikers I'm not generally alarmed by them, but this one seemed ornery. So I put on my Bland Face – a benign smile without much encouragement – and took a seat by the window.

The waitress laid down the menu and filled my glass with iced water. 'Can I help you?'

'Big question. What I'm really hanging out for is a nice, hot cup of tea.'

'Roger that. Something to eat?'

I glanced at the menu, 'Refried beans and a garden salad. But that tea. Do you have boiling water? Or do you use one of those wall heaters?'

'The water's pretty hot. It comes out of the tap.'

'Yeah. Is there any way you could heat it up a bit more? Maybe boil it?'

She sighed a little. She clearly didn't want to be rude but she was busy and I was making this hard for her, which I told her I understood. 'It's just, if the water's not boiling it doesn't come out right.'

'Okay. Boiling water. Got it.'

'And could you put the tea bag in the water?'

'You can't do that yourself?'

'By the time you bring it out, the water won't be boiling anymore.'

She looked at me with a flicker of irritation, followed by a softening smile. 'Sure, Hon, I live to serve.' She took my menu back and left to fill the order.

'I know I sound like a prat,' I called after her as she walked away.

I only asked because I was desperate. Tepid tea is such a cultural statement in most parts of America (the Boston Tea Party, War of Independence and all) that it almost seems insensitive to ask for it any other way. But let's face it, tea was the innocent bystander in their tale of tax and revenge, whereas it's my go-to comfort food. While others curl up with a bucket of ice cream and re-runs of *Sex and the City*, my existential crises are soothed by a nice cup of tea. And by 'nice', I mean piping hot, strong, and served with a side order of fresh, cold milk … *Damn.*

'Miss,' I called out as the waitress delivered food to another table, 'I forgot – can I have cold milk on the side as well, please?'

The biker craned around to look at me. *Trouble maker.*

Damn straight.

I had no idea what the problem was. Normally I find deserts recalibrating. The wonder of being is rarely as well-expressed as when you're standing on a bedrock plain with the whole world curving away from you to every horizon and nothing between you and the sun. If you want to know how important your problems are, put them in a desert and see how they stack up against eternity.

Mine stacked up fine.

At first I thought my anxiety was because I was travelling alone, but it wasn't that. I like my own company, and the experience in Tuba City would have been different if I had been travelling with anyone else.

I've always had difficulty asking for help. I nearly drowned once because I wouldn't accept help from a board-rider who could see I was caught in a rip. I was about ten years old, and only relented when he insisted *he'd* feel better if I at least held onto the back of his board while he paddled to shore.

Nothing's changed. If I had been travelling with someone else, I would never have asked for help, or at least not in the same way.

I wouldn't have met Laudable. Wouldn't have heard Bernard's stories. Being alone and vulnerable allowed others to be kind. It led me to make some valuable human connections. So that wasn't the problem. I could be grateful for being alone.

It was Monument Valley. My immediate emotion on entering it was one of awe. The closest thing I can compare it to would be Uluru, that solitary beating icon of the ancient Aboriginal community. Monument Valley has dozens of Ulurus scattered over the Colorado Plateau. Monstrous monoliths that dwarf everything near them. Crumbling mesas (the big square ones) and skinny buttes (the towers) strewn across the land like abandoned toys – and yet …

The sheer geography was overwhelming, but I couldn't feel it. Undeniable spirit country flashed by like postcards. The snow-capped mountains, the desert plains, the slow-moving rivers. I stopped, I marvelled, I meditated, but in the end they were just rocks.

Monument Valley is upstream of the Grand Canyon. The Colorado River ate away the soft stone until it hit the bedrock. Wind did the rest, eroding it one mesa and butte at a time. My life was like that. Family was the great Colorado River. Marriage was the wind. Everything I loved was being worn down by time. That mesa, the solid square table, was a monument to my mother carved by the great river. My grandfather was the solitary butte at the end, standing guard even in death. The shady one putting up a fight against time was my father. The five fingers in a mitten? My brothers and sister. But that crumbling one sinking back into dust? The one being eroded by the wind with only a fine land bridge holding it together …

When Pig first admitted that while he still loved me he was no longer 'in love' with me, I fell to the floor. I vomited. I wailed. My certainty in our love was so strong, so arrogant, so fucking smug I had no idea his leaving was even possible. It was as confounding as if Mum had said, 'I won't be your mother any longer. Call me Aunty Joy from now on.' This valley is a monument to all that unstoppable change – to all the impermanence that seems unreal. It will be there long after we're gone, and then it will go too. And when it's gone, the sand will collapse under its own weight and reform as rock, and the cycle will begin again. Dad was dead. Gran was dead. Poppy was dead. My marriage was dead. So it goes.

The waitress brought my beans and salad, and unloaded a mug of black tea with the bag still in it. 'Is that what you were hoping for?' she asked. 'I didn't know if I was supposed to put the milk in or not.'

It was exactly what I wanted. 'That is a thing of beauty,' I said, fishing out the tea bag, wrapping the string around my teaspoon and squashing the bag with the label. 'Thank you so much.'

So, hey, the tea worked its magic. It cleared my head enough for me to see that I had to leave the diner. The biker wouldn't stop staring at me, and his face was going purple with rage. Too much meth I expect, or maybe too much Gulf War, or maybe the whole *tea* thing was too precious for his thick skin. Either way, survival is the better part of paranoia, so I took my Bland Face and moved on.

I was aiming to drive to Mesa Verde to visit the Anasazi ruins that Laudable recommended, but after my fresh cuppa I decided to return with Sue on the way back instead. It felt like the sort of experience that should be shared with love. After consulting Misters Rand and McNally, I decided to visit Loveland in Colorado. I was looking for myself, and that sounded like the sort of place I might go.

And so it was that peace was restored to the kingdom of Betty. We were free to live once more in the fantasy of the real. Elbow out the window. The smell of sagebrush in my hair.

Growing up in Sydney's inner city, I'd always been what you'd call a dreamy kid, but practical – away with the fairies I didn't believe in. As an eight year old I wanted an imaginary friend for Christmas. Santa Claus was dead to me when he failed to deliver. We lived near Kings Cross, the red-light district of Sydney. All the kids I went to school with lived east, we lived west. This meant that most of my friends were adults, and that included the bouncers and prostitutes I passed on my way to the bus, and who waved at me during my blue-dawn rambles around the city on weekends.

I'm the youngest of five kids. There was a big age gap between the first three, but only 18 months between my youngest brother and I – so we were best friends growing up. During the school holidays, Mum would deposit us along with all our cousins at her parents' place. Her mother, Gran, had the sort of heart condition that meant she had to sit in her chair smoking Viscount cigarettes all day. (Prescribed by doctors in the 1920s.) My granddad, Poppy, was an energetic man, who was always out in the garage 'inventing' things. He'd been a newsreel cameraman in the days before TV and had some great stories, including one about tying himself to the wing of Charles Kingsford Smith's aeroplane to get an aerial shot, and discovering g-forces first hand.

On those holidays Poppy would deliver us kids sweet tea in bed before breakfast. It was an unimaginable treat, served in mismatched china cups, with two plain biscuits in the saucer.

I don't know if it's an Australian tradition, but delivering the morning cuppa runs strong in our family. Dad managed to keep Mum for thirty years by bringing her tea in bed before she went to work each morning. In the late 70s hers arrived in mugs with bright blue and yellow daisies on them.

My Aunty Penny (her red hair shiny like minted copper) loved her black tea 'weak as gnat's pee'. I was shocked because it was the only weak thing about her. In my imagination (some may say memory) dapper Uncle Brian delivered her tea in Marimekko cups with psychedelic poppies on them.

One of my first paid jobs was as personal assistant to my friend's father, Dick. He owned a coffee plantation in New Guinea, but I don't remember him ever drinking coffee. Instead, he introduced me to tea brewed super strong and super fast so that it had kick without bitterness.

Kick without Bitterness. I hope they say that about me one day.

Pig was a tea drinker (strong, milky, two sugars). His morning cuppa was the thing I missed the longest after he left. I found ways to do his half of everything else. When I cooked dinner, I'd freeze two portions so 'he' could cook every other night. I got a cleaner to do his half of the housework. I even bought myself flowers, but delivering myself a cup of tea in bed thwarted me until my friend Amanda bought me a Teasmade™. *Oh!* What a shining light of friendship when someone loves you so well. It was an original from the late 1930s with a ceramic pot and reading lamps on each side of an art deco clock face. I loved the chrome Goblin electric kettle out the back. Plug it in, set the alarm, and wake to the sound of boiling water pouring into the teapot.

The sun was setting when I left the truck stop. Cherubic clouds on the horizon marked the start of the Rocky Mountains. For a couple of hours, the dark blue sky spread from the centre until everything was black and it was night time. The road started to rise into the foothills.

After six hours, it was pitch black and I was on a steeply rising winding road. Small nocturnal animals came out in search of food, sometimes unannounced. Driving was becoming stressful. I felt lost. I was lost. I must have been lost.

How can you find yourself if you're not lost?

That thought made me laugh with its sharp thwack of epiphany. *If you're not going anywhere, then you can't get lost. If you're not lost, then you're found.* I found myself on the road to Loveland. It felt so good, I decided to give up any idea of a destination and stop for the night at the next place that was open.

It was around midnight when I pulled into Indian Springs, a mountain town built around a natural hot spa. The hotel was once grand, but now had a lunatic air about it. I didn't let any of that deter me from booking in.

The kid on reception handed me my keys. 'That one's for your room,' he said, 'and that's for the hot springs.'

It didn't make sense at first. They were giving me keys to the springs? 'I can go now? In the middle of the night?'

'Yes, ma'am. They're open twenty-four hours. Would you like a spare towel?'

'I would, I really would.' I took the towel and went straight down to the spa, expecting to be the only one bathing this late.

While the resort was in a state of nouveau-poor decay, the actual baths were pristine. They were set in a hundred-year-old mining shaft which had flooded a century ago. The walls were covered in thick, natural, dark brown moss – richer and more delicate than any wallpaper. The water was crystal clear and hot, almost boiling in places. And it was deep, well over my head, as I the descended the steps and embraced her watery arms.

There was mandatory nudity in the ladies' baths I shared with two other sucked, skinny, tense-looking white women. We draped ourselves on the cool, slippery surface of the white-tiled shelves spread around the alcoves. Without my glasses, the scene was a sensuous fusion of steam and rock and soft pink bodies. After a long drive, it was a total reward to succumb to the heat and humidity. To steep in my own fantasy of having everything taken out of my control.

Naked, I inhaled, sighed and floated away.

GOD DRIVES A BIG SHINY TRUCK

I woke up with the sort of heavy head that comes from sleeping with wet hair. It took a moment to remember where I was, and when I did, I was struck with the unshakeable feeling that I was utterly nowhere.

There wasn't a clock in the room, nor sunlight. Outside, a dank mossy wall was reflecting cool, but whether it was morning cool or afternoon cool was impossible to tell. The closest time reading I could get was 1945. The room was decorated with heavy dark furniture. There were muffled sounds of people walking distant corridors and the stale smell of old smokers. It wouldn't have surprised me to discover I was in a time warp.

Which turned out to be sort of true. Idaho Springs, the town next door, was a ridiculously cute cowboy toy-town smeared in time from the 1800s to the 1950s. Betty was wildly out of place next to the wide wooden verandas and hitching posts on Main Street. A barber's chair peeked from behind a red and white pole. Across the road, swinging bar-room doors waited to eject unruly patrons. A shopkeeper leaned in his doorway, dragging on a cigarette. A posse was due any moment. It wasn't a ghost town, but one haunted by economic rationalism and nostalgia.

Realistically I should've known I wasn't in the best of moods. I was disoriented. I hadn't eaten since the afternoon before. I had dropped my bundle and slept so deeply I didn't even know how to begin picking it up. All in all, an uncomfortable experience that I might've recognised as grief.

I was too late for breakfast at the spa and too early for lunch in town. If I had found a parking spot outside a cafe I would have stopped for a juice or something. Instead, in a flagrant fit of self-destructive behaviour, I barrelled out of town without so much as a grit between me and the rest of the day.

Ascending the winding road into the Rocky Mountain Park with neither destination nor breakfast was surreal. The sunny mountain tops were thick with snow in the middle of summer. My un-fed head was thick with nebulous irritation.

I became so completely absorbed by the quest to find hash browns and tea that I passed through the most achingly beautiful canyons (made of sheer granite hundreds of feet high) with only the vaguest acknowledgment of their grace.

I didn't admire the hundreds of colourful cyclists blocking the road.

I didn't admire the alpine meadows, nor the small groups of deer roaming in them.

I didn't marvel that I could have sung up the landscape to almost any John Denver song.

What I did was tailgate the chrome-plated truck in front of me. A bloody huge blockade travelling the curling road at perfectly the wrong speed. In America they have a 'turn out' rule. If you're driving with more than six cars behind you, you're obliged by law to slow down into a designated asphalt eddy and let everyone pass. There were no eddies in this alpine backwater. My frustration reached my accelerator foot, which tapped with agitation. My hungry head was thumping in time to the syncopating engine. I began shouting. Screaming. Wailing. Driving as close to the truck's bumper bar as was dangerously possible. The collapse of my marriage, the car breaking down, missing breakfast, being held back from driving as fast as I liked on an alpine road – it all bubbled over into idiotic rage.

'Why are you stopping me?' I shouted to no one. 'Where's my reward for action?'

No sooner were the magical words out, than the world opened up. With a slim glimmer of opportunity I accelerated to overtake the truck on the corner.

But no.

The fuming behemoth accelerated too. I was now travelling dangerously fast and insanely close as I pulled into the oncoming lane. With perverse insight, the truck *also* manoeuvred into the oncoming lane. Howling like a shrew, I slipped back behind the truck – as an instantaneous blast of cold air from an oncoming pantechnicon blew through Betty's windows.

My mouth ovalled into terror. I saw fear on the driver's face behind me. I slowed down.

Fine. Sure. Yes. I see that. Sun, meadow, Rocky Mountain, *Hi!*

Hash browns and tea are not worth dying for. Little pookie yellow flowers were dotting the future.

Pig's not worth dying for. The grassy meadows gave way to treeless snowfields as one by one the other drivers overtook or veered away.

Slow. Smooth. Grace. Know when you're being saved.

By the time I reached truck driver heaven, I was alone in a mountain lea with a diner twinkling like an ad for American values. A large flag flapped red, white and blue in the cloudless sky. Soft fairy lights winked in the snow-encrusted wall. Through the large picture window, a lone woman stared desolately out into the wilderness.

A red neon sign flashed, *Open,* but her face was closed and stained with tears.

She picked up some plates and moved away as I pushed through the door. Inside was fuggy and alive with the sound of *Wheel of Fortune.* A small child wandered from the TV as I took the woman's place in the window.

She returned some minutes later, blowing her nose. Terry would be my sad little waitress today. She had an ageless face – somewhere between high school and exhaustion.

'Sorry about that,' she said handing me the menu. 'I've worked two straight weeks and I don't believe this snow's ever going to stop. What can I get for you?'

'Am I too late for breakfast?'

'It's the middle of summer and we're still doing winter, may as well do breakfast too.'

'Then I'll have everything you've got: eggs, bacon, hash browns – the works. I nearly killed myself driving on an empty stomach.'

'Well that's no good. You need a trucker flask.' She went and came back with a wide-mouthed thermos. 'I'll fill it up with soup, throw in some bread and butter. You like that?'

It was my turn to well up. If I was stuck, Terry was snow-bound, and still she could reach out and show compassion. 'I really would, thank you.'

Women amaze me – family, friends, waitresses. I love belonging to this tribe. I love their ability to embrace and endure, to scoop up small broken things and fix them with food, wine and love. All over the world I received kindness from them, frequently with a great big side order of belly laughs. Like today, I was blessed in the mess.

Terry's hash browns and eggs were sublime. I ate. I drank. I left a large tip. I left feeling lucky. I had a big red car and a God who drove a shiny truck. Terry had a job which ended in spring, in a world of perpetual winter.

I slipped Sheila Chandra into the CD player and wove off into a magical, well-fuelled future.

If any good was to come from this breakup, it was that I knew how to be loved. That may sound absurd after being dumped and everything, but apart from the pitiful end, our relationship had been kind and loving. The most stressful thing for us as a couple had been doing IVF – although now that I see it written like that, I realise the infertility was worse.

Technically, it was all my fault.

A series of ectopic pregnancies resulted in the catastrophic loss of my fallopian tubes. Not only was that transcendently painful, but it came with a real risk of death by septicaemia. Ectopic pregnancies (pregnancy outside the womb) are rare, but if you've had one you're likely to have another. Having three was absurd, and only possible because of advances in micro-surgery. My doctor was able to repair the second tube the first time, but I lost them both in the end.

I think it's because women give birth that no major religion has ever been started by one. It's not just the magic of creation – that whole ten-toed-miracle-of-life thing – it's also the majesty of being and nothingness. *If God is within, why look for 'him' elsewhere?* After the birth of her first son, my friend Michele was surprised to discover the depth of her love for this brand new infant. She recognised the flip-side immediately. 'I've made something that can really hurt me,' she said. From the minute a child is born, the worst imaginable pain is them no longer existing. It's not only a death of the real, it's a death of all possible futures, and that's the pain of infertility – the death of all possible futures.

Fertility treatments like surrogacy, egg donation and IVF are miraculous, but they're also a black market in hope. Don't get me wrong, my respect for the whole medical team who helped us is unwavering. The only thing that separated them from God was their ability to create new life in me. We did eight full cycles, and more with frozen embryos. The process devastated my health, our finances and ultimately the marriage, because let's face it, there's nothing sexy about having a team of surgeons in bed with you.

In an attempt to assert some sort of control I tried every complementary therapy I could find: diet, exercise, psychoanalysis, hypnotherapy, aromatherapy, Chinese herbs, Bach flowers, acupuncture, reiki, tai chi, meditation, stress management, posture realignment. I read books on fertility, grieving, finding the child within, *The Cinderella Complex*, *The Road Less Travelled*, *Love Your Disease*, *Adult Children of Alcoholics* and *The Art of War*. As I became desperate, *Understanding the Midlife Crisis* and (at my lowest ebb) *How to Keep Your Man Monogamous*.

I found it difficult to stop doing the IVF when so many friends succeeded – and frequently succeeded at the point when they'd given up hope. Ultimately I was willing to try anything, including adoption. I'll spare you the full spit of bitter chips about that, but let's say I developed an intense hatred of social workers after hearing one of them refer to me at a parent preparation meeting by saying, 'Isn't she that chick off TV?'

Adoption didn't work either – unless it was supposed to weed out the unwilling. During our final 'induction' we were told we could expect to have a baby within eighteen months. A week later Pig announced he no longer believed in us as a couple, and that was it for me and kids.

Several hundred miles had lapsed as I detoured from back road to back road, until I was on a dirt track overlooking a wide grassy plain sprinkled with small farmhouses, smoke wafting from their chimneys like so many happy campers. Peter Gabriel was singing 'Washing of the Water' on the radio. It was the perfect requiem for our lost love. I turned up the music and sang along.

When the song finished, I cried until the car might rust. I know it's just pheromones coming down in the shower, but I love a good cry. That marvellous sense of dehydration. Hazy and woolly ebb in as urgency ebbs out.

I fossicked around and found the new thermos. Removing the lid revealed chicken noodle soup with real bits of chicken. Terry was like a Russian doll of love: at each new layer – the breakfast, the thermos, the tea, the soup – her kindness was freshly received.

I wouldn't get far if I stayed on the shoulder of Route 85 feeling sorry for myself. I consulted the road atlas and found I was still in Colorado, just south of Cheyenne in Wyoming. To the right of it, like an open palm on the map, were the grassy plains of Nebraska, with the Interstate 80 unfurling like an elegant finger, beckoning me into the green belly of middle America.

The great American prairie was just as advertised: hour after serene hour of nothing but an endless, hypnotic, undulating paddock. A vast ocean of grass. This was a land to get lost in. Without my noticing, without encouragement, Betty surged ahead – a wild filly finding her head. We'd be in Connecticut with Pipi in no time.

I saw the shiny black Mustang with fancy police logo speeding in the opposite direction. By the time he'd turned around and clocked me, I had slowed to five clicks off the limit, but he pulled me over anyway.

Ah yes, the boys love Betty.

A friend had warned me that in the event of such an unhappy turn, not to reach for my licence because the police might shoot me, thinking I was reaching for a gun. With this in mind, I turned off the engine and waited. But the car had electric windows, so when the officer approached I needed to re-start the engine to wind them down. That's when he drew his gun, thinking I was making a run for it. I put my hands in the air and pointed down to Betty's window button. He lowered his gun.

Generally speaking, there's plenty of goodwill for the Aussie accent. I think it sounds posh to Americans, and trustworthy, so I hoiked my vowels up into my nose, 'Moi, moi, moi, moi.'

'G'day, officer. You'll never sell ice cream at that speed.' *Ha ha ha.* Oh, look at me, flirting.

'Are you aware of how fast you were going?'

'Well, sir, I was doing 65 before overtaking the truck, so 75? That's not too bad is it?'

I was banking on being within ten clicks of the speed limit. Admitting to five seemed like hedging my bets but, in retrospect, if the officer had never met an Australian before, I probably sounded like a speed freak with a speech impediment. He asked to see my licence and registration.

I showed a great deal of leg while reaching into the back to find my paperwork. 'I like your car,' said shameless me. 'Is it special issue? Looks like a Maserati.'

Constable Morris was impervious to my lady chicanery. He booked me for not having a front licence plate.

'But, officer,' I whined, 'the car never had one. There's not even a space for it. I don't think that's even a law in California.'

'It's the law in Nebraska,' he said, ripping off a crisp new citation.

'But officer, I'm passing through. I'll only be here for a couple more miles. How wide is Nebraska anyway?'

Nothing. He gave me a fortnight to repair the problem. 'Get a front licence plate and return the citation signed by a police officer to prove you've done so. If not, we'll issue a warrant for your arrest.'

Oooh, was I mad. Firstly, he was being bloody spiteful. Secondly, I'd seen shows like *Cops*. If I got pulled over for some other misdemeanour (say, driving in Louisiana with an open container of alcohol on the back seat) they'd be able to send me down the river for traffic violations in Nebraska.

Utter bastardry.

That citation took hours to clear up. Weeks later, I went to the Department of Motor Vehicles in Norwalk, the capital of Connecticut, to get a new licence plate (which I intended to wear on my passenger sun visor) but they told me that I had to go to the DMV in California. *Man!* That was ten days' drive away.

I rang the DMV in California, but they told me I didn't need a licence plate. In the end, I put on a pretty, virginal white dress and a large straw hat. I parked Betty two blocks away and went to the Bridgeport Police station to confess everything.

Sergeant Johansson was cute. I mean, so cute I considered telling him I had an outstanding warrant in Nebraska and must be locked away forever. But I didn't. He had obscenely handsome blue eyes which didn't blink as I told my story. My whole story – about Pig, about Betty, about driving across America. I told him about the licence plate and the DMV and everything.

Without taking his eyes off me he signed the citation, saying, 'That's the strangest story I ever heard.'

Damned Aussie accent. Probably hadn't understood a word.

In Nebraska, I pulled back onto the freeway with a thumping sugar low and a crisp new hundred-dollar citation. The next exit was a quirky truck stop raised high on a manmade hill. I turned in to take stock of my situation. From high on that hill one thing was clear,

Nebraska was flat. Damn flat. No wonder it's sometimes called the 'Badlands'.

This exit was unusual in that it had character. Most 'service plazas' were franchised satellite towns (population: zero) made up of petrol stations, diners and chain motels – Unocal, Denny's and Motel 6. This one had a mom and pop feel, with wagon wheel décor.

Poring over the chilli beans and road maps, I observed that the exits were numbered from east to west, from state border to state border. This exit, 48, was forty-eight miles to the western border. The last exit was 454, so there was – *crap*, 415 miles left in Nebraska. I could either travel the surgical scar that was the Interstate 80 or turn off and take Highway 30, which ran parallel. That route was laced with country towns which sounded pretty, like they had their heyday in the thirties: Potter, Rownson, Colton, Lodgepole, Kimball. Betty and I could reconnect with the ideals of Route 66 and personally link some Main Streets of America. There were 12 more miles of Interstate 80 before I could turn off and take things gently, stay on the speed limit, watch the country slip by.

Across the plain a magnificent thunderhead was billowing on the horizon. It had a fiery charisma that seemed like a metaphor for my future. Forgetting I was in tornado country, I aimed Betty at that mighty cumulonimbus and set off for the next exit.

Within minutes, I was engulfed by a wind-driven sleet storm that sent Betty skidding like a dog on lino. The sodding LA roadcar didn't even bother pretending to grip as she was buffeted first into one lane, then another. Ice reduced my visibility to nil, common sense reduced my speed to 30. It was terrifying. Howling road trains overtook, spraying slushy plumes over the car. Finally I stopped on the shoulder of the freeway and waited for the storm to pass. There I noticed a handful of bison (aka buffalo) standing with their backs to the rain. I wound down the window and shouted, 'Roam, you bastards!'

The storm passed as quickly as it started. I imagine the locals thought it was a mere summer squall, but I was glad to be finally on the backstreets of middle America, where things were more sedate.

It's amazing how many things can kill you in this life, and how few do. Ectopic pregnancies didn't kill me. The truck didn't kill me. The tornado didn't kill me. My marriage wouldn't kill me. I wouldn't let it. I got a great quote from *Conan the Barbarian*: 'That which does not kill you, makes you stronger.' Seems Friedrich Nietzsche may have said it first, but that doesn't make it less true.

As part of my fertility treatment I'd done a lot of therapy and released a lot of demons. In those sessions, my father's alcoholism featured quite heavily, and how it ruined every holiday. Him driving home drunk in the VW Beetle with his cigarette ash blinding us kids in the back. There was one memorable time when he was sick of my whining and put me out of the car and drove off. I must have been six. Mum was steaming mad when they picked me up again. It was years before I realised it wasn't me she was angry with.

Like a lot of children of alcoholics, I suffered terrible anxiety. Would Good Dad or Bad Dad be on the verandah when I got home from school? Would my mother be harmed in the fight they were having? Once he fell down the stairs at home and passed out at the bottom, upside down unconscious. Mum checked his pulse and left him there. Later, my brother and I arrived home with a friend who, on seeing Dad, said, 'Oh, we have one of those at home.'

Until I met Pig, it never occurred to me that life could be different. That fathers could be different. That marriage could be different. Pig was different. He supported me through our attempts at fertility. He wept with my mother when I lost the babies. He worked hard and creatively and gave me my head to do the same, or not. Throughout it all he was my equal and my better half in love. He lost a lot, too, loving me.

The sun had long set when I realised I'd driven through yet another town that would be okay to stay in. I turned around and drove back through it again. Yeah, heaps of motels. As I slowed down to compare them, it became clear they were filling up. By the time I exited for the third time there was only one choice left, the Lazy K Motel: *twenty-two units, phone, colour cable TV, A/C, heated pool, coin-op laundry on premises and playground for kiddies.*

Only, *What the hell's a Lazy K?*

So I woke up in Ogallala, Nebraska. If Indian Springs was utterly nowhere, Ogallala was slightly east of it. That doesn't mean it was unattractive. It had retro charm in all senses of the word. The Prairie Cinema, the wide roads, the dressmaking shops, the checked shirts and hipster facial hair on the local farmers. It was all achingly old-school in a perfectly upright way.

I cruised Main Street looking for postcards. I bought four thirty-nine cent Jac-o-net hairnets instead, because I liked the 50s graphics on the packets. *Regular size, light brown, durable, invisible.* The perfect snapshot of Nebraska – and superlight, so cheap to post home.

The day was turning into some kind of perfect. It was crisp, blue and serene and so was I as I eased into the local diner (excellent hash browns and above average tea) and started planning my route for the day.

Because I wasn't yet fluent in Rand McNally, I booked a room in an Amish town called Amana, in Iowa, which was 24 inches away. This was twice as many inches as I had driven on the other days, but I figured if I made no stops, I could be there in ten or so hours.

Driving through the Badlands of middle America, I discovered the creative mind is like a cattle dog – you have to work it or you'll come home and find it's eaten the couch. Here, with no one but Betty for reason, my creative mind was sniffing around some pretty strange piles of poo:

Why don't we put hair conditioner on our pubes?

Do men think of tampons when they use tea bags?

Wouldn't it be embarrassing if you had a car accident while picking your nose, and pushed your finger into your brain?

Wouldn't it be great to set a reality show like Cops *out here where nothing ever happens?* We see cops catch up on their filing. Ed eats a pie.

Who paints the road pictures? Who designs the danger deer, the firemen wearing wee hats, the snow skidoos and the slow children – that enormous girl holding the hand of that proportionally peculiar boy?

I spent 40 miles trying to remember the name of 'Nessun Dorma'. I knew 'Ti Amo' was wrong. If only I could think of 'Pavarotti', I might remember the song, but it hovered out of reach on the edge of consciousness. *Come on, Sheridan, the fat guy with the hankie.*

One rotation of my music then I'd flick through the radio stations. Unbridled excitement was finding NPR (National Public Radio) – community-funded entertainment at its world best – varied, arcane and diverting, like travelling with an erudite friend. NPR was syndicated through regional radio stations so you'd never be certain what (or if) you'd find: international news, poetry, science. Happiness was hearing the words, 'This is Linda Wertheimer for *All Things Considered*,' and knowing you were in safe hands.

Prior to leaving LA, a colleague recommended listening to Garrison Keillor's *A Prairie Home Companion,* a compendium of big stories from small lives – home-town idiosyncrasies and the mixed nuts of everyday life. The show was set in Minnesota, but listening to it as I drove through the great prairieland of Nebraska invoked the world of Norwegian immigrants with their tall trees and flat vowels.

Fiddling with the fine tuning on Betty's stereo, local stations faded in and out as though they were being broadcast from underwater. Sometimes the sound would become crystal clear, and for an hour or so I'd listen to a local enthusiast discussing his record collection, or a 'swap-meet of the air' might result in the exchange of a couch for a club chair. Most often though it was the long, slow pain of white man's blues – country and western music.

Now I'm not prejudiced against the twang. Poppy was friends with Smoky Dawson and Chad Morgan, entertainers whose comedy hits, like their teeth, were cultural icons of my youth. I consider Lee Marvin's version of 'Wand'rin' Star' a classic, and Peter Allen's 'Tenterfield Saddler' brings me to tears every time. But dear God! Wall to wall lonesome cowboys yodelling their deepest feelings can start to grind your gears after a few hundred miles.

'You ain't so good looking since I quit drinking' was funny the first few times, but eventually the adolescent keening caused me to shout, 'Buck the fuck up,' at the radio. It's bad enough being dumped without having the whole thing underscored by crappy lyrics – 'take the "L" out of lover and it's over'? Take the 'S' out of stupid, it's still stupid.

My progress wasn't as fast as I expected. I drove and drove and drove but didn't get anywhere. After 12 hours I finally stopped for dinner and had a good look at my road atlas. It was then I discovered that the map scales were different from page to page. My 24 inches translated to nearly 700 miles. I'd be lucky to get to Amana before morning.

I went back onto the Interstate 80, and made a second horrible discovery. At night, the freeways of America are terrifying, with neither cat's eyes nor reflective highway paint to mark the interstate lanes and edges.

Worse, as the lights go out over middle America, the freeways are invaded by perambulating skyscrapers – awesomely huge trucks that bowl down on you at a thousand miles an hour. They have enormous headlights a hundred feet wide, and belch smoke from their chimneys as their foghorns wail to each other in the darkness.

Truck drivers keep their vehicles in flying formation so they can save petrol by being dragged along in each other's slipstreams. You haven't lived (or nearly died) until you've been stuck in a low-slung Chevy Camaro between three 'road trains' and a cement divider – barrelling down a highway together at 70 miles an hour in the dark.

At one point some poor defenceless animal about the size of a two year old wandered onto the road. I think it was a porcupine. All I saw was its bloodied body being spat out from under the truck in front, hitting Betty's pointy nose and bouncing off my windscreen. In my rear-vision mirror I saw the bloodied mass being consumed by the truck behind me.

It was ghastly. The whole thing was so brutal I started to scream – and scream. *What is this life? Where is my husband? Where are my babies? Where is the sense in any of it?* I lost it for a while. The trucks were so loud and frightening – it was satisfying to wail.

I didn't imagine anyone could hear me. I could barely hear myself over the trucks' crunching gears and stereophonic ten-tonne engines. But in this distracted scream, the driving formation began to ease. The truck in front and the truck next to me pulled away. The one behind accelerated, then overtook. It took the place of the truck in front of me.

I was now driving in a blind, screaming tantrum. What had

started with a bloodied porcupine had been absorbed into a demented state of unfocused grief and rage. *What did it matter if I drove and sang, or drove and laughed, or drove and screamed and screamed and screamed?*

I was inching closer to the truck in front – still crying, but coming down a note or two as I tried to absorb what the truck was doing. He seemed to be slowing, so I slowed. I stopped screaming. With that flash of girly annoyance – *Oh, what now?*

I looked at my speedometer: 80 miles an hour and slowing. The truck in front was slowing. We were both slowing down. *How fast had I been going?*

We settled around 50 miles per hour and drove like that for a while. He pulled ahead but held the speed so there were about five car lengths between us. It was pleasant. I could see what was happening on the road ahead by following his tail lights.

After about 45 minutes, he blew his horn and accelerated away from me.

He blew his horn.

Do you know how biblical that is? He blew his horn, and yea verily it came unto me that I had been blessed by an act of great kindness. A deliberate, premeditated, unremarked, unthanked act of decency and thoughtfulness.

I don't know how badly I was driving, but a complete stranger found me in pain and pulled in front for the express purpose of helping get my car back under control, like I was a distressed rider on a runaway horse.

For the second time in as many days, my sorry arse had been saved by an unknown truck driver. Someone should build them a monument.

↔

I finally limped, hoarse-throated into the Amish town of Amana at 3am. Even in the dark I could see it was the cutest little guest house fashioned out of a family home. The owners had left the back door open for me, with a welcoming note and my room key taped to the handle. It was adorable. Why bother with a key?

My room at the Die Heimat Country Inn was a symphony in simplicity. White hand-quilted Amish bedspread. Hand-hewn wooden bed. Plain white walls. Wooden roof. Oddly shaped room. There was a glass of milk and homemade shortbread in the shape of a heart on the side table. Maybe I had crashed and this was heaven.

I took a long hot shower and then sat up in bed, calmly eating my 'cookies and milk', thinking how weird life had become. My personality was completely out of kilter. Sometimes I felt like me, then I'd vacillate into hysterical demented abandonment. I was glad to be travelling alone. At least I didn't have to hide this beast which kept breaking out of me.

The shortbread was excellent. Half of the heart was coated in chocolate, which I picked off with my teeth. Better yet, when I bit the shortbread then took a sip of the milk, I could mix them together in my mouth by going *ziwoog, ziwoog, ziwoog*.

I don't think the madness was all mine. Some of it was this country, which has a dog whistle of brutality ringing through it – the guns, the violence, the sensationalism. But then that's counterpointed by the grace and grandeur of the landscape, the natural kindness of the average person, and the astonishing magnitude of the continent.

A spiritual calm washed over me.

The highway was a million light years away. The world was silent, except for the sighing of a nearby pine tree. Moving my feet under the sheets released the clean smell of sunshine. Until now my dominant emotion had been tension. The personal tension about my relationship and the stress of the driving, but something else as well. The same tension that informed the repeated question, 'Aren't you afraid you'll be murdered?' This is the dog-whistle weirdness that pervades this place.

Do all Americans have first-hand experience of violence to get this mindset, or is it media based? I mean, how many adrenaline-packed, reality shows can you watch before you start to think that is life? How many news shows and *CSIs* does it take before you believe you're going to die in a blaze of unpredictable violence?

This isn't a purely American phenomenon, but it may be an American invention. We no longer have rituals for coping with death. Our society has become so consumer-youth-fun-based that we never even talk about it in a meaningful way. Death, once the domain of the church, has been sidelined along with our declining faith. Psychotherapy may offer consolation or counselling, but as long as social responses fail to meet our personal experiences, death will remain a frightening and fascinating taboo.

As with sex in Victorian times, curiosity and fear meet repression, and a taboo is turned into pornography. News and current affairs are the pornography of death. We turn them on and our whole culture slows down to check the daily roadkill, and it's frightening people in a deeply disturbing and paralysing way.

You know what started this thought? For the first time since I got to this country, I felt completely safe. The Amish seem to have created a media shadow – one of those places where television doesn't get a good reception. Maybe it was the cookies and milk talking, but I felt safe driving through Amana. I felt safe entering the house. And there in my bed, I felt serenely and perfectly safe to sleep. It was such a glorious indulgence, I didn't put it off for a moment more.

7

THE BADLANDS

One of my personal missions in America was to find God. Not necessarily in a religious sense, although I was open to any epiphany that might strike me on the road to Damascus (which, being located 55 miles south east of Cleveland, would be a perfectly viable detour). No, the particular God I sought was more of the American sideshow variety. That leathery old Calvinist with his pitchfork and dour wife were high on my hit list, as was the snappily dressed black preacher with a great gospel choir.

Part of my rationale for choosing Amana (a million light years ago when 24 inches rolled out like a stroll on the Parkway) was that it was knee-deep in Amish country, the handcrafted buckle of America's Bible Belt.

In reality, that religious demographic accessory is ten states wide and five states deep, but this part of the country was hewn out of history by nuggetty, disenfranchised Quakers (Shakers, Ravers, Mennonites, Baptists and their husbands). On a sunny summer's morning after a glorious night's sleep, it was easy to believe I was truly in God's country, and it was only as wide as the Interstate 80.

My rather ad hoc plan was to drive around until I found a church with a couple of buggies hitched outside – a sure sign, I figured, that some old-order Anabaptist hallelujah was not far away.

By the time I stumbled out of bed and out of the shower it was well past 10.30. Around these parts Yahweh carries a clock and frowns on slackers. Or so said the kind man at reception. I'd be lucky if I could rustle up a Billy Graham cracker this late, much less a morning church service. I'd have to set my sights on a more casual God.

Hunched over more shortbread and tea (delivered by the owner's wife because everything else was 'off') I pulled out my own good book, the now dog-eared Rand McNally, to see if there were any other Great American Icons between me and Chicago. And there she was, winking at me with the little green dots which spell 'scenic'. The great Mississippi River. *M. I. Double S. I. Double S. I. Double P. I.* I learned to spell that at school and by God I was going to see something I'd spent that long spelling. Somewhere between Muscatine and Buffalo there'd be breakfast, lunch, or salvation.

Setting out with Betty, I resolved to let go of my anger and grief. All I was achieving with my pent-up hurt was a one-way ticket to a bad mental state. Frankly, I didn't want to go there anymore. I filled my thermos, bought a bag of shortbread biscuits and drove into the day feeling wise.

Back in the 1950s, psychiatrist Elisabeth Kübler-Ross outlined the stages of grief as Anger, Bargaining, Denial, something, something, something. I couldn't remember what the others were. Sneezy, Dopey and Doc, perhaps? There's no doubt I was experiencing Grief, but attempting to square up to my feelings and place them 'with the people and in the places where they belong' was exhausting. It'd be so much better if we could check the stages off like a to-do list. Anger, Bargaining, Castration, Regret.

I know, I know, life doesn't work like that. Instead, we're left alone to bounce around in grotesque splurges of emotion. Yesterday was Anger (Rage, Fury, Insanity, Tears). Today I was due for a little Bargaining. *But oh! Would you look at that.* The sky was blue and the clouds were fluffy. No. This day was perfect for Denial.

The dust of Amana had barely blown off Betty's bonnet before the epiphany of the Midwest was rendered to me in all its simple glory. Nothing much matters when you have a belly full of shortbread and milk.

I never did find the church and buggies. It turns out the Amish don't actually go to 'church'. They have autonomous congregations who meet in members' homes. When a congregation gets above seventy-five people they split and form a new one. But, hey! Betty was my home and I was an autonomous congregation of one, so maybe I was filled with the Amish spirit after all.

It was in this state of ecstasy (the 'Miracle of Shortbread') that I managed to somehow miss Muscatine, my first proposed breakfast destination. Instead I was on back roads and dirt tracks, marvelling at the rich farmland neatly carved out of rolling plains, with wooden fences and large, leafy windbreaks which smacked of generations of hard work and abstinence.

The asphalt ebbed and flowed. I found myself travelling gingerly down neatly graded dirt roads and private laneways. As I came over one small hillock, my way was blocked by a family of ten, mainly adolescent-looking bison. Up close they're big buggers, bigger than bulls but shaggy like a mammoth. I got out of the car to see what would happen, but the largest one looked at me with intense rhetorical eyes that asked, 'You are not serious?'

What a wise old bison. I quietly got back into the car and slowly reversed away.

The unfolding miles revealed scores of exquisitely ordered homesteads. Each had a hand-hewn quality which reflected a personality as demure as the community's reputation. Large, rambling white farmhouses shrouded in English trees, with symmetrical red barns that looked like a child's drawing.

I blipped through West Liberty, wondering if I would ever come to Liberty. I didn't. Nearing the river, the farms got smaller. The rhythm of passing white houses and red barns became faster. White House. Red Barn. White House. Red Barn. Like a meditation. My mind began to wander. Why house? Why barn? Why white? Why red? *Maybe the Amish paint them different colours so they don't sleep with the sheep when they come home drunk.* That sad little joke amused me all the way to Toolesboro, where I pulled up at the Bait and Bullet shop, the first place open in 91 miles. Maybe they'd have a glass of lemonade for a hypoglycaemic traveller in need of a sugar hard-on.

Is it just me, or do you ever wonder where in God's name you've placed your brain? They sold Bait, and they sold Bullets.

The dust-encrusted flyscreen slammed behind me, and three pinched male faces looked up through the gloom with studied nonchalance. My guess is they had already checked Betty out, and now the crazy looking guy behind the counter had a shotgun pointed at me through the plywood. You know, in case I was a drug runner from *Cal-eye-forn-eye-ay.* Okay, that's paranoia talking, but my instincts had little alarm bells ringing like Tinkerbell on speed. 'Don't suppose you have any food, do you?'

'No, lady,' said the gun-toting owner, 'we have bait, and we have bullets.'

'And beer,' added the customer to his left, 'you also have beer.'

From where I was standing, I could see a colourful array of handmade fishing flies in the dusty glass case. Maybe this was a workshop for fly fishermen. Maybe if I'd stopped longer I'd have discovered a unique artform or contraband lemonade being consumed in brown paper bags under the counter. But we'll never know, because the third guy (the one who hadn't said anything yet) had really bad body language. He was walking towards me for no apparent reason.

Betty and I squealed a hasty retreat in a dramatic spray of dust and gravel, to the sound of brown dogs barking from the back of their pickup trucks.

Back on the road, I felt I'd overreacted. Rationally speaking, you wouldn't get away with much in Toolesboro. It's not like there was a restaurant, bar or nightclub within a hundred miles on which you could cast suspicion. No, they were merely three bored locals who liked to shoot fish, because …

… around the next corner there she was – the empress of high-school geography. The third-longest river in the world. Old Man River? Give me a break. The Mississippi's a woman, wide-hipped and reassuring. The dowager duchess of a nation, lazing around in a majestic arc.

Food could wait. For the moment something much more precious was flowing through me. Something like silence, but softer. Peace, maybe. Intransigence? Permanence? Something which is always changing but always the same. The rhythm of the water as it flowed between the trees and the stones. The gentle counterpoint of dragonflies and plopping fish. What would they be? Trout? Catfish? It was a symphony in sigh.

A barge carrying coal was floating downstream. Old-fashioned smoke rings blew through a small stovepipe poking out the cabin roof. A nation flowed on this, the original American highway. Homewares, farm produce, Mississippi gamblers, Huckleberry Finn. A passage to freedom, a passage to slavery, all shunted along her brown enigma.

The passing coal barge blew its whistle. How many generations have heard that sound? Maybe I should wade out into her deep, wide embrace. Be cleansed of my rage, and washed anew.

Ah, there he is again – that silent presence, that loving force, that spent energy.

I heard somewhere that every cell in your body is regenerated over seven years. I've forgotten which ones take the longest – spinal cord, maybe? Liver? Some parts are fresh every couple of days, others take years. Since Pig and I had been together my whole body has completely reinvented itself. There wasn't a single cell in me that hadn't known his touch, his smell. How long before he's passed from me, before he's gone with the flow?

I waded out into the river and sank down into her muddy arms, the cool, fresh water combing my hair out into a fan. *I am now part Mississippi.* There's no point fighting the tide when you're part of the third-longest river in the world.

Among the tips and contacts I was given in LA were some phone numbers for friendly people who might give me a meal or put me up for the night. One was in Chicago, so I cracked it open and dialled it. When the soon-to-be friend didn't answer, I left a message and booked myself into the pleasant-sounding Mansion Youth Hostel, 'close to town on the south side of the city'. Having worked all my life, I'd missed the gap-year-shared-accommodation-backpacking thing. By booking into a youth hostel, maybe I could reclaim a little lost youth. Mine, right?

With a destination secured, I unrolled my treasure map. I wasn't going to fall for that pesky ol' miles per inch trick ever again. I carefully weighed up the full 200 miles to Chicago. It was already 3pm (I don't know, it just goes) but with these glorious northern summer evenings there was still daylight until 9pm. I was near the Interstate 80, so I could make good time. It would take about four hours to get there, five for getting lost. So, *yay!* There was a chance I might actually get to see where I was going this time.

←→

On the outskirts of suburban Chicago, John Lee Hooker's song 'Boom Boom' came on the radio. I was in Sunday night traffic crawling past Joliet, the maximum security jail which featured at the start of *The Blues Brothers* film. It seemed like a good omen, so I turned up the radio and set my mood to high beam optimism.

I was looking forward to Chicago. I couldn't decide if I'd spend my night with comedy or music. It is, after all, home to both the Chicago blues and the comedy venue The Second City.

The Second City is famous for showcasing the young talents of John Belushi, Dan Aykroyd, Bill Murray, Tina Fey, Amy Poehler, Julia Louis-Dreyfus and every funny American you ever heard of. Several other places opened in its shadow until Chicago officially became the laughing stock of America. Perhaps I could buy a standing room ticket? Maybe one of the youths from the hostel might join me? Winding through the skyscrapers downtown, I was looking forward to meeting these new human beings. I turned up the volume and sang along to give my 'out-loud' voice a bit of practise.

The description of my South Side accommodation was of 'a stately home with luxurious gardens'. I drove past the address, unconvinced I'd found the right place. To be fair, it was a stately home. Once. Now it had all the earmarks of a squat. There was a mattress on the footpath, a council garbage bin on fire and a car on the driveway in a thousand unmarked pieces. From somewhere nearby a domestic blew through the windows.

I reread the instructions and retraced my steps. The suburb looked like an episode of *America's Most Wanted* – boarded-up shops, patrolling squad cars, police sorting out a dispute, kids sitting on the steps of brownstone houses. I drove around the block again.

Yep. Those police are definitely arresting that man, and drawing a pretty good crowd too.

Chicago's South Side gets a bad rap for violence. The historical context draws a long line from the Industrial Revolution to the Civil Rights Movement. During the 19th century, the area was upwardly mobile, with plenty of housing being built for the burgeoning middle classes. That continued well into the 20th century when Frank Lloyd Wright built Robie House here.

After the Civil War, millions of freed slaves were attracted by the prospect of work in the factories. They brought with them preachers and the blues. The South Side remains a devoutly Christian area, famous for its gospel choirs. It makes sense that it's been home to politicians like Jesse Jackson and Barack Obama. During the American Apartheid, residents challenged segregated housing laws and won, laying claim to the title of 'Home of the Civil Rights Movement'.

After the collapse of manufacturing in America, unemployment in the area skyrocketed. The community struggled to maintain basic amenities like health and education, all of which combined to create an unruly reputation. To be fair though, in the same period it was also home to Frankie Knuckles and the birth of 'four on the floor' house music, so a lot of love's been made here too.

It wasn't until Betty and I got stuck in a dead-end alley with a bunch of kids distracted from their basketball game ('Ooh, look at that car,') that I thought maybe I should return to the first place I visited, the one that looked like a squat with the car in pieces outside.

The door was unlocked, and an affable bloke called Fats was expecting me. He indicated to come in and passed me the register, the key to my room and a can of mace without getting up from his couch.

I declined the mace, took the key and signed the register.

My room was on the ground floor between the kitchen and Fats' lounge. As I slipped the key into the lock, I saw a petulant-looking man reading a book in the kitchen. He lifted his eyes, so I waved.

The room was fine. Clean sheets were folded on the single bunk bed. The towel, though scratchy, was fresh. Excellent value at twenty-three dollars per night.

When I came back out, the book-reader was standing solicitously by my door. His name was Rick. Up close he was handsome, from the Leni Riefenstahl school of good looks, which is to say blond hair, blue eyes and crazy like a Nazi youth. He appeared to be living in the D-range – although I had yet to decide which quarter.

Rick introduced himself. He showed me where to park; carried my bags; offered me beer and cigarettes. He even cooked hamburgers for dinner and included me in his headcount – all upstanding American hospitality. If only he'd blink, maybe I could relax.

After dinner the three of us settled in front of the telly to watch my first ever game of ice hockey. Chicago was playing. I was excited to be having what I saw as an authentic American experience – a bunch of blokes, way too much beer, and well-armed sport on the teev.

'I played hockey at school,' I informed my host. 'Once. I sized up Avril Wynne for my first ever serve.' I demonstrated. 'Hockey One. Hockey Two. And, *pow!* Broke her nose with a textbook golf swing.'

Little did I know how well I had grasped the sport.

'You'll enjoy this then,' said Fats. 'Beating each other up is so much a part of hockey, there's a joke to go with it: "I went to a fight last night and a hockey game broke out."'

We were rooting for the Blackhawks (Chicago). I misheard and thought our team was the 'Black Cocks'. Rick and Fats gurgled like drains while Scarlett O'Red-Face sat primly on the couch mumbling, 'What's so funny about a team named after roosters?'

Halftime was reserved for getting-to-know-you chitchat. Fats was funny. 'There's not much to tell. I was born on this davenport.' (He was so much a part of his couch, it seemed possible.) Fats was in the enviable position of having achieved his life's ambition. He'd found a way to make the world revolve around him – a beached American lying on his lounge, watching television and eating refined carbohydrates. 'Never trust anything that says *lite.*' I think that might have been his family motto.

Rick, on the other hand, had missed out on a world of opportunity. He was a good-looking man from a middle-class family. He dropped out of uni and couldn't get a job and didn't know why. Obviously it was because of the Crazy Man waving at everyone from behind his eyeballs, but how to tell him that?

Rick wanted a dog and was wheedling Fats to buy one. 'Why would I do that?' asked Fats. 'Dogs are dirty.'

'No, they're not. You just don't want to get off the couch to feed it.'

'How about a pig?' I suggested, my Freudian slip showing. 'They're clean and smart.'

'And if you don't like it, you can eat it,' added Rick.

'There, that,' said Fats, pointing at Rick, 'that's the sort of joke that makes people nervous around you.'

'It's not a joke. Pigs are tasty. Pork, bacon, rinds …'

Fats looked to me for backup.

'Would've been funny if he was joking,' was all I could think to say.

During the second half of the ice hockey, a fellow Australian arrived. Mike was also driving across America. He'd taken a corporate option where, for the price of petrol, you could transport someone's car interstate. His contract gave him five days to cross the country and limited mileage to prohibit sightseeing. Mike had done a calculation of his own, then detoured to the Grand Canyon. He was doing well until arriving here. He mistook Interstate 55 for Exit 55 and drove 70 miles and two hours out of his way.

'You want me to put the billy on?' I asked, and Mike almost wept with gratitude.

Rick felt threatened by the mysterious connection which made Mike and me instant friends. Our connection won't surprise Australians. I had tea bags from home and was willing to share. To add piquancy to Rick's discomfort, Mike had been in high school when I was on TV. He thought he knew me and couldn't work out from where.

I would've put him out of his misery, but having already done renditions of Blanche DuBois and Scarlett O'Hara that night, I chose not to throw in scenes from *Sweet Bird of Youth*. Instead, I mentioned I was thinking of going into town to catch some comedy if he wanted to come. Mike was too tired, but Rick was enthusiastic. 'I could do with a laugh,' he said.

Fats, who was sitting behind him, shook his head softly. I cocked mine, and he repeated the gesture – a clear message that Rick was not to be trusted.

So, that's who the mace is for.

'You know what,' I said handing over my tea bags to Mike, 'I've got an early start in the morning. I might call it a night too.'

In my room I discovered the door didn't lock. I went to the kitchen to get a chair to stuff under the handle, but the boys were sitting on them, arguing about Rick's book, *Fatherland* (a fantasy about what the world would be like if Hitler had won the war) I looked around and saw that Fats was still parked on the couch outside my room. He'd be my chivalrous sentinel for the night, so I was probably safe.

Back in my room without a chair, I dangled wire coat hangers over the doorknob and window lock. That way if Rick snuck in, I'd wake up before I found him staring at me from the end of my bunk.

↔

Miraculously, I slept well and was up early the next morning, ready to go. Not early enough though. Fats was fast asleep on the couch, but Rick was at the kitchen table wearing Desert Storm camouflage.

Okay, don't panic. All you have to do is have a shower and leave. Yes?

No.

No sooner had my door cracked open than Rick was bounding over asking, 'How do you like your eggs in the morning?'

'Unfertilised' was the word that sprang to mind, but I smiled and said, 'In a cafe. You Americans have really mastered breakfast.'

'Cool,' he replied, unfazed, 'I'll come with you.' He picked up the peaked cap which matched his army dungarees.

'I've got to shower first,' I said, then hesitated when he moved towards the bathroom as though I'd invited him to join me. I nipped in and slammed the door before he could follow.

Christ, I thought, *this must be what it's like to be in a* Pepé Le Pew *cartoon.*

In the shower I considered my options. I could phone the friend of a friend I'd messaged the night before – make a lunch arrangement, then make it clear to Rick that people were expecting me. That I would be missed. That I had places to go and people to see. Sure. That might work.

When I was dressed and ready, I broached the subject of getting rid of him. 'You know,' I said, 'I don't really have much time for breakfast. I'm meeting friends for lunch.'

'Great. I'll show you how to get there.'

'I have a map.'

'I know the city. Where are you going?'

Damn. I didn't know the name of a single place to say. 'Breakfast first,' I replied, thereby inviting Rick to go out with me.

This was the only time Fats got off the couch. He levered himself up, waddled across the room and with great concern whispered, 'Be careful around Rick.'

'No shit, Sherlock,' I hissed back. 'How?'

'Just don't drink with him.'

There ensued a brief moment of total connection while Fats looked into my eyes – maybe making a mental impression to give to the police in the future. I laughed at that thought, and he smiled, shook my hand and wishing me luck as Rick proprietorially touched my back to walk me outside to Betty.

Breakfast in the South Side diner was tense. 'I know a great bar near here where Al Capone used to sell hooch,' he said.

'It's eight o'clock in the morning.'

He shrugged. 'It must be five o'clock somewhere. Aren't you curious to see the city? Not much of an adventurer, are you?'

'I'm meeting friends for brunch.'

'Where? What are their names, maybe I know them?'

'You know, I'd better ring them and find out.' I excused myself and went to use a phone I'd spotted near the till.

I dialled, silently willing someone to pick up. When they did, I was so relieved I pointed the receiver out to Rick – an idiot saying, 'See, I do have friends.'

I introduced myself to the woman on the other end of the line and explained my situation. 'God, I am so sorry,' she replied. 'I've got back-to-back meetings all day. Do you want to come to dinner?'

'That's nice of you, but what I really need is some way to shake this guy. What do you think I should do? I'm desperate!'

'Do you need me to call the police or something?' she asked.

'No. Not that sort of desperate. Perhaps you can suggest somewhere public I can pretend we're going to meet up?' This was an all-time nutty phone call.

'Can't you be straight with him? Tell him to go away. You might be making this more complicated than it needs to be.'

'Yes. That's perfectly sensible, but I've already got myself nipple-deep in nonsense. If you give me the name of somewhere public, I'll pretend we're meeting there.'

She suggested the restaurant on top of the Sears Tower on Adams Street. 'It's always popular with tourists. But one thing – you must phone me later and tell me everything's turned out okay, or I absolutely will ring the police this evening.'

There's a small gap between histrionics and humour into which her words tumbled. I was grateful for her investment of concern, and promised to phone her and leave a message when I was clear of Rick.

Armed with my newly minted lie, I returned. 'Judy Schneider is meeting me at the top of the Sears Tower for brunch at 10.45,' I said, adding all the extraneous details that usually indicate a lie.

He asked if he could come too.

I told him, 'No.'

He asked if I could drop him off downtown.

I said, 'Yes, I can do that,' and regretted it instantly. Now I had a six-foot Neo-Nazi to eject from my car.

'I might go to Sears myself,' he said, plainly not believing anything I'd said. 'I don't have to go with you. I just could sit at the next table. Make sure no crazies bother you.'

Despairing of what to do next, I pulled Betty over to the curb and resorted to the truth. 'Rick, I don't want you to come. Now get out of the car.'

It was that simple.

The last I saw of my erstwhile suitor was in the rear-vision mirror – a forlorn figure in camouflage, blending into the grimy beige of an Illinois street corner as I hit the accelerator pedal.

I felt mean for not recommending he visit the Bait and Bullet in Toolesboro. He might have made some new friends. They could have gone shooting fish together.

THE BETTERLANDS

The joy of escape! For once I didn't consult my trusty navigator. I did a couple of (almost intentional) laps of the city and was soon burning down the Chicago Skyway singing, 'Chicago, Chicago. I'm gonna get me outta thar-go.'

There was a brief flash of water which, if I'm not mistaken, was a Great Lake.

I slipped El Torta's *Colores Morenos* into the CD player and set the car on cruise control while wily Andalusians applauded my progress into the industrial wasteland. The enthusiastic Spanish clapping was a little at odds with the cement and steel scenery. *Bravo!* Endless miles of telegraph poles. *Encore!* Thousands of newly manufactured cars parked underneath them like post-industrial mushrooms.

A wave of irrational optimism washed over me.

When Pig left, I thought the quickest way to get over him was to start hating him, but I couldn't do it. I loved him and felt compassion for his crisis. Growing up is hard. Loving one person for the rest of your life is hard. Being freelance. Motivating yourself every day. Fighting inertia. The competition, the complexity, the clients who don't pay. All that clamouring ambition snapping at your heels.

Worse, how could I hate him when he'd been so much fun to live with? Nobody could make me laugh like Pig. Even at our worst, after the ectopic pregnancies. Even on our first date when nothing went right. Even sitting in an empty cinema watching a film I'd directed but nobody turned up to see. Even at the end, when our fights were so loud that neighbours opened their windows and told us to shut up – even then he could make me laugh. Not scoff or chuckle, but deep belly laughs of weeping joy.

Travelling through the long, soft afternoon was soothing. The man in the moon eventually rose. He was so fat with summer love that he had to use both elbows to heave himself over the horizon. And there he was, his head tilted into an unfamiliar expression. It was such a happiness to see his big yellow face and realise that all those I loved were bathed in his benign gaze as he slipped around the world.

When a truck stop appeared that was surrounded by the number of long-haul semis that indicates good food and friendly service (more than four), Betty and I stopped to refuel.

Inside, the decor was comforting like a big ol' toolshed. Everything was in jumbo sizes except for the skinny aisles, which may have been designed as a social experiment to help lonely truckers get some human contact.

For the most part the truckers dressed in singlets and tracksuit pants or shorts. There was the odd young buck in Western drag – you know, fancy shirt with a fringe, arse-tight jeans and a belt with a buckle as big as Texas. 'Shit, man, how much money you makin'?' They all seemed to know each other, or know about each other. A few sat in groups, gossiping good-naturedly, 'She was giving him all sorts of bad medicine …'

There was a pay phone on every table. Even in the middle of the day, guys were dotted around the yellow-lit dining room, sharing the break with loved ones. Well, I presumed it was with loved ones. They were picking at their food with a fork in one hand and cooing long distance love into the other. 'Of course I miss you, honey, it's bad without you.' Each table had a golden thread home.

I telephoned Judy in Chicago and left a message to let her know that I had escaped safely. 'You can call off the bloodhounds,' I joked. 'I took your advice, and the truth set me free.' Then hung up and played with the salt shaker while I considered who else I could talk to.

To those of you who have travelled before me down love's highway to divorce, I apologise. Had you known what I was about to do, you'd have sent in an intervention SWAT team. I hear them arriving now. *Hep hep hep.* Forty-year-old divorcees in Capri pants and stilettos are rappelling down from the roof to stop me.

I rang Pig and told him I missed him.

It didn't go well. Someone was with him. It wasn't a fight, it was a passive-aggressive spit fest. In the end I gave him an ultimatum with an address. 'If you value our friendship,' I said, 'you'll send me a letter with some real emotions in it so I can understand what you're going through.' Not an email. Not a fax. Not a text. An old-school, handwritten, pen-to-paper letter that would reveal his tears as they melted the ink.

The address I gave was for my old school friend, Pipi, who I would be staying with in Connecticut. 'Or you could send it to Michele in London. I'm flying there in a week.'

'Oh, why are you doing that?' he whined. 'We agreed to not make our friends choose.'

'I haven't asked her to choose. This doesn't change anything.'

'You say that, but then you girls get together with your great big goblets of drama. And Mark's been so sick. He doesn't need you dumping all of this.'

'I'm not *dump*ing.'

Pig and Michele were friends from school. They'd been flatmates when we met. She'd moved to the other side of the planet where her husband worked as a journalist. He'd become critically ill on assignment, and the last two years had been spent in a state of emergency as his health deteriorated.

Back in Sydney, I used to ring Michele in the middle of the night when my existential crises came to get me. It was the middle of her afternoon in London and she always took my calls. I wanted to thank her for that, as well as see how they were doing, before flying back to New York to pick up Sue.

Invoking Michele's friendship was unworthy. She knew all our secrets but never traded any of Pig's with me. She hadn't said a bad word about him, but by dropping her name in this way I laid a little turd in his ear. I hung up, regretting the call entirely.

Why does the moon look so big on the horizon, but so small in the sky?

No. He'd send the letter to Pipi's house. Our friendship was on the line, and for all our troubles I knew that meant something to him. *This letter – the letter that will be there waiting for me – will communicate all of that. In it he'll be vulnerable and funny and infinitely forgivable.*

Yeah, the Nile is more than a river in Egypt.

I arrived in Sandusky after the sun left the sky. I hurried further east to secure a front-row view of light on water. Somewhere around Ruggles Beach I parked the car and, without a clear plan, wandered through backyards to the waterfront.

The pinks and apricots were lifting off the water, leaving a thick band of blue to blend the horizon into the sky. So much water. A warm breeze lightly stirred the surface. As the breeze made it to my brain, I discovered that what looked like an ocean smelled like a river. I put my hand in to taste it. Fresh water.

The 'Great Lakes' are no understatement. They're enormous. A freshwater aquifer in the middle of America. HOMES: Huron, Ontario, Michigan, Erie and Superior. So which was this? *If that's Lake Erie, this must be Friday.*

I wondered what my friends at home were doing. Each year at work we wrote a list of goals and aspirations. Mostly it was practical stuff about what we wanted to achieve in business. Back in January, in a state of uncertainty and despair, all I wrote was *June.* That was as much future as I could envisage.

Today the sun was rising and setting on the 13th of June. Miraculously, and without fanfare, I had achieved my primary goal in life. With this realisation, a glow of infinite possibility ripped through my pall of grief.

If you could be anyone in the world, who would you be?

If you could be with anyone in the world, who would it be?

What do you need to change about yourself to become that person?

Sometimes we put ourselves on hold in a relationship while working towards a common goal – kids, parents, property, business, health – even another person's happiness. And that's all good. They're the things we do because love is also a verb. But sometimes we put ourselves on hold because we're frightened, depressed or too timid to assert ourselves. To get biblical about it, we hide our light under a bushel.

Alright. Yes. It's me again. I'm the one who's been doing all that.

I'd been bending my personality and making choices to support my marriage. That's not bad in itself, but bending myself out of shape, pretending to be less than I was to make someone else feel good, that's bad. It's actively self-destructive. The Bible said it, Shakespeare said it, even the rap group 2nd II None said it: 'To thine own self be true.' Whatever string or chain had tethered me to my marriage was broken. And forsaking all others, I was free.

Tabula rasa. Clean slate. What did I want to do with all this shiny, brand-new me?

The soft apricot light was traded for blue over the water, and then the blue for black in the sky. Dew began to settle around me. It was time to find a wooden verandah and put my feet up for the night. I looked around and saw that someone had set fairy lights in the bushes. They twinkled so prettily. Welcoming. Perhaps this would be a good place to stay?

I couldn't see anywhere nearby. The houses on the waterfront were bigger than cabins and set back from the water's edge. But someone had gone to a lot of trouble with these fairy lights. So pretty moving in the breeze ... moving up into the air ... detaching from the bushes and flying towards me?

Fireflies! The air was full of them.

I was too enchanted to be a spectator. I got up and chased them until I caught one. Up close, the firefly was a perfect fairy, with the finest wings and body. Their little fly legs supported a translucent abdomen that stuck up into the air and twinkled the morse code of entomological love.

Pure. Magic. A sign, I thought, that I was welcome here.

I returned to the car and drove around looking for the weatherboard cottage of my dreams – something on the waterfront with a verandah and a shingle out front. In fact, there were quite a few. Most of them said, *Summer Accommodation,* or *Cabins.* I stopped about 100 metres down the road where an actual couple were on their porch. They were a cute-looking pair of grey heads with a welcoming manner. The price was good. The place was pretty as pecan pie, but it wasn't on the actual water, so I drove on by.

Picky. Or as they like to say in France, *idiot.*

Soon the road curved away from the lake. At the next cabin, Ma or Pa (it can be hard to tell after a certain age) was replacing the

Vacancy sign with one that now read, *No.*

By Vermillion (some ten dawdling miles away) that's all the signs said. I stopped around Lorain at a cement block of toilets with a neon Vacancy sign. It was on the highway, facing what appeared to be a combined Target and correctional facility.

The receptionist was housed in a bulletproof cubicle. His television was tuned to a game show, and I was keeping him from the 'fast-paced magic minute'. Through the muffling glass he conveyed that he had a bridal suite on offer for $135. *Shit.* What sad marriage would start there? I wasn't bridal, and I wasn't paying $135.

At a bar further on I was told accommodation was scarce because the American Open (a big golf thingy) was in town, and they couldn't make me dinner because they were closing.

Shit. Shit. It was past midnight.

I got onto the Interstate 90. Cleveland was full. Motel 6 was full. *No Vacancy* signs were appearing on the off-ramps to the exits. *Don't even think about it.*

East Cleveland, Euclid and Mentor became Exit 200, 212 and 218.

Shit. Shit. Shit. They were all full.

For the first time I wished I had someone in the car with me. I was tired, and my personal brand of stupidity was pissing me off. I'd be seeing Pipi soon. She was an old-growth friend. After twenty years of shared experiences, she'd screw my head on straight.

Pipi and I met in high school. She came from England and said 'book' so it rhymed with 'souk'. *Boo-k.* I practically swooned every time she said it. At age fourteen she also had the most glorious Titian-red hair. Turned out she dyed it that colour, but who expects that of a fourteen year old? It only made her seem more worldly and sophisticated.

She introduced me to music by David Bowie and English parlour games. Her mother, who was only thirty-two at the time and drop-dead gorgeous, used to give me hickeys to get me into trouble at home. But it never really worked because Mum always believed me when I told her that Charlotte (naughty, glamorous Austrian Charlotte) had given them to me.

When I had my first ectopic pregnancy at seventeen, Pipi came to visit me in hospital, even though I was a high school pariah. (Try blame that on someone else's mother.) After we finished school, her parents returned to Britain and Pipi came to live with us in Sydney. She was footloose, broke and brutally lonely. She was also still a baby, so Mum finally wrote to Charlotte in London and suggested she take Pipi home.

After she returned to Britain she married a handsome man and they made five perfect babies. They moved to Connecticut and she sent me Christmas cards each year. She also remembered my mother, and returned our hospitality more kindly than we ever gave it. When Pig left, she sent a heartfelt letter and offered her home and friendship, which was now only two sleeps away – if I could find a bloody bed to have one of them in.

It was 3am when I pulled into Kingsville, 420 miles from Chicago. When I arrived there was only one motel with its lights on. They had one vacancy. It was the Bridal Suite. It cost $135. I took the room. I took the little packets of coffee, biscuits and fake milk. I was grateful.

Pragmatically, they could've called it the Suicide Suite. It smelled of cigarettes and stale humans. I turned on the rumbling air conditioner to drown out the sound of trucks barrelling down the highway. My eye ran around the room, looking for a gentle place to spend the night. There was none.

What led anyone to think that orange curtains, drab olive carpet and a print of a flamenco dancer were creative choices? Who in their right mind said, 'I like the sad guy with the mandolin, but I think the flamenco dancer is better for the bridal suite'? Maybe there was a

1-800-MOTEL number you could phone: 'I want 150 mauve vanity units, 45,000 beige tiles. Do you have any with pasta on them?'

But how much of life is really dictated by choice? Would I ever choose the flamenco dancer? Would I choose Kingsville? Would I trade any of it in for anything else at this precise moment? Thing is, you close your eyes and the whole ugly mess disappears. Except for the roar of the air conditioner and the foul smell of air-freshener (a rare, single-word oxymoron) I could have been in a cottage with a wooden verandah in the lap of Lake Erie.

Once upon a place, in a time far, far away, you could stand still and hear your food. It's like Laudable said in Tuba City, those trucks I could hear from my bed, the ones driven by angels, were all stuffed full of cornflakes and coffee and buffalo wings. Tell that to your grandchildren, and we'll all be Indians at heart.

I awoke to the shrill scream of a telephone. My sleep had been deep and dreamless, and I answered in a state of confusion.

'Hi there. I'm ringing to see how you are.'

How am I? Who am I? 'Who is this?'

It was Rebecca at reception. Apparently the maids had been knocking on my door for over an hour and were concerned. 'Most of our customers are gone by nine. We got a little worried when you didn't answer the door at ten.'

Shit, the Suicide Suite. 'No, I'm fine. What time is it?'

When I finally left my room it was close to midday. I was the last to vacate. The cleaning staff gathered to give me the openly curious stare usually reserved for heads of state caught in flagrante. They weren't pissed off that I'd made them wait – more morally curious. *Who the hell spends that long in the Kingsville Bridal Suite by themselves?*

I apologised for making them worry, as Betty and I demurely rumbled back onto the Interstate 90 heading towards Pennsylvania – which was good, because that's where we were going.

Maybe this whole trip was a journey into becoming unmarried. I'd separated, broken the wedding presents, slept in the Suicide Suite. Maybe it was time to celebrate my singlehood. Marry myself. Become a family of one. Cook food I liked. Buy girly things. Give all the love I had inside me to myself.

As though being rewarded for my insight and compassion, I crossed into New York State a whole day ahead of schedule. *Finally* I'd misread the map in my favour. Exactly how a journey of 300 miles passed so timelessly, who knows? Maybe I drove further in the night than I thought. If I could be *way* wrong, why not *way* right? I slipped Sheila Chandra into the CD player and sang up the landscape.

About forty minutes into this quixotic journey I passed an exit to Dunkirk, followed by a signpost to Sheridan. Now this may be a British/Australian perspective, but imagine you're driving in a foreign land at 70 miles per hour, humming a Hindu mantra, and the highway starts talking to you. Personally. It says your name and Dunkirk. Is that a good message, or a bad message?

I was heading to Canada.

New York State has an itty bitty dog leg, and I had travelled north over it. Two hours in the wrong direction. So much for 'even numbers are left to right, and odd numbers up and down'. I was now overdue by three days, lost by two whole states and damned near in the wrong country.

I turned around, and by late afternoon I was back on track in Pennsylvania.

The towns blipped by in a kindly heat haze of honeyed love. Every fenceless backyard was draped with an American flag. It was almost unbearably innocent and patriotic to see young children kicking up dust on their slide to home base under the gentle flapping of Old Glory.

I was awash with peace when out of this utopia floated an Aladdin's cave of treasures. *A yard sale.* An entire elegant life was up for grabs on the grassy verge of a stately clinker-built mansion. Oil paintings, a dinner service, silverware, Venetian glass. After Crockery Nacht I was due for some new cups and saucers, and here was a whole world to choose from.

As a kid I totally fell in love with my Aunty Patty's harlequin tea set. I thought it was the epitome of elegance. A harlequin service is one with cups, saucers and plates from different makers. In my aunt's case, each set commemorated a moment in her life: her first job, 21st birthday, a gift from her grandmother. When they came together (usually at baby showers and kitchen teas) they created a crockery quilt of her life, a biography in fine bone china.

I loved this idea so much when I was sixteen, I bought Poppy a Royal Albert trio (cup, saucer and plate) covered in fine, pale blue forget-me-nots. Even the name was chintzy: *Memory Lane.* I gave it to him for his seventieth birthday and inherited it soon after his seventy-first.

I would have added it to Gran's Winton Welbecks (the original chintz in yellow with pale pink roses) but Mum threw them out. My mother was a believer in using the best china every day. Gran preferred to eat from supermarket crockery for fear of chipping The Good Stuff. Accordingly, the Wellbecks had no meaning to Mum, who threw out two whole table settings for eight people. No one else in my family mourned their passing. They were deemed too Edna Everage by the boys, but I regret the loss of every one of those 124 pieces every time I see a trio for sale on eBay for hundreds of dollars more than I can afford.

If I got the habit of collecting china from my aunt, I got the attitude of using the 'good stuff' from Mum. According to my friend Amanda (she of the Teasmade), one of her earliest memories of me is arriving at her apartment with a china cup and saucer of piping hot tea, and a taxi waiting downstairs. It was this robust usage which caused so much of my crockery to be chipped and cracked, and why my grandfather's Memory Lane had been among those I smashed.

I was bereft about losing Poppy's cup – something he'd brushed with his lips. To console me at the time, my aunt told this story about the sentimental value of teacups:

A friend of hers locked himself in his home after the death of his wife. My aunt became concerned about the widower's wellbeing, and eventually turned up at his door with a casserole, and insisted on coming in to watch him eat it. Over dinner he told her that after the wake he'd broken one of his wife's teacups. His wife had been collecting the dinner service since before their engagement, and breaking one was the final straw of his grief. A madness overtook him. In a fit of furious loss he destroyed the lot – smashed *all* the cups, saucers, plates and dishes. His remorse was instant. In destroying her treasured possessions, his love had died all over again. He swept the pieces together and took the remains out into the garden – where he built a mosaic fountain from the shards – and that was why he hadn't left the house.

I was willing to forego the permanent memorial to Pig, but I wanted to rebuild my tea service. Now was as good a time as any. The yard sale presented two cups made from fine bone china. They were smaller than I normally like, only the size of my fist, rather than the five-inch English breakfast cups I prefer, but they were beautifully hand decorated. My favourite, the one I allocated to Sue (who paid for half the car and was joining me for the return journey) was a bright yellow Royal Adderley Floral with a single Flanders poppy and forget-me-not in its basin.

The other cup was a 19th-century white Royal Stuart with a scalloped edge and dainty spring flowers on the outside. Choosing two was as much a symbol of my future filled with friendship as it was a desire to snack on the road. Already these cups had stories, and soon we'd be ladies together, sipping tea on the banks of the M.I.S.S.I.S.S.I.P.P.I.

I paid for my treasures, and commented on the ubiquitous flag lolling over the table. The seller told me it was National Flag Day.

Of course it was.

Nearing the east coast, the towns and cities grew denser and closer together, and NPR became my constant companion on the radio. Today there was a program about Heinrich Schliemann, the father of modern archaeology. The German-born American was fascinated by Homer's *Iliad*. Around 1870 these stories were considered fairy tales, so it was amid much scepticism that the young man mounted an expedition to trace the itinerary of the Greek fleet described in the epic poem. When Schliemann and his friend Frank Calvert discovered the ancient city of Troy, they were feted as heroes and a whole new science was launched.

Weirdly, I was wearing a t-shirt with the cover of James Joyce's *Ulysses* printed on it. Originally I bought it as a joke to wear in the gym, but every time I did some smart-arse asked, 'Have you read it?' I'd reply, 'There are only seven words, of course I have.' But I felt such a fraud, I bought the book and read the whole damn thing. Who says exercise doesn't expand your mind?

Now, here I was in the middle of nowhere, wearing the t-shirt, listening to a story about the man who followed the journey of Ulysses, and starting to think about somewhere to stay for the night, when I passed the Susquehannock Lodge and Trail Centre. As though God knew I was hard of hearing, he gave me an additional sign. It said *Ulysses, Pennsylvania.*

Stop!

You've read the book, you've heard the stories, you're wearing the t-shirt – now stop and stay for the night.

After Ogallala, Kingsville and just about every other city on this journey, I didn't hesitate to book a log cabin for the evening. It came with a fireplace and a slice of bucolic happiness out back called the Allegheny National Park.

After ten straight days in a car I was ready for a walk in the forest. I prepared a picnic to christen my new un-wedding presents. Taking the bedspread to sit on, I walked deep into the forest – okay, you're onto me. I stumbled a couple of hundred metres and then set everything up before it could get cold.

I went full crazy-lady with the tableware. China cups and saucers, hot tea, fresh milk, cake and sandwiches served on dainty side dishes. Anyone driving by would have thought someone was playing grownups. And they'd have been right.

It was achingly pretty in the forest. The shivering birch trees were in full green-dappled cool. The forest floor was soft with the mulch of winter. If this had been Australia, rowdy eucalypts would be jeering the birch from a vast wilderness. But here, sitting in this glade, it was so still you could hear the trees breathing …

… and the soft clicking of food nearby.

About twenty feet in front of me, a short tree moved – sort of shivered, and walked away. A young doe was trying to hide by standing as still as her fear would allow. She was showing me her hind, white and brown like two stunted birch trees.

It was like all the strands of my life were coming together – I was rewarded for action. I was rewarded for sitting still. I sipped hot tea from my new cup, looking forward to the old-growth friendship that was waiting for me in Connecticut.

BEAUTIFUL LIVES GLIMPSED AT HIGH SPEED

The last 332 miles to the East Coast were, frankly, a blur. The journey may well be the journey, but at this precise moment my destination was achievable. It was so long since I'd felt even the possibility of attaining a goal, I wasn't about to waste the moment on the moment. I was savouring the future, the total glory of victory over inertia.

I was so damned excited I didn't even bother to navigate. Like a sailor smelling land, I was a landlubber smelling the sea. No star or misplaced northern hemisphere sun was required. I followed my nose as it dragged me east over the last three states towards the Atlantic Ocean. Granted, my nose was mistaken at Lawrenceville, Canoe Camp, Scranton and Port Jervis (all the way to Danbury). It also prescribed a strange little victory dance around New Canaan, Darien, Norwalk and Fairfield. Bizarrely, my nose also required that I perform a lengthy lap of honour around Westport itself, the town where Pipi lived with her family, before I vetoed any further adventures and rang to ask for directions. I believed until this point that if I drove around long enough I'd just, you know, find Pipi's house even though I'd never been there.

I was a block from her home.

Pipi was completely unfazed that I was three days late. So unfazed, she'd taken the kids to New York for the night and left instructions with her cleaner about how to find her parents' house.

It was an unexpected bonus to be visiting Charlotte and Hugh. They were the youngest (by a decade) of my friends' parents when we were growing up. Given that I had the oldest folks, there was nearly a generation between them. Mum was reasonably sanguine about the time I spent at their house, because while Charlotte and Hugh were cool, we the children weren't. All we did was flop around their house playing parlour games and loud music. Even then the music didn't get much louder than Elton John.

I don't know if my understanding about how Charlotte and Hugh met is fact or adolescent fantasy. I suspect the latter, so this may be a romantic interpretation of their world, but … Charlotte was a Hapsburg, a rooly trooly Austrian countess. As a girl, she'd been wild enough to get expelled from schools all over Europe. By the time she was seventeen, her parents despaired of her wilful spirit and she was being home-tutored. Escapology was her best subject.

On one of her illicit forays she met Hugh, a tall, dark, handsome Englishman with an artistic disposition. They fell madly in love. As a commoner, Hugh was unable to date – much less marry – the aristocratic Charlotte, so they eloped to Spain (or Gretna Green, which I thought was in Spain). My friend Pipi was born a year later, which if my memory is true, means when Charlotte was my age she had three children aged seventeen and under.

It was nearly twenty years since I'd seen them. Charlotte was still rambunctious like a Great Dane puppy, and Hugh the serene Englishman. They welcomed me into their lush home, an elegant slice of Europe with oil paintings, pot plants and feature walls in bright colours. They also prepared the best bedroom I'd slept in since Amana.

We sat up late drinking Harvey's Bristol Cream and talking about my adventures. I spared them my late night rants and dead porcupines, telling them instead about Laudable Adams, the diners of Route 66 and my attempts to catch fireflies on the banks of Lake Erie. Pipi later told me they enjoyed my stories so much that they took the journey themselves.

As teenagers, Pipi and I had been inseparable, but since her marriage to Colin they'd lived around the world and I hadn't seen her as much as I'd have liked. We'd caught up at key moments like the birth of their babies, who seemed to come both late and quickly.

Around the time child number four was due, Colin was called away on business in another state. Because none of their children arrived on time, neither Pipi nor Colin were concerned as she waved him off. An hour later, however, she rang his office to find out if they could catch him before the flight, saying, 'I think I've gone into labour.' Another contraction overtook her and she hung up. As far as Pipi was concerned that was that. She phoned a taxi to take her to hospital.

Now, this was the week before Christmas and goodwill was running high, because as they taxied for take-off Colin was called to the cockpit. His assistant had relayed Pipi's message, and the pilot laid the situation out for him. 'Your wife's gone into labour. Would you like us to turn the plane around?'

Colin was stunned. 'Can you do that?'

With the casual Chuck Yeager tone admired by pilots worldwide, he announced on the intercom, 'Ladies and gentlemen, we have a young man here whose wife has gone into labour. I'd like to turn the plane around so he can join her at the hospital, but I need your approval to do this.' The plane erupted into applause and they returned to JFK. As family legend has it, a tardy businessman was standing at the gate enraptured that his plane had returned for him.

Colin was waiting for Pipi when she arrived at the hospital. Nora Ephron wouldn't have been that audacious.

Pipi picked me up from her mother's house with three of her five cubs at heel. They arrived like pink and pretty flies buzzing around her on invisible string. Her eldest son, Teddy, was due to play his end-of-school baseball game, so we all piled into our cars and drove to the local diamond.

It was so idyllic, it was almost painful. Unlike the lady of England who still said *boo-k* and *loo-k*, Pipi's children rolled their Rs and put a surprise W in words like *cwoffee*. Wearing sunscreen and a straw hat, Pipi brought deck chairs for us to sit and watch the game, and enough sandwiches and cordial to feed both teams.

It was a family crowd, including plenty of fathers striding the sidelines in tailored suits, clapping their hands saying, 'Rah, rah, rah.' Two had loosened their ties and were smoking cigars. They were all in their thirties. *How in God's name did these people get to be so grown up?*

I noted that some psychology was at play in the makeup of the teams and Pipi shushed me with a low hand. 'This is a friendly group from Teddy's school. We're hoping to teach him team spirit.'

There was one small kid with glasses who was frightened of the ball. He stood at the plate having a panic attack as it whizzed past him. The coach chose him to bat fourth, because nine year olds can't pitch for shit. What happens when a kid doesn't swing and the bases are loaded? He walked like a hero.

Then, with a man on every plate, the coach called out Teddy. At age nine, Teddy was already head and shoulders above everyone else. He swaggered onto the field like Paul Bunyan coming to chop down trees.

He hit the ball.

It flew out of the field.

He strode the bases to four more points and victory.

After the game, we drove to a county fair to celebrate the start of summer holidays. Some of Teddy's teammates came with us, and they all wanted to drive with me!

Oh, alright, they wanted to drive with Betty.

I turned the radio on and rumbled after Pipi in her people-mover. We made quite a spectacle in the backstreets of Connecticut, a sure-fire threat to hold up a lolly shop.

'What type of car is she?' asked one shiny nine year old.

'A Camaro'

'Is that as good as a Ferrari?'

'Yes, it is.'

'Jeremy's dad has a Ferrari.'

'Then Jeremy's dad will be jealous when he learns you've gone for a drive in a Camaro.'

The county fair was set in a grassy field between two lightly wooded hills. The smell of frying onions lured us through a jingle-jungle of food stalls selling hamburgers, hot dogs, popcorn and fairy floss – cotton candy – handmade from spun toffee that tasted of childhood.

Yards of colourfully striped canvas were decorated with miles of delicate lights. There were squealing rides, a Ferris wheel and knock 'em down concessions where everyone was a winner. The crowd was cashmered and emolliated with the smooth veneer of the very rich, and connecting it all was the golden thread of childhood unleashed.

At one point, Pipi's two younger kids begged Teddy to ride with them. They'd chosen an aeroplane merry-go-round which was way too small for overgrown Teddy, but he got on to please them. It had gone magic hour, when the last light renders the sky a deep cerulean blue. I didn't have a camera so I've taken a mind snap. In it, the colourful bulbs are lighting the children in blinking yellow and pink. They're flying in the air. Teddy, twice their size, is seated between his brother and sister in a toy aeroplane and they are suspended in perfect happiness above us all. Secure, sure and loved.

It was late when we got home. The kids were revved on sugar and whinged off to bed with an accepting clump. I put the kettle on while Pipi started preparing for the next day. 'You want one?' I asked.

'Sure, Polly,' she said, using my teenage nickname, 'still putting the kettle on.'

'I'm a natural born tea maker.'

I opened her neat cupboards looking for tea bags. Inside, the doors were covered with Post-it notes – management memos to a busy mother:

- *Stay calm.*
- *Set limits with empathy.*
- *Connection before correction.*

I read one out loud, '*Keep the loving cup full.* Isn't that a country song?'

'Gotta have a cup of love,' she said, 'or you can't pour love into others.'

'Deep.' I ferreted until I found her stash of herbal teas, 'Kava Stress Relief? Sleepytime Extra? Tension Tamer? I'm sensing a theme here.'

'I'll have the Rooiboos Superfruit. It's too late for caffeine.'

I rejoiced at finding a squashed box of PG Tips. 'Real tea. With tea in it.'

I fiddled with the makings – finding her plain white mugs and arranging them for when the water boiled. 'Is every day like this? Your life is a slice of heaven.'

She spun the dial on her washing machine and didn't look up. 'Are you mocking me?'

'No, that was worldclass street theatre out there today.' I was ready to discuss the nuances of each performance, but her expression was one of eloquent disbelief. 'Seriously. How good was today?' I asked.

'I know you want children, but don't be fooled. This is work. This is training for the Olympics every single day. Do you know what I was doing in Manhattan? Burrowing through the garbage out back of McDonalds. One of those great big industrial bins, filled to the top.'

'How did that happen?'

'We'd gone to the Golden Arches as a treat. Vicky, who's self-conscious about being twelve, wrapped her retainer in a napkin and *accidentally* threw it out. The damn thing cost like eight hundred bucks, so I wasn't about to leave it. There I was, me, waist-deep in half-mauled burgers. And I found it. Waved it triumphantly. Took it home and boiled it. And you know what? The little minx wouldn't wear it. Refused to put it in her mouth.' She laughed, now that hindsight was having its way with her. 'It was gross, apparently.'

Pipi was talking while preparing for the day that was rushing up to greet us. After loading the wash, she arranged the kids' school bags, checking off a list of various planned activities. She found corresponding uniforms: Gap jeans, Nike trainers, mitts, goggles, the baby's blue comforter. She sterilised bottles and made up formula. She collected strewn toys into orderly piles.

I pushed a cup of herbal tea to her while she talked. She flipped a pile of baby blankets into squares like a seasoned shop-girl. 'When you're pregnant, you worry you'll be some doe-eyed hormonal cow for the rest of your life. By the time you come to, when the kids start daycare, the only way back to who you used to be is by following the trail of soft toys and wailing children.'

'Christ, you could print that on a t-shirt and use it as a contraceptive.'

'But I love being a parent. I loved being pregnant. I love the children. I love the chaos and mayhem. I even love the permission it gives you to see soppy family films and cuddle soft toys in posh cafes.'

She pitched toys into various plastic storage bins, *pow, pow, pow*. They landed one after the other, and she turned to make sure I'd seen. *Yes!*

'You make it look easy.'

'I've reached my fighting weight. You should've seen me in the beginning. I was made of rage.'

'You've all turned out alright.'

'I got help. The local pastor introduced me to peaceful parenting classes. It's about mindfulness – allowing emotions to take hold without acting on them. Airlines tell you to put oxygen masks on before helping others because kids can't save themselves. Peaceful parenting is like that. Learning to control negative emotions, and teaching the kids to do the same.'

'*Only love today.*'

'That's in the loo,' she said. 'I sometimes hide in there when I think I'm going to explode. It says *Stop, Drop, Breathe* by my bed. That's the one I live by, but thirteen years and five kids later and I still need to remind myself every day.'

'Stop, drop, breathe. I could use some of that.'

Pipi remembered she had some letters for me. 'Old-school,' she said.

'Living in the moment,' I replied.

I knew she'd have mail, and I was looking forward to savouring the letters as a gift from home. One was from Mum, the other from Justin. There was no letter from Pig. My disappointment was so involuntary, tears sprang to my eyes.

Pipi shifted from one foot to the other. I didn't have to tell her why I was upset. Hell, I'd probably already told her. Probably left a message on her answer machine, or had an aeroplane write it in the sky.

'The time's good,' she offered gently, 'why don't you ring him? I'm sure he'd have sent something if he said he would.' She was right, of course, and it's testimony to his good nature that she knew that.

There was a click at the back door as Pipi's husband, Colin, arrived home looking quite the executive in his corporate drag. Thirty-five years old and more mature than any adult in my family. He put his leather satchel on the kitchen counter and kissed his wife.

'That's a long day,' I said as he greeted me with a smile and a hug.

'Sure is when you consider I caught the six o'clock train this morning.'

'The only way we can keep this up is by sticking to our plan,' said Pipi. 'Bed by ten or we're both wrecked in the morning.' She kissed me good night, and they went upstairs, leaving me alone with the phone.

So I rang Pig.

He was out.

I left a message.

I checked the address I'd given him in the truck stop. It was wrong. I'd left off the street name. His letter would have gone to Westport Street, Connecticut. *Fut.* Typical. Crossed wires and vexed packages were a motif of this bust-up. On our last wedding anniversary he sent me flowers. The message read, *Dear Chloe, One year to go. Good luck. Love Adam.* I tried to make sense of it before reconciling the fact that the florist had attached the wrong card. This time was my fault.

How could we ever make it home if we didn't know the address?

I rang the local post office to see what might have happened to the letter. They said if it had a return address they'd return it.

If not, they'd open it for clues, and if there weren't any, they'd destroy it.

While looking in the local directory for the Post Office phone number I saw that *Marriage* was next to *Martial Arts*. Sounds about right.

I took my letters to bed. Mum gives good correspondence, full of life at home: *After you left, there was a ring at the bell (I had to get my leg working to open the door because of my footballer's knee) and there was your aunt, laden with flowers and misery like a muster of the vultures. Apparently she misses you terribly, and it's only been a month.*

Justin sent me the poem I liked so much and a weird story called 'Life in a Texas Whorehouse' instead of a covering note. It was nicely written in a 50s style of Beat misanthropy. Maybe he perceived it as a self-portrait, or the ideal tone for my adventure. Either way, reading it in Pipi's daughter's pretty-in-pink girly room made the whole experience seem sordid and twisted. When I later learned that the story was written by Charles Bukowski I was even more intrigued as to why he sent it, but there was no return address so I'll never know.

In order for me to conclude the coast to coast journey that started in Venice Beach, California, Pipi took me to Cedar Point, Connecticut, to look out over the Atlantic. Actually, we looked over Long Island Sound but the Atlantic Ocean flows through it, and that was good enough for me to declare this leg of the journey done.

The sky and sea were evening into the impenetrable deep green of the Atlantic. Across the middle, a Rothko was writ large upon the world. The vast shoreline was awash with seashells and broken glass. The expanse of dark water seemed exposed and unpredictable, as though there might be sharks or submarines in the undertow – but it smelled like the ocean, and by God I'd missed that salty breeze.

I still needed to resolve the outstanding traffic citation from Nebraska, so Colin drew up directions to the local police station. They were easy to follow and my mission was successful. However, returning home I went the wrong way around a roundabout into oncoming traffic. Luckily, the only thing I hit was bad language. It rattled me though, and soon I was lost in the neighbouring town of Norwalk before I realised I was no longer heading to Westport.

It made me crazy.

The last four signposts said *Westport,* and then at the critical junction – nothing. I no longer had the information I needed to proceed. I was shouting to no one in particular, 'How do you expect me to understand this if you only give me half the information?'

Then it hit me. Insight. *That's how it is with me and Pig. I'm completely paralysed by the fact that I only have half the information. I only have my side of the story because he can't, doesn't or won't tell me his.*

Ever since he left, ever since he told me he was unhappy, I'd been trying to make sense of it. How would he view the end of our marriage by the time it passed into anecdote? How would he phrase it? 'I stopped loving her', 'a mid-life crisis', 'a mistake'?

In not getting that letter to me he'd set me free. It may have been my fault, but the fact remained – his letter didn't come. He didn't come. I was alone with only half the information to make decisions about us as a couple, but I had all the information to make decisions about me.

I am lovable. I am free.

The revelation of the wrong way roundabout was this: I may never know what happened to our love. There was a real possibility he didn't know either. Maybe the signposts were missing for both of us.

Finally I could accept that I might never know what he'd been through, but more than that, I realised it was completely irrelevant to me.

I believed in our love. Nothing changes that. All that changed was how we expressed it. Friends, lovers, family. It's all love. I wouldn't wallow in my attachment a moment longer. There was a universe waiting to reward me for doing something. I was excited to see what that would be. I parked Betty with Charlotte and Hugh, and boarded a flight to Britain.

Time to let this little birdie fly.

THE ENGLISH ARE KISSING

Arriving at Heathrow Airport, the only thing I had to declare was an unusually high level of optimism. I hoisted my duffel bag onto my back and strode out of the airport and into an English Summer of Love.

My previous visits to the UK had been work-related and the overall impression I got was that Britain was a country which liked a jolly good spanking. The London I was disgorged into this time was totally different. Piccadilly was in the full flowery bloom of a hot European summer. Every window box and street lamp was bucolic with petunias, pansies and impatiens. The cloudless sky was beaming with such benevolence it wasn't even necessary to squint.

Irreconcilable with memory, the English were smiling. Some were even kissing. In the street. England seemed young and frisky and it was infectious. To quote a man passing by, 'Oh yeah, that makes your gonads tingle'.

There have been times in my life when overworked or lacking confidence, just knowing I would soon see my good friend Michele was enough to make me feel like Noddy going to visit Big Ears. May the censors also ban me for waking up and feeling a little queer, but I was excited.

Michele answered the door to her Primrose Hill home and we fell on each other like puppies. She grabbed my head in both hands and squeezed her signature air-kisses into me, 'Ah moom, moom, moom, moom.' Then held me at arm's length, 'Look at you. So slim.'

'The Dumpee Diet,' I replied, following her inside. 'It involves throwing up for a fortnight, then being too angry to eat for a year. It's not Weight Watchers but it does have its own distinctive lack of charm.'

'Well, you look great.'

Michele is ageless. She's five years older than me and ten years younger. She also has a great arse, which I followed up her precipitous stairs. 'You're looking pretty good yourself,' I observed.

'Hmm. You should see the world from this side. Dancing 'til four in the morning. What was I thinking?'

When younger son Will started kindergarten, Michele returned to university and chose philosophy to get some perspective on her life. Her husband Mark had been in and out of hospital and she was enjoying academic problems as a relief from existential ones. With her first year of study behind her, she'd taken a night off to celebrate.

'Was it worth it?'

She nodded emphatically, 'You have to go dancing while you're here. I forgot how cute twenty year olds are. Little babies jumping up and down.'

The summer school holidays had started and Mark had taken their boys away so Michele could have some childfree time to revise for her exams and then catch up with me. *What a gift!*

Over a cup of tea, Michele pulled a box of Marlboro Gold cigarettes from its hiding place behind a row of cookbooks. 'That's pathetic, Michele. You hid them from your parents, now you're hiding them from your children?'

'Yeah. Want one?'

I gave up smoking years ago, but Michele, who had been away from Australia even longer, didn't know. Even though giving up was among the hardest and most unpleasant things I've ever done, I leaned forward on an adolescent impulse and took one. Lit it. Inhaled. Then exhaled with a long, contented sigh. *Oh baby, where have you been all my life?*

If my year had been emotionally fraught, Mark and Michele's was hell. We had a lot to catch up on and unleashed a conversation that raged all over London.

Literally.

We strode up Primrose Hill and down Regent's Park. We marched along Marylebone High Street, around the Regency architecture via Oxford Street and into Soho. We paraded through Piccadilly, Trafalgar Square and passed Buckingham Palace. We circled back towards Bloomsbury so she could show me where she studied at Birkbeck – a prestigious college within the University of London.

Michele talked so fast they'd pull her over for speeding in Nebraska. Her wild blonde hair seemed to move independently, as though animated by ideas from within. 'Philosophy's a way for us to approach the really big questions.'

'To swallow, or not to swallow?' I asked.

Caught by surprise, she laughed. 'An absolutely vital philosophical question about the nature of being.'

'Whether it is nobler to suffer the gagging and distaste, or spit and wash the sheets?'

'A serious issue. Do you have the necessary and sufficient conditions for swallowing? Can you justify a true belief of the state of mind of the swallowing?'

'Honour, love and, um, convenience?'

And so we went, careening from love to death to blow jobs as we ploughed our way back up Primrose Hill.

All the letters I could possibly want were waiting for me back at Michele's. The one from Pig made me cry for all its easy, loving friendship: *I think of you every day and hope that the wind is blowing around you and nourishing your great spirit and gentle soul.* Clearly our friendship mattered.

'What am I going to do with him?' I asked Michele. 'Or without him, as the case seems to be.'

There was no need to show her the letter. She knew how it was. 'You ever read *The Unquiet Grave* by Cyril Connolly?' she asked. 'He understood the crazy jujitsu that keeps a couple in a state of lingering decay. You do it by leaving but not leaving.'

'Pig's in Sydney and I'm in London. I couldn't go any further without starting to come back.'

'What goes around, goes around and around,' she said wisely.

I woke up with my first smoke-over in years. It's just like a hangover, only worse. I crawled into the kitchen where Michele was fielding phone calls while bringing muesli and fruit together. I asked her which food group she thought tobacco belonged to and she looked scandalised. 'You addict. I can't believe you. No.'

She was right. Ten years without a fag and there I was hanging out for a burning hair of the dog. My resolve held in the short term but the vacuum had broken on the seal and there was no stuffing that genie back in its pack.

Michele's phone was ringing hot. She was organising an end-of-exam party at her university and invited me to be her date. I was looking forward to it, imagining fine Byronic men drinking Pimm's and discussing things from high up their brow. I jokingly nicknamed it 'The Philosopher's Ball'.

'I wish,' she said. 'It'll probably be more like the Philosopher's Balls-up.'

For the last term they'd been studying Edmund Gettier's theory of 'justified true belief'. His short paper observed that a person could have justifiable reasons to believe something was real or correct, and still be wrong. Ironically, for a problem about what is or isn't knowable, one of the questions in the exam had been ambiguous, and a number of students were boycotting the party to send a message to their professors. Michele was trying to soothe ruffled feathers.

'You study philosophy, Michele, but it's always psychology with you.'

'*Ha.* You can talk. You might like philosophy. It has a rigour to making sense of the world that discounts the emotional.'

Listening to her talk about her studies was like listening to any geek. I was interested. I wanted to share her enthusiasm, but the information bounced off my brain as though I were philosophy-proof. The more I lost my way, the more insistently she'd try another route.

'The example Gettier gives is about fake barns. Imagine a film crew has erected the façade of a barn in a field for a shot. You're driving through the country, nothing to do with the film crew, but you see their barn in a field. You're in the country. Barns are in the country. You've seen other barns like this one. You have all the necessary information to justify your belief in the barn – but you're wrong.' That last bit was said triumphantly.

'Well, what's the name of the film?'

I saw the inexhaustible run out. I saw her deflate and it made me sad. I wasn't trying to be obtuse. Funny, maybe, but not mean. I could even see at its core the Gettier problem was the same as the one I had in my marriage. Everything had looked real, but it wasn't.

I'd been justified in my belief that we were okay, but we weren't. The human heart is a world in which you might sometimes want to question what is true.

'Okay,' I said hoping to win back some respect. 'What you can and can't know. You see a pair of sunglasses. They're designer glasses. They have the look. They have the logo. They have the price. But they're rip-offs from Thailand and the only way you can tell is the misspelled name, *Jean Paul Gettier*.'

She clapped her hands. 'And you, Cinderella, can go to the Philosopher's Ball.'

'It was during the next twenty minutes that there occurred one of those tiny incidents which revolutionises the whole course of our life and alter the face of history. Truly we are the playthings of enormous fates.'

Cyril Connolly, *The Unquiet Grave*

'You don't know from one phone call to the next where life will take you.'

Joy Jobbins, mother of the author

The party was outdoors on a pretty summer's evening. Around 9pm the slowly setting sun left us standing under a deepening sky criss-crossed by glowing apricot vapour trails. Vibrant young things were talking animatedly about – who knows? Philosophy, probably.

Michele, after her initial reluctance, arrived on gossamer wings, her hands and hair flitting with particular nervous energy. She introduced me to her friend Scott, who was the other half of the Philosophical Society steering committee. He was talking to a fellow student, Soren. Michele handed me a drink and disappeared into the crowd.

I sat on a wooden bench next to Scott, listening to Soren nut out an argument about one of their exam questions. I was concentrating. Really, I was. I was concentrating on Soren's practical workman's shirt, his European good looks, the intensity and intelligence with which he spoke.

Scott, who was closer, smelled nice. Not perfumed, but sweet. He had a calm profile, a handsome, strong nose, and a serene brow swept by fine blond hair. *He's going to lose that,* I thought.

They were sufficiently intent on their conversation that I could get away with staring at them openly by just looking interested in what they were saying. Occasionally a word or phrase snuck into my cranium and bounced around. 'Epistemology'. 'Justified'. 'Sheep'. 'Barn'. 'Induction'.

Scott politely turned to ensure I was interested. Frankly, I had been day-dreaming, but managed to chop the air with my right hand and say, 'Ah, Gettier …' in what I hoped was a definitive manner.

His face lit up, 'What do you think?'

I thought this man had beautiful eyes – deep, intelligent, good humoured brown eyes – which I searched for clues as to what might be the right answer. 'Sheep and barns,' I said, 'I guess there's a limit to what you can know.'

They both laughed, so that was nice. I'd made a joke. He asked me where I was from and what I was doing in London and, after a courteous pause, went back to his conversation with Soren.

I went back to daydreaming about his peachy skin. The nape of his neck was almost blue. *How do you get skin that white?* And how do you get such a perfectly formed welt in the middle of your forehead?

When Scott turned to look at me, I saw he had a very new, very angry sore in the middle of his brow. It was surrounded by an equally angry swelling, which inferred a recent impact. The whole blossoming flower was set off by light bruising. Plainly, something hard, flat and fast had hit him in the middle of his head.

Eventually the party dispersed. Michele gathered me up to get something to eat. Scott asked if he could tag along, and the three of us went to get some Indian food.

In the street I asked him about a word he used a lot in his conversation with Soren. It sounded like something belonging to electricity, like conduction. I'd been struggling to fit it into philosophy. 'What does induction mean?'

Scott looked at me with genuine surprise, then rolled over his ankle into the gutter.

'You're quite clumsy, aren't you?' I said, helping him to stand upright.

'You don't know what induction is?' he asked, ignoring the fact he'd probably just sprained his ankle and was now limping in pain. 'I thought you were one of Michele's philosophy friends from Australia.'

'No. I'm a film maker.'

'Blagger.'

Turns out 'induction' is a Philosophy 101 word. Something they issue in a list on the first day you turn up to school. It means learning from observation. The sun rises every day, therefore you can *induce* the sun will rise today. It's a relative of deduction, but without needing to connect a missing fact. Importantly, it's *the* central concept of the Gettier problem, so Scott was onto me. I knew shit about philosophy, and since blagging was local slang for bullshitting, he had me there, too.

Dinner was in a heaving Indian restaurant in Covent Garden. Scott ordered a vegetarian thali, a dozen mini-meals served on itty bitty metal dishes.

'This can't be a fancy restaurant if they serve TV dinners,' I said.

He smiled at my joke and I wondered why I'd never heard of a male English Rose before. (Although, it transpired he was from Wales, not England.) Scott was studying philosophy part-time. His Clark Kent day job was as a technical designer in the cartography department of Dorling Kindersley. 'You wouldn't think there was a lot of room for design in maps,' I said, teasing him, 'most of the continents being finished and all.'

'There's always room for adding a little filigree to the fjords, an island or two to the archipelagoes.'

I pointed at the sore in the middle of his head, 'So what great idea struck you so hard?'

He touched his brow with an open hand and groaned. He'd been one of the babies Michele had been dancing with after their exams. Scott, however, had to work the next day. When he got home at 4am, he hadn't so much gone to bed as fallen across it. When his alarm rang at seven, he sat bolt upright – into the wall next to his bed.

'Of all the ways I imagined you doing that, it never occurred to me it could be a sleep injury.'

The juxtaposition between the elegant, urbane cartographer who studied philosophy in his free time, and the (probably) concussed party animal telling stories of his own excruciating clumsiness was adorable. Strange to think he was probably only ten years old when I started dating Pig.

We finished dinner and went out into Leicester Square. Michele and I were walking home, and Scott was going to meet some friends at a nightclub. Scott asked if we'd mind taking some papers he'd collected from the philosophy office. He was speaking to Michele, but handed them to me. 'I'll come over and pick them up in a day or two.'

Michele teased me about it all the way home. 'He likes you. He gave you his homework so he could see you again.'

'No, he gave me the papers because he didn't want to dance around them like a sad old fart at Fellowship.'

'No, he likes you. You should follow that up. He's really sweet, and very bright.'

'Don't be absurd. He's way too young. I felt positively geriatric standing next to him.'

'He's not that young. He's nearly thirty.'

'He is not.'

'He's twenty-six or twenty-seven – something like that. This is his *third* uni degree.'

'Really? He looks about twenty. Wouldn't you kill for that English skin?'

'You probably won't have to.'

'I meant on me.'

'So did I.'

'Michele! There is no world in which that man would find me attractive.'

The next day Mark returned home with the boys, and they circled me in their loving arms. It was good to see my friend upright and moving through the world unassisted, even though he was still frail.

As to their sons, Nick and Will, the last time I saw them, Will had been a baby. Now he was every bit the young boy. 'Where's baby Will gone?' I asked the five year old.

'I ate him,' he replied proudly.

Okay.

'It's a game,' said Michele, 'now you tickle him and he throws up baby Will.' She demonstrated, and Will and Nick were soon writhing on the floor in fits of laughter.

Over dinner, Michele was as happy as I'd ever seen her, talking animatedly about her exams. A summer storm broke, and she flung open the windows to let the cool air rush around us. 'A southerly buster!' she joked, which, for those of you not from Sydney, is a summer wind not found in London.

Mark bundled the kids up and they went to bed, leaving Michele and me alone to retrieve the naughty cigarettes. We crawled out onto the roof to smoke them under an orange night sky washed clean by the storm.

'So now you're single, where do you stand on dating?' my friend asked.

'I don't. I had three official dates before I got married and they were all disasters. I've sworn off them forever.'

'Meaningless sex, then?'

'No such thing, is there? Long after you roll out of the wet patch, you're still in the emotional mess you made to get there.'

'So celibacy it is.'

The small orange pinpoint of her cigarette tip lit up. 'How bad were these dates of yours?'

'Oh, they were bad. On one, when I was sixteen or seventeen, I filled a sock with talcum powder and put it in my pocket so I could squeeze it when I got nervous.'

'Okay, that's weird.'

'My hands get really clammy when I'm anxious, and we were going to see *Jaws*. Every time Bruce, the mechanical shark, appeared I squeezed the sock. Job done. Dry hands.'

'Squeezed the sock. That's not a euphemism, is it?'

'Ha ha. No. When Bruce made his move, so did the guy.'

'In for the kill.'

'I was totally complicit. Pashing, necking, petting, whatever – that part was fun, but when we emerged into the blinking daylight after the film, my brand new boyfriend and his black sloppy joe were covered, and I mean encrusted, with my white talcum handprints.'

'Oh, that's painful.'

'That wasn't even the most embarrassing one. That prize went to the Crows Nest Boys High School formal. I was about fourteen, all awkward new tits and dental braces. My Aunty Penny took pity and pimped me out to her neighbour's son who also had braces. She was so excited, she bought me a pretty cheesecloth dress with an empire line and daisies embroidered on it. I thought I looked like Lady Guinevere.

'So this kid turned up, and he was gorgeous – a total schoolyard god with blond hair, green eyes and, well, braces. We went to his school dance, and everyone else was wearing jeans and black leather. But that was okay. My date seemed to think I looked nice.

'Some friends of his invited us down to the back of the playground for a cigarette and a drink. I primly refused both, but accepted my date's offer of a kiss. My first kiss. A gentle kiss. For two kids wearing braces, a loving, respectful kiss. Which made it super confusing when my "ups" got caught in his cross-wires. We had no idea. I started to pull away and there was this moment of claustrophobic agony. We were totally joined by our front teeth.

'We negotiated our way through the schoolyard. Through the dance hall. Through the dancers. Past the band, to the St John's Ambulance men – who couldn't help us because they were laughing too hard.

'Eventually the older of the two ambulance men cut my date's wires with some pliers, which freed me, but imagine the humiliation of explaining what happened to your braces to your parents?'

It took Michele a while to compose herself. When she did, she asked, 'You said three dates. How bad was the last one?'

'So bad I had to marry him. He spilled more than one rum and coke on me, lost my teapot and sat on the cat. There's no way he can ever go on another date. All I have to do is wait for this to pass, then I'll pounce.'

'Really?'

'No, probably not.'

I was only in London for a few days. Among the things I wanted to do was visit the legendary Turner collection at the Tate gallery.

The exhibition was a knockout, but not in the way I expected. The paintings were laid out in chronological order. By standing in the middle of the room you could spin around and watch an artist mature. Clear, precise, mythical expressions slowly unfolded into highly emotional abstractions.

One painting, of a ship in a snow storm, was so impressionistic I couldn't imagine what gave Turner the courage to defy his generation and create something so original. It wasn't just the picture, which was lively and chaotic, it was that he painted it when he was old and half-blind. Maturity doesn't mean setting yourself in stone, or hardening the resolution of who you are. It can also be a wild abandonment of constraint, a surrender to change.

While I was having this revelation, that I would age better if I gave in to chaos, two suits from the city were using the otherwise empty room to discuss a large and delicate financial transaction. One turned to his reluctant cohort and said, 'You're safe, it's only change.'

Sitting outside smoking a cigarette afterwards, I felt deflated. Not exactly lost, but like that ship at sea in the snow storm. My life was chaotic and uncontrollable, and the future was hard to see. Who knew what could come from surrendering to it? Maybe pain and uncertainty. Or maybe it would lead to the path with heart.

You're safe, it's only change. It's curiously soothing to say out loud.

I wondered whether it was true or not, what I'd said to Michele about waiting for Pig. How long can you wait? It'd been eighteen months already. He'd moved on. Why couldn't I?

You're safe, it's only change.

Maybe it was time for me to repeat the mantra that brought Betty into my life. 'Whatever is perfect for me, in a perfect and balanced way, let it happen now, with thanks.' I then added, 'And, God? If you could throw in a little healthy, happy bonking, well, that'd be real nice.'

When I got home Michele had dinner underway and six places set at the table. Scott was dropping by to pick up the papers he'd left with us the other night.

THE SACRED RECYCLING BINS OF PRIMROSE HILL

Sometimes, like a good Rolling Stones song, you don't always get what you want but, if you ask very nicely, you might possibly get what you need.

Dinner was Australian-rowdy, an undignified hodgepodge of shouting and laughter counterpointed by serious points of view. The company (a pair of philosophers, two journalists and a couple of kids) was excellent and blew through me like fresh humanity.

Now that Michele had pointed out the bleeding obvious, I could see that Scott was a lot older than I first thought but I still doubted her assessment that he found me attractive.

Three courses included rack of lamb, too much wine, and poached fruit with ice cream. Afterwards there was a clatter of dishes up and down the stairs to the kitchen, and the kissing of children for bed time. Then suddenly Scott and I were alone.

It was past ten o'clock when we stepped out onto the balcony and pulled the glass door closed behind us. The warm summer sky had descended into the deep Prussian blue of a European night. A pale green thumbnail rimmed the horizon. Scott offered me a cigarette from a ten-pack.

'That's so cute. Is it a child's portion?'

I took the cigarette, and he lit a match for me with both hands cupped around the flame like a farmer. As he leaned over to present it to me, the light caught the gentle arc of his brow and etched his fine, strong nose against the night.

We talked for a bit about what I was doing in London. How I was in the middle of a road trip across America. About my ex. It was all framed in the sort of light banter which ends up with two grownups flicking cigarette butts from the parapets like a pair of delinquents. Scott won butts-down. His sailed across the road after a single-handed, thumb-over-forefinger, marbles-style flick. While mine, flicked like a booger, barely made it out of the sphere of gravity.

Scott stood back to watch me flick my butt. I smiled helplessly as it hit the pavement. 'I have three brothers, I really should do better than that.'

We stood there looking at each other for a moment. A hopeful breeze shifted the eddies of warmth on my skin. Someone nearby had soft music playing through summer-night windows.

'You're so beautiful,' he said unexpectedly, 'I'm completely stupid in your presence.'

It was the nicest compliment anyone has ever paid me, but under the circumstances of a butt-flicking contest, I laughed.

'I'm sorry I sound so clumsy,' he continued, trying to make up for my gaff, 'but if I don't say something now, you'll be gone and everything will be impossible.'

He didn't sound clumsy. He sounded like he'd thought about it. Like he'd thought about me and the fact that I was leaving soon.

I don't know what I expected when I asked the universe for romance: a film maker, an older man, a raconteur – one of my usual suspects. Instead, standing in front of me, lit by the living-room lights shining through the glass door, was an absolutely astonishing

… what? Cartographer, designer, philosopher, klutz. Someone impossibly romantic burning with curiosity.

He stepped forward and kissed me. He kissed me with such rare excitement he quite literally took my breath away. As in, I had to put my hand out to steady myself, and then sit down before I fainted.

I'm safe, it's only change.

He looked concerned, perhaps thinking I'd sunk to the floor in disappointment. But it was neither. It was a potent dose of Edwardian romance. He kissed me and I swooned. I actually swooned.

He sat down next to me, 'Are you alright?'

Maybe love is a symptom of low blood pressure. My response was totally physical and it involved my perception of reality dissolving and becoming something unfamiliar. I felt something, and it was in his kiss.

We talked for a bit. We kissed a bit more. He wanted to know what I wanted to do, but I didn't know. 'Do you want to come back to my place?'

I did, but I also didn't trust what was happening. 'In principle, yes. It's just – can I think about it?'

We agreed to go on a picnic the next night and work it out from there.

The next morning at breakfast, Michele was looking at me with her best mother's expression, as if to say, *And what have you been up to, young lady?*

I returned the look with my best adolescent, *Why are you looking at me in that rather peculiar fashion? Don't you know it's putting unflattering lines on your forehead?*

Once we'd completed a repertoire of nonverbal dialogue, I submitted to the underlying interrogation. 'Oh, he's cute, that's all.

And "cute" isn't right either. He's attractive, but honestly, where can this go?'

'Too right,' she replied, 'I make a point never to date anyone prettier than me.'

I laughed, then pointed out her historical inaccuracy.

'So is that, that?' she asked.

'No, we're all going on a picnic this evening. My treat.'

Michele and Mark had other plans and couldn't come. I didn't want the pressure of a simple evening turning into a *date*, and gladly accepted their request to babysit Will. He could be our chaperone.

Also, Michele had double booked with another colleague, Henry, an Oxford don who was a world expert in very small numbers, so he was bunged into the mix. My uncomplicated idea of a family picnic had disintegrated and then reformed into something weirder – a double date with two men and a baby chaperone.

Michele said Scott was a vegetarian. As I wandered the aisles of the local Sainsbury's choosing dips and cheeses, the idea of a date with a much younger man bounced around my head like a pachinko ball. (Seriously, a pachinko ball.) I'd asked the universe for romance and this was what I was given. It would be churlish to turn him down. I didn't want to turn him down. What would sleeping with him mean? Could I enjoy a holiday romance? What had I asked for? Meaningless, happy bonking? Is that what this was? Was I ready for that? Was I ready to become that person again?

This is what I knew: he was handsome, he was bright, he was the friend of a friend (so he wasn't an axe murderer), he had a confidence that spoke of good self-esteem, he liked me. Here is something else I knew: in Sainsbury's I was just another mad lady with a shopping trolley talking to herself.

↔

The day was sunny and warm, and the evening long-grassed and honey-scented. I never imagined that London could be so pretty. We agreed to meet at Mark and Michele's then walk to Parliament Hill on Hampstead Heath.

I was standing on the balcony (smoking) and got a good look at Scott as he walked down Chalcot Road. He was clicking his heels like Granddad used to. I loved the way Poppy walked like a flamenco dancer. It made my heart leap. Scott walked like a good man.

Michele's friend Henry turned out to be another handsome, smart Englishman. He arrived wearing grey Oxford bags held up with braces, and a collarless shirt. Scott was wearing a hemp shirt with a tan waistcoat. I have a photo from the evening. In it Scott, Henry and Will have turned to me (with the camera) for approval of the picnic site. Except for Will's bright red running shoes, we look like we're picnicking in an E.M. Forster novel.

Both men brought wine and glasses. Neither brought food, but it wasn't a problem, I'd catered for the Last Supper: quiches, pies, salads, olives, dolmades, avocadoes, breads, cheeses. Michele filled a thermos with tea, and packed a sponge cake for dessert. It was a feast.

Henry was a good foil for the first date tension. He was older and already had his PhD, which offered an unspoken challenge to Scott. While they didn't exactly fight over me, there was certainly some lively banter. Henry was particularly funny when talking about statistics and very small numbers. For example, did you know that most people have more arms than is statistically normal? It's because many people lose half an arm, but rarely have three.

Dinner was a triumph. By 9.30 it wasn't even dark but Will needed to be home. Henry decided he could make it back to Oxford if he rushed to catch the last bus, and ran away shouting out an invitation for us to visit him there on the weekend.

Us. Like we were a couple.

The best time in a relationship is when both parties are all dressed up with somewhere to go. If I had all the time in the world, I'd stretch that moment out forever. I'd live in the space between the beats of the clock, where everything that is anticipated is good and exciting. But I only had three more days, and one was almost over. Unsure of the next move, I tried to catch a glimpse of the 'real' Scott. I read meaning into his hand that lingered too long when brushing mine. I felt the air arcing between us, sex the unspoken subtext.

Back in Primrose Hill, Michele and Mark were waiting. Michele put Will to bed while Mark put the kettle on, and we all sat up with a nightcap.

It was about midnight when I finally said, 'Well, it's been a lovely evening. Scott and I are off now.' It was later than we'd sat up on all the other nights, so it was probably time for them to turn in anyway.

'We're going?' asked Scott in a bewildered voice. 'Where are we going?'

'To your place. I'll get my bag.' I'd packed a little rucksack with some essentials for the morning. Underwear, makeup remover, makeup.

I felt I was being rude to my hosts in leaving like that but, well, they were grownups. Mark realised we'd be walking past the recycling bins and gave us several bags of empty bottles to deposit on our way.

After lots of hugs and kisses and promises of returning tomorrow, Scott and I finally left. I was really pleased with myself. I felt that I'd extracted us with a degree of dignity – although I wasn't sure Mark was comfortable with it. Michele had some time to get used to the idea of me being separated from Pig, but this was a seismic shift for Mark, to whom I'd barely spoken of my feelings. It felt a bit like leaving their house with the wrong man. But they were gracious and waved us off seeming mildly amused rather than alarmed.

'Well,' I said with a self-satisfied sigh as we chinked and clanked down the high street, 'that went well.'

'No, really,' asked Scott, 'where are we going?'

I looked at him and smiled a broad, this-is-a-fun-game smile, 'Your place.'

'Why are we going to my place?' His tone was stubborn.

'Because you invited me.'

'When did I invite you?'

The blood was starting to pump a little harder, sending a red blush of annoyance to my cheeks. 'Last night. You invited me last night.'

'But that invitation was *for* last night.'

'So, what? I'm not invited now?'

'Well, no. I'd like to invite you, but I haven't invited you.'

'Oh crap. Well that takes the cake,' I said, handing him my bags of bottles. I was going back to Mark and Michele's. 'Put these in the bins, would you?'

'Hang on. I'd like to ask you to my place. But I'd like to, you know, ask you.'

I sighed. 'So was that it? Did you just ask me?'

'No,' he said, walking towards me and leaning forward to give me a kiss. A gentle, soft kiss. The bags of bottles lightly bumping my thigh. 'You wanna come back to my place?'

'Yes,' I said petulantly.

I took my two bags of bottles back and we walked down the street to the rhythm of their clanking. 'Well, how were you planning to get us out of there?' I finally asked, still feeling injured.

'I don't know. I would have asked you after they'd gone to bed.'

'And I would have snuck off?'

'Sure. You could have left a note, or sneaked back in before they got up.' He was teasing me now.

We came to the railway bridge where the recycling bins sat – large black dumpsters with small round holes for squeezing bottles through. Each bottle made a satisfying smash as it plummeted to its death. When a train passed underneath us the world became a roaring, smashing wall of noise.

'*Waaaaaaaa*,' I shouted, drowned out by the cacophony. Scott looked surprised, then joined in. After the trains had passed and the bottles were broken, Scott pulled me to him and gave me another of his delicious kisses. In this strange hothouse romance we'd had our first fight and made up. The recycling bins on the Primrose Hill overpass are now a sacred site of love and healing.

As we walked along the busy road towards Scott's place in Camden, the trees thinned out, the age of the crowd lowered and the noise levels rose. Camden was a vibrant, dirty place full of nightclubs with queues spilling out onto the pavement. Late at night you could get anything you wanted there – drugs, girls, *minicabs*.

Scott's home looked grand from the outside but was one of several maisonettes carved from a much larger house. Inside had all the earmarks of communal living. There was a ubiquitous brown couch facing an excellent television set, baby-poo coloured carpet, and every cup, pot and saucer was stored in the dripping sink – only these boys were classy, *their* dishes were washed.

The toilet was on the landing, a remnant from London of the sixties – an old-fashioned water closet with flock wallpaper, a red light and a tasselled cord for the flush. The bathroom proper was the scene of an ongoing battle with lime scale. The lime scale was winning.

During my guided tour I fiddled with my overnight bag like it was a talisman of connectedness and identity. When I had a moment alone with it, I discovered I had only packed crap. I had an eyelash curler, but no toothbrush. Lip gloss, but no undies.

Scott proudly presented me with a purple Tek toothbrush fresh from its wrapper. I chose to think he had it for visitors who vacationed here over the summers. I suspected it was for the endless stream of girls arriving with neither eyelash curler nor undies.

I thanked him.

I brushed my teeth.

I looked at myself in the mirror.

What the hell are you doing, woman?

Half of Scott's room was taken up with a freestanding stereo he'd built for himself. The speakers looked like they belonged to our 1930s picnic. Given the men in my family are witty but useless, this seemed like a remarkable achievement. The other half of the room was a comfortable display of turn-of-the-century Ikea furniture: Billy bookcase, Dombås desk, and a Kugakaatcha double bed with Milf throw cushions.

I felt like a cat (an alley cat) who couldn't find a place to settle. I checked the books. (Studious philosophical tomes.) I twiddled the knobs on the stereo. (Loud, soft, loud.) I checked out the closet. (Clothes.)

The bed was recessed into a small alcove that would provide a perfect striking position should you choose to pass out sideways. 'Is this where the battle for your brains took place?' I asked.

'Yes. You see, I lay down like this,' he demonstrated how he had concussed himself, 'and when the alarm rang. *Wham.* Knock me out before you go-go.'

Yeah. Awkward.

The only place to sit was on the bed, so I was circling. A little plane without a landing strip. Among the papers on his desk was a portfolio of graphic design work. I brought it over to the bed and opened it on my lap.

'How romantic,' he said, 'just like a job interview.'

His artwork was sophisticated. A final year piece about Schopenhauer looked like an album cover. He'd used it to apply to Birkbeck; no wonder they were impressed.

While I flipped through the pages, he put Leftfield on the stereo. *Leftism*. It sounded like London as another planet – a young man's world where people express ideas and make art. The music was nice. Sexy, but not self-conscious. A well-considered antidote for how I was feeling.

Well, that's about it. I'm taking the fifth from here. As I throw you out of our bedroom, I offer you one parting glimpse: Scott had the only natural sixpack I have ever seen in striking distance.

OXFORD DREAMING

Scott's alarm went off at 7.30, blaring the BBC Radio 1 News. Frankly, it was shocking. The house snapped awake with the sound of showers and the smell of cooking toast. It was Thursday morning, a traditional workday of celebration as the world revolved towards the weekend.

There wasn't time for romance. The day started with rollerskates on. Scott gave me a crusty towel, showed me how the bathroom worked, and waited until my eyelashes were curled before walking me to the Tube.

We made a plan to meet after work, and I left him on Camden Town platform with a mixture of amazement and the weird awkwardness of feeling like everyone knew I'd just had sex. We've all done the walk of shame in last night's evening dress but, wow, there's something super weird about returning to your friend's home when your friends know you've been sleeping with their friends.

Mark and Michele greeted me with a message from Sue. So how's this for divine intervention? She had made a detour from Sydney via Seoul and had phoned to see if we could move our meet-up in New York from Friday to Monday night. *Yes.* I'd have the weekend in London. I may have been feeling squeamish about my morals, but the universe approved. I changed my flight and turned the day over to my hosts.

Mark wasn't working that day and Michele was going to a conference in Liverpool, so we carried her bags to Euston Station and waved her off. Then Mark and I went to lunch in Soho so we could finally catch up properly and I could find out more about his health.

Two years earlier Mark had contracted a rare autoimmune disease – a virus that his immune system mistook for his own body. 'Once it killed the virus,' he said, 'it then set about killing everything else: tissue, organs, bones. The doctors are treating it the way they do cancer, with steroids and chemotherapy. It's under control for the moment, but it's been pretty hideous. I think I've blotted out the worst of it.'

Always the master of understatement – Mark had died a few times and been resuscitated. It was a miracle that he was living in a city with one of the best rare and tropical disease hospitals in the world. 'But the real shock,' he said, 'was you two. What happened? Was there no chance to be had?'

Mark and Pig were friends, or at least friendly, so I unpacked the story for him with as much respect for their relationship as possible. As we sifted through it, I wondered whether my marriage had maybe suffered some sort of emotional autoimmune disease. 'Maybe our edges had become so blurred that his reinvention ate through the both of us.'

'Perhaps it will all make sense in retrospect.'

'Do you really think so?'

'No, I was hoping to sound sage.'

I told Mark about my visit to the Tate and the marvellous revelation of Turner's ship in a snow storm. That maybe things don't make sense in the way we hope they will when we're children. 'I think the only way to negotiate chaos is to surrender to it.'

'No. If I was surrendering to my body's chaos, I'm pretty sure

I'd be dead by now.' He suggested, instead, we go to the National Gallery, where he'd show me his favourite painting.

The Arnolfini Portrait by Dutch master Jan van Eyck is a painting of a droll couple standing in their Amsterdam bedroom. When he pointed it out to me amid all the other classical works I was surprised my friend rated it so highly. 'Why?'

'Well, there are all the technicalities – the quality of light, the metal chandelier, his use of oils.' He pointed out the bits. 'But mostly I like the drama of the pose.'

'What drama? They're stern and staid.'

'The intimacies,' he said. 'Look. Is the wife pregnant? Is the master of the house greeting us, blessing us, or telling us to wait a moment? See her slippers – are we supposed to imagine her bare feet? Imagine her nude? But, really, I just like that they have such a great sense of humour.'

It was me laughing now. Surely he was taking the piss. 'They're a couple of medieval nouveau richies showing off their stuff.'

'Maybe, but they're doing it lightly. Look in the mirror,' he said, pointing to the back wall. 'The painter's in it, and someone else is watching over his shoulder. And the signature, an ornate inscription, *Jan van Eyck was here 1434* – like graffiti. It's hard to imagine such dour looking people having a sense of humour, but I really think they do. I think they're all in on it. It's a 15th-century selfie and they're mugging for the painter. I like them for that.'

Viewed this way, he was right – it really was a lively picture, and by showing it to me he wrote himself into Scott and my story. This was our van Eyck moment. Scott and I holding hands in Mark and Michele's Primrose Hill home, with our friends observing our meeting, and now you guys piling in to jump up and down on the mattress while van Eyck and I finish the portrait of a five-day romance.

Yes, five days. That's all we had from beginning to end. Having decided to dive in, there was no slowing the headlong rush.

↔

Scott and I met after work and went to dinner in Covent Garden. I showed him a snap of Betty. 'She's glorious, can I keep this for my wallet?'

'Let's not rush things, huh?' I snatched the photo back. 'I was able to change my flight to Monday morning,' I added casually.

'You did that for me?'

'Hmm,' I mumbled, using the universal sound for not actually dissembling. 'Can I move my things over to your place? Thought I'd better ask this time.' He leaned over and kissed me – the universal symbol of assent.

The best thing about such a short fling is that even the bad times are good. We went to the movies. My choice. I chose unwisely. We sat through a cloying romance starring Johnny Depp. Fortunately I hated it more than Scott.

'Well, that's a relief,' he said, 'I was thinking I'd have to dump you right there in the cinema.'

'Tough, but fair. Maybe we should drink to forget it.'

I redeemed myself by introducing Scott to Rolling Rock, an American pale ale sold in a dinky green bottle. 'It's a legacy of their enormous German population,' I told him, sounding more like a children's TV host than ever. 'Most people don't know this, but back in the 1700s, English was chosen over German as the official American language by only one vote.'

'I'm surprised that's not used in a campaign about how every vote counts.'

We went back to his place and made out. I had sincerely forgotten how gorgeous twenty-six is. Twenty six needs to be defined as the perfect age for a man. It's the age of an Etruscan warrior, a ballet dancer, or a rockstar in his prime. In Scott's case, it's the age of a young man of classical proportions with the romantic expression of a Rodin sculpture. *Ha!* You need me to tell you I was smitten? He was gorgeous.

Laying with my head on his chest was irresistible. 'I love you,' I said. It was a weird thing to say – *way* too soon. I simply didn't know him, except in the biblical sense, so I added, 'Nothing personal.' And he laughed.

The next morning, I went to Mark and Michele's to pick up my luggage and say goodbye. I was supposed to be leaving, but not to Camden Town. My friends couldn't have been kinder, but it all seemed so rash.

I dropped my bags at Scott's place. They didn't fit in his room so I parked them outside his door where they looked suss, like I was moving in, like I was a bunny boiler going from naught to everything in forty-eight hours. 'I'm not moving in,' I explained to his flatmates, 'I'm just here for the sex.'

We went out for brunch. It was pure bliss drinking coffee and reading the papers like Europeans. It was hard not drawing comparisons to my marriage. I tried not to make them out loud, but everything that happened could be held up against eleven years of routine. Like, Pig and I never went out for breakfast. The cafe revolution annoyed him. He saw it as a pretentious adjunct to people who used the wrong yardsticks to measure character. An inveterate tea drinker, he even resented the fact that everyone aspired to be a connoisseur of the bean while only he understood the leaf.

Scott, on the other hand, really liked coffee. I'm tempted to say he was an aficionado, but I'm worried that may betray a little of Pig's prejudices.

'Australia was saved from British cooking by the Italians and the Greeks,' I told Scott. 'The Chinese and the Thai helped too, but the Italians gave us great coffee.'

'That's quite a claim. I'm pretty sure I can take you to the best coffee shop in the world.'

'Are you challenging me to a coffee-drinking taste test?'

'If you can think up a way to hold up your end of the bargain.' He had a point. My idea of a good coffee was instant, made with milk boiled in the microwave.

He took me to the Monmouth Coffee shop in Covent Garden, a phone-box sized outlet which roasts its own beans and pioneered the single-origin revolution.

'That's my office,' he said, pointing to a fire escape on the building behind the cafe. 'The smell of roasting coffee is so enticing. We should be paid a loading for the amount of money we spend here.'

He was greeted like a regular. Over the years he'd sampled all their blends and settled on a favourite – Huehuetenango Cuchumatán. It's a Guatemalan bean. Scott preferred the medium roast, prepared as a filtered coffee. I can't comment on the taste, other than it was nice coffee, but I can recommend the merits in learning to say its name, '*Hue-hue-tenango coochu-matan*.' It seems to be a spell for summoning sophisticated men.

As I was the tourist in town, Scott gave me the choice of the day. I wanted to go to Kenwood House – the neoclassical museum deep in the woods of Hampstead Heath – and see some Gainsborough paintings. They're icons of English culture and I'd never seen one in the pigment. I still haven't. Somehow the day ran away from us and it was already past 5pm. Although the house was closed, it wasn't a total loss. Through the window I glimpsed a huge skinny woman in a blue frock. She looked like she could do with a good feed.

A large crowd was gathering in the gardens for an evening of opera. The rich folks had tickets close enough to see something, while we plebs sat for free on a big lawn overlooking the duck pond. On a perfect summer's evening, it was too wonderful.

We lay in the long grass and waited for the concert to start. I have a mental snapshot of Scott. I'm lying in a field of long grass looking up at him looking down – blue sky and fair-weather clouds behind him. He looks so handsome – backlit, red sunshine bouncing off my dress and onto him. Youthful self-consciousness framed by a lock of long blond hair sweeping his gaze.

We left before the opera started.

When we got home, Scott's flatmates were watching television in the lounge. Malcolm and Paul were nursing 'stonking' hangovers by watching football (soccer) on TV. Barnsley were playing and Paul, who was the most passionate on the subject, tried to explain the rules to me. That's a subject for another lifetime, but the enduring result from that meeting is when asked who I follow he told me to say, 'Barnsley and anyone playing Arsenal', which apparently relates to an incident in 1919 that saw Barnsley relegated from the premier league. Grudges run deep in football.

We'd picked up some hot chips on the way home. Scott took them into the kitchen and 'plated' them with tomato sauce and mayonnaise artistically daubing the rim. It was funny, this gorgeous boy trying to create a dining experience – hell, cuisine – out of hot chips and 'dead horse'.

In Scott's room we listened to Leftfield, Talk Talk, Anita Baker and Paul Weller: the comfort zone to which he took this new foreign woman.

He put Talk Talk on first, *Spirit of Eden*, and we lay in the dark watching the ambient light from outside play around the room. Mark Hollis's voice was hauntingly vulnerable, like someone unaware of his audience. I found myself relaxing into a place that was both intimate and foreign. I was at home, but everything had been rearranged. I started softly crying, because time was running out, and because beginnings are like endings when you're lying with a stranger.

On Sunday, we took up Henry's invitation to go punting in Oxford. The day was so picturesque it was almost corny, all dappled light and ducklings, sunshine, rainbows and willow trees draping their leaves in the water. And time was slow, like it had taken a holiday. Mum used to have a *New Yorker* cartoon by Alan Dunn stuck to our fridge, it was of a suburban couple floating in a swan through the Elysian Fields. The caption read, *What was the name of that tranquiliser we took?* Sunday on the River Cherwell was like that.

Henry began punting with charming ease, sliding the long quant between his hands like a Venetian gondolier. Pushing us down the river.

'That's Parson's Pleasure,' he said, pointing out some picnickers on the bank. 'It used to be reserved for nude bathing by the dons.' Another push, another surge down the river. 'A habit they continued even after women were admitted. One day, the dons were caught by a woman floating by, like us. They covered their privates, all except one don who covered his face. When asked why, he said, "I don't know about you, gentlemen, but I'm known by my face."'

I asked if I could have a turn driving the boat. Henry handed me the pole, 'Remember to pull the stick out of the mud.' It sounded like unnecessary instruction – until I started punting. He'd made it look simple, but I struggled not to fall in. I also struggled not to lose the pole. It's possible to push the quant in and sail away from it.

But I didn't, so there we all were – me in my pretty red floral dress, punting two twenty-something young men along the River

Cherwell on a sunny Sunday afternoon. I've never seen straight guys more willing to look gay than the Brits.

↔

It was dark by the time Scott and I boarded the last bus to London. As Oxford rolled away from us, there was a claustrophobic tightening of time. Sunday night has always had an end-of-freedom feel, but this was different. In less than twelve hours, all this would be over. I wasn't ready for it to end. Wasn't ready to break up with someone I'd barely met.

I was fashing about trying to work out some way to reschedule, or stay, or do things differently. 'I could ring Sue and put her off for another week.'

'No,' said Scott, 'I don't want to be chasing time with you.' There was a simple truth to the way he said that. It caught me by surprise. 'If this is meant to work, there'll be all the time in the world for us.'

If this is meant to work? Was this ever going to be anything more than a holiday romance?

'Sue's a big girl. I'm sure she can spend a few days in New York on her own.'

'No,' he said firmly, 'I can't do anything about my deadlines next week, and nothing's to be gained but desperation over a few fleeting hours.'

It's so rare to be living in a movie moment, but that's what it felt like. All the midday movies I'd watched with my mother during rainy school holidays – *Waterloo Bridge, Casablanca, Now Voyager.* Here I was with my own Gary Cooper saying if we had any future at all, we had all the time in the world.

But we didn't. Did we?

↔

Scott's urgent deadline was a computer training course at Mac University. Yes, as in the computer company. He had dreams of publishing an online philosophy magazine and creating a revolution in knowledge. I suggest to you he'll be the world's first Geek Philosopher.

His course didn't start till eleven. My plane didn't go till one. There was still a little time for us to share the morning. Everyone else made their ritual bolt for work and we had the house to ourselves. As a special treat, Scott took me to the other bathroom. The *secret* bathroom.

It turned out Scott had a third flatmate, a policeman I hadn't met, who had an en suite for which he paid extra rent. Technically it was off limits to us mere mortals but since no one was around, so we snuck in.

It was much nicer than Limescale Hollow – modern, with a power shower, black slate floors and a towel rack that heated your towels. There was also a light dusting of talcum powder on the floor. I noticed it as we left, our double footprints marking our progress in and out of the room. I pointed this out to Scott, who said his flatmate was studying to become a detective, so we cleaned up after ourselves and re-set the booby trap with a fine new layer of talcum powder.

Scott decided we should take a taxi to the airport. I was scandalised by the expense, but he insisted it would give us extra time.

'You know, if I had the money I'd ask you to come,' I told him from deep down in the bucket backseat of the black cab.

'What? Drive across America with you?'

'Yes, and Sue. Although as it is I can't afford it myself. We'll have to camp wherever possible.'

We sat holding hands as the M4 blinked past at high speed. A spirit of urgency was underscoring everything. We weren't chasing days, we were chasing minutes. I felt an imperative to give him something of myself that was true and valuable. 'You know the other night, when we were lying in bed. I was crying.'

He looked at me for a moment. He knew, but he hadn't said anything. 'Did you cry because I seemed uninterested?'

'No, it wasn't that,' I said, while wondering if maybe it was. The English landscape which looked so verdant before now seemed dank and suburban. 'I don't think it was indifference,' I added, 'but the intimacy of the silence. It made our beginning feel like an ending. That's how it felt with my ex at the end. Lying in bed with a stranger.'

But I had rolled over and held him, and we made love, because Scott is Scott and this was a beginning, not an ending, and because I don't know what he's thinking when he's quiet in the dark.

Talking about it in the taxi wasn't much in the sea of love, but it was a single vulnerable truth that made me feel while I wasn't taking much away, the little I was taking was precious, and real, and healing.

MY FRIEND THE FIRECRACKER

Arriving at JFK Airport was like being disgorged into a Social Security claims department. Everyone was rendered jetlagged under the green neon lights and throwback linoleum décor. It was quite a comedown from the Summer of Love.

I scanned the sea of faces for my friend, but Sue was nowhere to be seen. I read the cardboard signs displayed by chauffeurs. None were for me. I went to the message board and checked under all the possible letters of my name. Nil. Nothing. Nada.

Because we'd made plans in the ad hoc elation of Friday's phone call, I had no idea where Sue was staying, or where she'd be if she wasn't here. I didn't even have a phone number in Seoul to find out if she left on time.

It was 9pm in London, borderline late to ring Mark and Michele, but I did anyway to make sure that Sue hadn't left a late message about her plans. The answer machine was on, so I said I'd arrived safely at JFK and thanked them for their hospitality.

I checked the buses to New York. There was one in an hour, so I booked onto it figuring if Sue wasn't here by then, I probably should leave anyway.

I'm safe. It's only change.

Having done all the logical things, I did the emotional thing and telephoned Scott. He answered, and I was grateful to hear his voice. I wanted to inhale him one last time before stepping back into my life and told him so.

'How can I get in touch with you while you're on the road?' he asked.

The idea he wanted to stay in touch seemed to soothe everything. Suddenly it was okay to be lost in New York. I was okay. I was where I was meant to be.

I gave him Marc's details in LA. 'It's my sister's ex-husband. I phone him every three days when I'm on the road in case the bogeyman gets me.'

I had planned to give up smoking on the eight-hour flight, but after the phone call I went outside to a loading dock and lit up. I now remembered what sealed my conviction to quit last time – giving up is hard. Seated on a bench in the undercover driveway, I opened a book and started reading.

I'd finished the cigarette when my attention was caught by a blurring figure emerging from the blinding sunlight. A small, familiar, duck-footed, bum-in-the-air, tippy-toe trot, coming down the driveway like a ballerina making her entrance in *Swan Lake*.

'Sheri! Sheri! There you are! I've been trying to work out how to get in.'

Sue couldn't explain how she came to be running down this random driveway, or how she'd found me without looking. She was flustered because New York had been tricky and unwilling to help her. She'd booked into a hotel but couldn't get clear directions from the staff about how to return to the airport to meet me. 'I can usually flirt my way around these things,' she said, 'but the man at reception was a cyborg.'

'They pay them to be like that here,' I replied. 'The fun bit is, you're supposed to be just as rude back.'

'He made me feel old, and that's unforgiveable. All I wanted were directions. He could barely be civil to me.'

'Poor Sue,' I said, giving her a warm embrace. 'Did your flirt gun fail?'

'It did. You don't think it runs out at fifty, do you?'

'No, love, it runs out at thirty-five. It's a miracle yours has lasted this long.'

We bought her a ticket for the downtown bus and piled onto it.

I have loved New York since I was a child growing up in Sydney's Elizabeth Bay. The smell of saltwater on the summer breeze mingling with onions cooking at dusk always made me nostalgic for New York, even though I'd never been there. Imagine the thrill when I finally arrived and it smelled exactly the way I imagined.

Sue had booked us into a fancy hotel, way fancier than my finances could afford. It had chintz wallpaper, chintz bedspreads, chintz curtains. It may well have had chintz toilet paper. No wonder Sue felt old, the décor ganged up on her – because you need to know, there's nothing old about Sue. Her age is utterly irrelevant. She's a firecracker. A spectacular Catherine wheel that whistles and crackles and makes you go *oohhh*. I felt lucky to be with her, like girl-Tarzan, swinging on vines of friendship from one soft landing to another.

Being the owner of a successful restaurant gave Sue's trip a secondary purpose. A worldwide food expo was in town and she wanted to check out the competition. She was also going to visit New York's fashionable nosheries, and I could be her assistant in this food fest. *How lucky am I?*

The first restaurant we tried was Nobu in its original incarnation as the partnership between actor Robert De Niro, chef Nobuyuki Matsuhisa and Tribeca Grill restaurateur Drew Nieporent.

Deluxe.

Nobu the venue was a glamorous fusion of Japanese minimalism within the fin de siècle architecture New York's famous for. Nobuyuki the chef was gracious and good natured. Chefs must have a common language, because one word from Sue and we were honoured with a degustation of twenty itty bitty sushi – including one made with beluga caviar and another wrapped in gold leaf. Each mouthful dissolved in a puff of culinary magic. Divine.

The bill was also out of this world. Astronomical, even. Like, nearly a thousand dollars. It was so expensive we got the giggles and had to hide in the bathroom while we worked out how to pay for it. I didn't have anything like that sort of money.

'I could stick my fingers down my throat and regurgitate if that helps,' I offered.

In the end, Sue paid for it on a canasta hand of credit cards, but that was the end of our fancy food budget. We decided to save my door price at the expo by letting Sue go alone while I returned to Connecticut to pick up Betty.

Pipi was waiting for me when the train pulled into Westport. She took me up to Hugh and Charlotte's, where Betty looked shiny but forlorn in the street. I opened her heavy steel doors and felt the satisfying crump as she folded her arms around me. I swear the car was happy to see me. Her deep black leather seats sighed under my weight.

Elegant Hugh came down to ensure everything was alright, and apologised for not driving her. 'I'm sorry to say, I found her a little dramatic,' he said. He'd started her engine each day but her rumbling, throaty sound was a growling menace in the manicured cul-de-sac. 'One felt one should dress in purple and wear a watch with diamonds to do her justice.'

'I know what you mean,' I replied sympathetically. 'My sister had a dog like that, once.'

I gave Pipi a final grateful hug, and then Betty and I made our way back to Manhattan.

Safety is joy, said a road sign on the freeway. My mother, Joy, would have approved. Hell, she probably paid to have it installed.

'She's fucking enormous,' said Sue on seeing Betty. 'You really don't do things by half, do you?'

She wasn't wrong. Driving through the canyons of New York was like floating a liner down a canal. I was swimming against the tide of morning traffic, flowing along one-way boulevards, being jostled by throngs of marauding yellow taxis, past absurdly handsome police on their mounted horses. I swear I could hear Jimi Hendrix's guitar strike up the *Star-Spangled Banner*.

If you have any affection for computer games, you really have to try driving in New York. Bicycle couriers, jaywalkers, cars weaving in and out. The streets were a test of nerves – one magnificent obstacle course. Pipi warned me that I shouldn't take anything other drivers said personally, but I was still surprised when a New York taxi driver yelled (little flecks of invective hitting the inside of his window), 'Get back across the river!'

'Thank you,' I replied cheerily, thinking I was being mistaken for a local.

Sue got to be designated tourist while I concentrated on the traffic. 'The street signs are hilarious,' she said in her mellifluous

Welsh accent, reading them aloud to me. '*No parking, no standing, no stopping, no kidding.* And that one says, *No parking, not five minutes, not one, not ever.*'

Staying in New York was financially unsupportable. Apart from the fabulously expensive Nobu, Betty's room (the overnight parking attached to our fancy hotel) cost more than anything I'd pay for myself. Sue had generously picked up our tab, but it was time for me to start pulling my weight financially.

'Okay,' said Sue, opening the Rand McNally wondermap, 'where are we going?'

'I thought we might drive down through New Jersey, into Maryland and then to Washington DC, and then turn right.'

'How long will that take?'

'To Washington? About three hours.'

'You don't have a plan, do you?'

'I booked some accommodation in DC if that counts.' I did have a plan, but it was a touchy-feely sort of thing. 'I figured we'd make our way south to New Orleans, then diagonally north through Texas and west into New Mexico – I want to show you Mesa Verde and the Grand Canyon. I'll research the fine print when we get to Washington.'

With that half-arsed itinerary sorted, we trickled out of New York on the New Jersey Turnpike. After about an hour we pulled into the 'service plaza' outside Woodbridge and filled up with petrol, hot tea and chocolate chip Otis Spunkmeyer cookies.

'Guess the secret ingredient in a *Spunk*meyer biscuit?' I asked Sue, who doubled over into a satisfying fit of puerile giggles. (My life will be complete when I can get her to snort liquids out of her nose in surprise.)

'Okay,' I said, brushing the crumbs off my lap and getting out of the car, 'time for you to take the wheel.'

'I can't.'

'You paid for half, you get your money's worth.'

'But I can't see over the bonnet.'

'You want pillows? Use my duffel bag.'

'But how will I reach the pedals?'

'Logistics. Always with logistics.'

We made a pillow for her and moved the seat closer to the steering wheel. She plunged the key into the ignition and Betty roared into life. 'Oh, fuck!' she said, followed by, 'Shit! I promised your mother I wouldn't swear.' Sue may have been a cautious little short arse, but her language was that of a seasoned trucker.

It was her first time driving on the wrong side of the road and from Woodbridge to Washington she did a brilliant job, while I learned some cunning new ways to say, 'Whooopsadaisy.'

Trying to make up for lost money, I'd booked us into a B&B in a fashionable part of town. Of course, which fashion … I rang ahead for directions, and they were delivered with the fine granulation preferred by very old people. I wrote as our hostess spoke. 'Delaware Interstate 95. Maryland near Baltimore. Two tunnels – choose Fort McHenry. Exit 27. Interstate 495.'

As the meticulousness inferred, we were greeted by a well-heeled woman in her early hundreds called Mavis. The bed and breakfast was in her family home. It was a personal museum, filled with photos, prizes and ornaments from people and places which don't exist anymore.

We were to sleep in a child's bedroom, in which no child had lived for over a generation. It had twin single beds with chenille bedspreads, a shiny linoleum floor, and was clean in the way where nothing dirty ever happened. I had inadvertently trapped us in someone else's past and a claustrophobic panic began to rise. It was like drowning in potpourri.

To make things worse, or more punishingly shameful, Mavis was completely innocent. Her home was safe and lovingly tended. Hearing our accents, she mistook us for being English (which was nearly right – Sue was Welsh a million years ago) and offered us tea, which we gratefully accepted.

We were set down in her formal dining room, in front of her best china, with homemade biscuits on a side plate, while she went to the kitchen to put the kettle on.

'Aliens invade Planet Grandma,' Sue whispered playfully when Mavis was out of earshot. 'Take me to your lederhosen.'

'I forgot to tell you,' I hissed back. 'We're prisoners of hospitality. The accommodation fee is actually a bond subject to *very* good behaviour.'

Social anxiety caused a fit of the giggles so intense, and so contagious, that Sue and I could only contain our mirth by not looking at each other. As such, our conversation turned to admiring, in some detail, two framed needlework samplers on opposing walls.

'Jesus loves me,' whispered Sue, reading hers.

'That's nice,' I whispered back, 'because everyone else thinks you're a cunt.' It was so appallingly inappropriate, we convulsed with barely contained laughter. The reality that we were about to insult this very respectable old lady just made everything worse. And by worse, I mean more hysterically funny, because it was hysteria.

'I feel like we're cheating on my mother by staying here.'

'Bags not telling Joy you've dumped her for someone else's mother.'

Our cantilevered mood was due in some part to the news Sue had received before leaving New York. Her friend Gareth had recently discovered a shadow on his lung and was scheduled to undergo urgent medical tests. Sue desperately wanted to talk to him, but not only was there was no internet, the only phone Mavis had was a reconditioned pay phone stuck to the wall in the hallway – no way suitable for such an intimate and potentially upsetting call.

On the upside, Mavis made an excellent cup of tea. Over it, I introduced the notion that I'd erred by booking us into a private home when we needed the facilities of a large hotel. Mavis, as anticipated, was bewildered and mortified. She was also fabulously stubborn. We could only leave if we paid her in full for our three-day booking.

I paid.

While repacking the car, I found US $500 cash that I'd hidden in the bible. I was delighted to show Sue what I saw to be instant karma. Mavis and Sue were astounded by what they saw to be a bible.

Sue booked us into the absurdly posh Stouffer Mayflower Hotel. 'This award-winning luxury hotel is the second-best address in Washington.' Apparently the White House was full.

As soon as we arrived Sue was on the phone. From her body language I could tell the news about Gareth was grim. Cancer was spreading voraciously through his body. He was dying.

We sat for a while after she hung up, the rich silence of the room rising out of the deep pile carpet. 'Where do you suppose all that life will go?' asked Sue, deeply shocked by the news. 'What will happen to his sense of humour? He has a degree in Medieval French from the Sorbonne. Where does all that learning go when he's gone?'

Sue and Gareth were friends from high school in Wales. Their lives had travelled different paths to Australia, where they met again as married people with children. 'He knew my father. Do you know how rare that is at my age?'

'I can barely imagine.' Pipi had met my father, but he was gone by the time everyone else came into my life. 'It really underlines the fact that life and love are one thing, doesn't it?'

There was no question what Sue wanted and needed. We spent the afternoon on the phone arranging an urgent flight home. Qantas showed compassion and changed her LA to Sydney ticket for one in two days' time. Now, how to get her to the other side of the country?

A quick check revealed that a last-minute, one-way flight to LA was punishingly expensive. But having driven across the country, I still had a magical stray leg on my ticket. If Sue was prepared to fly under my name, she was welcome to use it.

'Is that legal?'

'No, but it's domestic, so as long as I pick up the ticket and walk you to the gate …'

She was frantic to get home, and this seemed like a solution. She'd go from one gate to the other in LA with a couple of hours to spare.

I'm embarrassed to observe that, given what was going on in Sue's life, for me it was all about *me*. I needed to work out what to do without my travel partner. I had spent my money on the way over, and was relying on Sue to match the travel costs. Also, I wasn't sure I wanted to spend another fortnight on my own.

My life was at a crossroads – or rather, one of those multi-junction roundabouts where it's easy to go the wrong way. So I wrote a list of my options:

- Drive to LA anyway (hang the expense)
- Ship car to UK (hang the driving)
- Sell the car (hang it all)
- Amtrak (see America by train)
- Return to London
- Work for Peter Gabriel
- Mind Michele's house while they're on summer holidays

- Bring Scott over – drive with him
- Camp in Montana – write
- Work for MTV
- Make documentaries
- Work for children's television

It's brilliantly delusional. In what world would Peter Gabriel want me as his assistant? Camping in Montana? Maybe I could join their militia as well. Mainly though, the list revealed my truculent resistance to returning to Australia, and a strong pull towards London. I wanted to kickstart my life, but couldn't see how to do that in Sydney.

My most ridiculous idea was to 'Bring Scott over'. *With what?* I had totally maxed out my credit card. I was sleeping on Sue's goodwill and eating her largesse. I was excited to find five hundred dollars because it was pretty well my last five hundred dollars in the world. Sue had offered to pay for the plane ticket. If that happened, I could buy a little more time to work out what to do next.

The actual real-world thing to do, the one not on the list, was to phone friends of Mark and Michele's who lived and worked in Washington. Maybe Sarah and Tony could put me up when Sue returned home.

'Oh God, we're stuffed to the gunnels with Australians,' said a refined English voice. She was British, he was Australian, they had houseguests. 'Do you need somewhere tonight? We could make room on the floor.'

I was touched that Sarah rose to my emergency without hesitation, but it was plainly an imposition. Hopefully she could give me some tips on where to find a cheap place to stay after the weekend.

She perked up when I told her about Betty. 'I'm ill, and Tony's working. It would be an act of mercy to all of us if you could show our Australian friend around Washington.'

Their friend, Matt, turned out to be a type of Australian who both conformed to stereotypes and broke them. He was a tall, handsome Queenslander, a country lad who was fit and handy. He was also a professional actor with a taste for urbane culture, who looked like the American actor Matt Damon. Not a little bit, not similar to, but pass-me-my-glasses he *looked* like Matt Damon. Given they shared the same first name, let's just say we got great service everywhere we went with him.

Since Sue couldn't fly out for two days, the three of us did the Washington circuit. We piled into Betty and cruised around the White House, the Smithsonian, and the Memorials Lincoln and Vietnam Vets. We drove past the Arlington National Cemetery and over the Arlington Bridge with its glorious golden statues of horses. Each time we crossed that bridge I felt compelled to say, 'My, that's a fine set of buttocks.' It remains an enduring monument to horses' arses.

Matt took us to vintage record shops. I'm indebted to him for talking me into buying a Curtis Mayfield CD, but it would have been nice if he'd issued a content warning. As soon as we were back in Betty, I put it on and turned up the volume.

Picture this: three white people rumbling through downtown Washington DC in a fine red Chevy Camaro. It's the height of hot summer and the windows are down. Out of the stereo blasts the mighty rumbling voice of Mayfield calling his nation to arms, '*Alright you niggers …*'

When we returned to the hotel, I phoned my brother-out-law Marc in LA to let him know I was in the country and back on the road, and to check whether I had any messages. He was convivial and warm as he told me that Scott would be arriving in Washington in ten days' time.

Oooh, aah. Didn't see that one coming.

When I hung up and spoke to Sue about it, she was pleased. I'd have company now that she was returning home.

'But he doesn't know that,' I said petulantly. 'What if you were still coming? Where does he think we'd all fit in that itty bitty car?'

In case you need a map, I am not an easy person. I'm more prickly than pear. This was my adventure and I was equally pleased and peeved about Scott's decision to come on it with me.

'He's chucked in his job, bought a ticket, he's literally crossing an ocean to be with you.'

'Yes, yes, yes – it's absurdly romantic.' What else could I say? Sue was taking Scott's side. 'It's also incredibly presumptuous.'

'Aren't you the one who invited yourself to his house?'

'That's a completely different order of magnitude.'

'Aren't you the one who put his coming over on a list of options?'

'He doesn't know that.'

You don't need hindsight to see his arrival stuck a burr in my saddle, but at the time I told myself I was antsy because I hadn't had a cigarette since the airport and nicotine was withdrawing from my body kicking and screaming. Matt was a smoker. Each time he inhaled, I wanted to reach over, grab his ears and suck the smoke out of his lungs. Eventually I succumbed and asked him for a puff. One little puff. Then I snuck out and bought a packet of American Spirits. It really is a most insidious drug.

After phoning Marc I went downstairs for a fag. I must have been gone for a while because Sue came to find me. Seeing me smoke, Sue gave me a jolly good lecture that culminated with her demanding, 'What do you have to say for yourself?' Mum would have been proud.

'I seem to be indulging in a little self-destructive behaviour that I am unable to control at the moment.'

'I'm leaving early because Gareth is dying of lung cancer, and you stand there blowing smoke in my face.'

'*Wow.* I really can be a most insensitive prat.' I stubbed the cigarette out. 'Sorry, Sue.'

Back in our room, I rang Scott and was pleased to hear his voice. His enthusiasm for the adventure was completely winning. He'd booked a ticket and presented his office with the fait accompli. He was going to America and would resign if necessary. His romantic gesture wasn't in the least bit diminished by the fact that they didn't accept his resignation. Instead, they gave him a month off without pay. This was going to be the longest third date ever.

'I don't have any money, you know,' I told him. 'We'll have to camp if we're going to eat.'

'I have a tent I bought for Glastonbury.'

'Is that like Stonehenge?'

He laughed, then realised I wasn't joking. 'Erm, no. It's a music festival. A four-day mud fest in a field. It's a two-man tent, but there were three of us last year.'

'Kinky.'

'No. I slept with Malc and Paul.'

'Kinkier'

'Well, we certainly got to know each other even better, but it's going to be big enough for you and me.'

I was surprised to find that I felt emotionally raw. I hadn't formulated a real picture of Scott. He was currently tantalising. Nothing else. It was validating to have a bright young man chase me halfway across the world, but mostly it was daunting.

Sue thought it was hilarious. She'd come on this wild American adventure with me, and we'd ended up in a swanky bar in the best hotel in Washington. To celebrate, I dressed in my tiny black cocktail frock to play Boopsie, Sue's (imaginary) big-titted personal assistant. Sue put on her power Armani and we asked the concierge to take our photo. He framed the shot in the marble entrance way with a glamorous bohemian crystal chandelier behind us and an enormous spray of flowers growing out of our heads.

Mrs Burrows and Boopsie: camping in the great American indoors.

Sarah was an investigative journalist and world-class researcher. I asked her for suggestions about where to stay, and she gave me a list of vacant student quarters where we could apply for summer accommodation using Scott's accreditation from his philosophy course. *Totally awesome.*

This led to a small hotel between P and Q Streets, where forty dollars a night bought a modest but charming room with a view onto a quiet, leafy street. The Church of the Pilgrims was across the road and on Thursdays and Sundays they chimed their bells in a reassuringly European way.

Washington is famous for its long, dry, hot spells. This particular summer was a scorcher. As temperatures rose above 40 degrees every day (that's 104 degrees in the old money) Sue and I went to the movies to get out of the heat.

Ironically, *Smoke* was screening in the local art house cinema. The film was an air-conditioned treatise on the joys of smoking. Sue and I loved it. When we came out she stretched and yawned. 'That was good,' she said. 'I think you need a fag.'

After the movie we visited Matt for a nightcap. He was hoping to see more of the country, including getting down to New Orleans to visit friends.

'I haven't formulated a clear plan yet,' I told him, 'but I'm thinking of visiting New Orleans if you want to drive down with me.'

'What about Scott?' Sue blurted out in surprise.

'There's plenty of room in the car for three. That's what he's expecting anyway.'

Matt was keen on the idea, and we considered it set.

When we were alone outside, walking back to our hotel, Sue asked what I thought I was doing.

'I know, I know, I know,' was all I could offer in my defence.

'Scott's what, twenty-six years old? And you're putting him in a car with a forty-something actor? That's cruel.'

'I *know*.'

I didn't have the language for what was bothering me, all I knew was there was more to my plan than merely sticking pins in Scott's firm young arse. None of us had enough money. Matt was willing to contribute to food and petrol. Also, I didn't ask Scott to come on this trip. While I thought he was cute and all, I didn't ask him to throw in his job, life and expectations to come with me on my journey of self-discovery. Explaining all that was out of the reach of my reasoning, so all I could say to Sue was, 'I'm simply not ready for a 3000-mile date on my own with him.'

She looked at her shoes thoughtfully. 'Fair enough,' she said with a passable Australian drawl. 'It's not like Matt's handsome, independent, funny, or anything.' Matt, of course, was all those things.

'It's not the kindest thing I've ever done, but I'm not prepared to start moulding my personality and expectations for strangers. If Scott doesn't like it, well, he can go home.'

Sue nodded with a wry smile. 'This is gonna be a whole new sort of car crash.'

←→

Sunday came around too soon. Next thing I knew, I was checking out of luxury and into reality. Sue was gone, away on her twinkling toes, devoured by the departure lounge doors. There was still a week before Scott arrived. I would be waiting for him in Washington longer than we'd been together in London.

It was the week before my birthday, so I sent my bank details home and suggested if anyone wanted to give me a present, they could post it care of my Visa account.

God, it's hot.

I discovered the Francis swimming pool down the road from the hotel. It was a vibrant family place, shrill and lively. Pinned out on the cement concourse, dripping wet and burning under the summer sun, I had time alone to review my position with Pig. I was homesick for my friend as much as anything. Matt was funny, but not as smart as Pig. Scott was smarter, but not as funny. All three men had an arcane love of music and technology. If they met without me, they'd probably bond over that and be friends for life.

I felt with Scott's decision to come to America, I was being lured into another relationship when I hadn't finished grieving for my marriage. While I was ready to window shop (slip into the changing room and try a few on) I wasn't ready to buy. Scott's decision to come to America would be the end of my marriage. There'd be no turning back. Thinking all of this didn't make me a bad person, but it did make me anxious, and anxiety made me mean.

Scott wrote every day. He was working hard to get his project (a world atlas) to a good place where he could leave it. His use of language was so formal, like a teenage boy on a first date – his words were dripping carnations of self-consciousness: *If you ever wish to indulge yourself in the meticulous presentation of my contribution to design, project, and technical management, which occasionally reveals an aptitude for pedantry in the service of clarity and functional ease, here is a work for you.*

Poor love. He had no idea who he was working himself into the ground for.

Matt and I went to a camping store and bought mats, ground sheets, sleeping liners, lights and insect candles for the grand adventure. When I saw the prices of the tents, I was glad Scott was bringing his along. The ones in the shop were fantastic, but even the cheapest cost hundreds of dollars.

We went to a second-hand store to buy some eating irons and there I saw it. *Oh, treasure.* A commemorative plate featuring Ike and Mamie Eisenhower. He was wearing a blue serge suit, and she had the most lavish 'bangs' I've ever seen on a human head. I hadn't even known to dream about such an object. It was perfect kitsch, ideal for finger food and a great addition to the new crockery quilt of my life.

I also found a pretty bargain – three dollars for a dainty teacup and saucer by Phoenix China (Thomas Forester & Sons). From the logo, it was probably made in Britain around 1912. It had a white fluted rim with a soft-shaded pink interior and hand decorated gold trim. This cup never expected to have the adventure it did – you can tell by the fact that no sooner did it hit the road and have hot water poured into it than it instantly crazed. Snap, crackle and stain. As for the phoenix, rising from the ashes of a dead relationship, I had found my perfect teacup for my adventure.

As the weekend got closer, I became excited about Scott's arrival. (Ambivalence is good like that, it works both ways.) I sent him an itinerary of our trip. I worked hard on it too, taking into account how far I'd travelled on the way over and what was possible in a day. I even booked accommodation at the Grand Canyon so we could hike all the way to the bottom.

The one thing I didn't do was tell Scott that Matt would be travelling with us.

↔

My birthday arrived in a flurry of emails, faxes and phone calls from home as all my girlfriends poured love into my ears and money into my adventure like I was their favourite charity.

My mother rang. She'd picked Sue up from the airport and been told all about Betty and Scott. 'Darling, I know you've wanted to have a baby, but is dating one the answer?'

Best of all, my office rang to say that the ABC had picked up our miniseries. This was a big deal for our small production company. We'd been developing a drama about Australian politics for over a year, and finally someone wanted to produce it with us. The best part for me was that they didn't want us to start until September. That gave me six more weeks before I was needed back at my desk in Australia.

I was well loved, and you'd think such good news would be the cherry on my happiness, but none of it made up for the fact that Pig forgot my birthday. There was nothing new in this. Eleven years and he never got the date right. The real shock was how hurt and angry I felt – so self-pitying that instead of celebrating my good fortune, I cried for my lost life, for my lost love. I was amazed to discover, yet again, that I thought I had moved on, and I hadn't.

Over and over I think I've let him go, but I haven't.

NEW BOY IN TOWN

It didn't start well. I was freaked out. Scott was exhausted. We were both unbelievably nervous.

I had been excited the morning of his arrival. So excited I'd gone to Dean & DeLuca's, a spectacular and punishingly expensive delicatessen Sue introduced me to, and bought tapenade, stinky blue vein cheese, figs that looked like they came from the Garden of Eden, and guacamole with fresh garlic and a touch of chili.

As I sped along the freeway to pick Scott up from the airport, I could smell the cheese curdling in the sun that was beating through every window. By the time I was at the arrivals gate my excitement had peaked into panic. *What the hell was I doing? Embarking on a four week camping trip with a complete stranger?* This was stark, raving madness.

Scott arrived with a fancy new haircut, but no tent.

He said he had another look at the one he shared with his flatmates, and it wasn't good enough. I bristled under the idea that this might be a style issue, rather than an economic one. All he'd bought for the trip were a new pair of glasses (Armani, no less) and a 35 mm Nikon camera with attachments. He also brought me a birthday present, and was so excited he insisted I open it in the desolate car park.

The day had turned white hot and airless. Even the trees were holding their breath. The heat radiated off the tarmac beside Betty as I unwrapped Scott's thoughtful gift. His upturned face, shining with love, watched me open a small leather box to reveal a pair of pearl earrings set in the finest silver filigree. My grandmother had a pair just like them. I held them in my hand trying to find something nice to say, 'Pearls, huh?'

'You wear that necklace all the time.' A simple gold chain with 21 matching pearls hanging from it.

'It's a gift from my mother. She gave me a pearl each year for my birthday, and the necklace for my 21st.'

'I love it on you.'

'Pearls are a symbol of tears. I figure it's alright from Mum, because her name's Joy. So they're tears of joy.'

'You don't like the earrings, do you?'

They were brimming with all his youthful optimism. I could imagine him standing in the shop, thinking of me, loving me, but they made me feel old – they were motherly. 'They're so thoughtful.' I would rather have had a tent. I was swallowing my words, looking for a way to reject the gift but keep the giver. 'It's such a shame I don't have pierced ears.'

'You don't?'

'No.' It was horrible, whipping that innocent puppy in the godforsaken car park. 'Can you take them back?'

He took the little box from me. 'Maybe I can exchange them?'

'For a brooch, perhaps? I don't wear earrings.'

Freak Out. Freak In.

Even Betty looked at me sideways as we packed his modest luggage into the boot. *What the hell's going on?*

What was going on was an out-of-body experience. I was floating above it all, mechanically moving my limbs, hoping to vibrate through the weirdness of the situation and into another dimension. 'How about we go for a drive? Show you the city.'

Betty and I took Scott sightseeing, retracing all the good times we'd had with Matt and Sue.

'My, that's a fine set of buttocks,' I said as we crossed the Arlington Bridge.

'What is?'

'On the bridge. The horses … Never mind.'

Scott photographed everything. We made a lap of inner Washington, and he made a complete record of it.

EXHIBIT A: In this photo I'm in front of the Washington Memorial, smiling and frowning at the same time. I've just explained that the memorial (a pointy elevator shaft in front of a long wading pool) created negative chi for the American capital.

'They seem to be coping,' Scott replied as he took the photo.

EXHIBIT B: The Lincoln Memorial. Tony and Sarah asked us to settle a debate: Does anything on the monument indicate whether the Civil War was over slavery or something else?

Scott and I were working on this question like it was a school project. For the record, the memorial clearly states that the war was about the right for all men to live freely and equally: i.e. without slavery. The autonomy of the states from central government is also mentioned, but the autonomy they wanted was the right to maintain slaves. We concluded, therefore, that the two issues which caused the Civil War were both about the abolition of slavery.

EXHIBIT C: Lincoln on his pedestal. The framing is dreadful, but the photographers are in better balance.

EXHIBIT D: The Pool of Remembrance and the Bad Chi Thingy from the other end. This time it's nicely framed.

EXHIBITS E – I: Several photos of the Vietnam Veterans Memorial. (So many names etched into its polished black façade.)

EXHIBIT J: Scott reflected behind the names on the wall, included with the fallen. You can buy a poster depicting a young soldier reaching out from within the roll of honour to an aging comrade in civvies. I liked it, but Scott thought it was laughably sentimental. He wouldn't even allow its artistic merits to be tabled in conversation.

EXHIBIT K: Oh, dear. This photo could be of a river anywhere, but it's the Potomac running through Washington. We're midway through our deluxe picnic with teacups. You can see Mrs Eisenhower poking out from under a cupcake. Scott is mid-mouthful. He's frowning like a dog taking a crap. A small strand of (newly cut) hair has fallen foppishly over his brow.

This photo requires further consideration. It's of a heart-shaped head with a widow's peak (which I adore). He has even features and a fine, straight nose. He's wearing a collarless shirt, rolled up above the elbow revealing strong forearms and elegant hands. He's looking at me with an intense expression that's all pink and exposed – a confident man who hasn't developed a shell and is out of his element for the first time.

It's not a flattering photo. His expression has fear and amusement in equal parts. The food might be disgusting or delicious. He may be about to laugh or spit. Everything about the world in this photo is rough and smooth at the same time. It's a photo of my love as a chili sorbet. It's not in focus, and nor is he.

EXHIBIT … Z: There's no photo of me putting my foot down at the Jefferson Memorial.

'I work in television,' I said, hoping that didn't sound too grand. 'I make pictures for a living. It's no coincidence that I don't have a camera on this journey. I don't want it to be an extension of work, or the world viewed through a screen.'

Scott blinked at me, trying to work out if I was joking or not. 'But it's not a screen, it's a reflex camera.'

'I tell you what, I won't inveigle you to design any maps if you don't include me in any photographs.'

'That seems unfair. This is my holiday as well. Can I record sound maybe?'

So Scott's got pushback. I like that. 'What sound?'

'That high-pitched buzzing. It's fascinating and revolting at the same time.'

'You don't have cicadas in Britain? That's what Christmas sounds like in Australia.'

'Cicadas? Their harmonics are hurting my ears.'

'The sound amplifies in the skull – some people hear them as pain.'

He cocked his head at me curiously.

'I worked in children's television. I know a lot of useless stuff about animals. Like, they used to think the sound was made by the cicadas rubbing their wings on their legs, but it turns out it's from rattling their rib cage.'

'Like a wobble board?'

'More like little yogis doing magical breathing. How are you thinking to record it?' He riffled in his bag and pulled out a digital audio recorder. 'You carry a dat with you?' (It's a professional machine used in film making.) 'What sort of geek are you?'

'An audiophile. I like sound.'

Okay. That's cute. Cute enough to pull me up. It was patently unfair to stop him doing something he was passionate about, but I felt passionate about living in the moment, if only for the moment. 'I'm not convinced that recording sound is any better than taking photos. It all smacks of bad film making.'

'Maybe we could make mnemonics. Have you heard of the Russian mnemonist, "S"?'

'Is that a Keanu Reeves movie?'

'Maybe. A mnemonist is a person with a great memory. S had a condition known as synaesthesia – the boundaries of his senses blurred, so he tasted sounds and heard colours.'

'Orange.'

'Sure, but what does it sound like?'

'Cicadas?'

'Maybe.'

'You say "maybe" a lot.'

'I live in a world of infinite possibilities.' The stress was leaching out from between us as we walked around the bronze statue of Jefferson, talking about sound, memory and cicadas.

'So this man, S, was studied for years by a psychologist called Alexander Luria, who discovered that synaesthesia gave S a phenomenal memory. One of the tests saw him walk around the city and then recall everything he'd seen in minute detail. His memory was perfect.'

'Was it a trick?'

'Sort of. He used to hang numbers as he walked around. One day he recalled an image incorrectly and it was so unusual that Luria asked him to explain what went wrong.' Scott was enjoying the story so much that he needed to pause for the punch-line. 'S said he'd hung his number in a shady spot and missed it.'

It would be another 500 miles before I got the joke – before I finally understood that S had only *imagined* hanging the numbers as he walked around, so he only *imagined* hanging the number in a shady spot. For now, I smiled politely, figuring it was another of those sheep and barns things. *Move along*, I said to my brain, *nothing to see here.*

Scott decided that the perfect compromise between our ideals would be to make a mnemonic recording of the sounds on our trip. 'We'll memorise the good times and number the moments like S did. Number one, for instance, is right now. Let's record the cicadas here at the Jefferson Memorial.'

My favourite moment in film making is when the crew stands still at the end of a location to let the sound recordist capture a couple of minutes of 'atmosphere'. Every place has its own unique vibrations – the rustle of wind, the whir of fans, the soft breathing of bodies in space. Those minutes always seem holy to me. Sometimes it involves as many as a hundred people standing in peaceful contemplation of what has happened, what will happen, and what is still in the moment.

Scott's suggestion to create a mnemonic recording was a perfect conciliation between my desire to be in the moment and his desire to remember it. And so we stood outside the Jefferson Memorial for thirty seconds of companionable silence, listening to the nuances of the humming cicadas, the soft voices of other tourists – their feet crunching on the gravel pathway.

There was a distant wash of traffic and a light summer breeze in the trees. The evening was settling into night. The sky was an iridescent blue. He was standing so close, I could feel his warmth next to me. In that mnemonic I am so pleased Scott has come to Washington to be with me.

↔

If Scott was disappointed about our accommodation he didn't show it. He seemed delighted to shed the flight in a shower. By this time I was excited again, and happy to see him.

Hmm, what would a lie detector make of that one? I was freaked out *and* excited to see him. I was glad he was there, and terrified and unsure. I had no idea what it meant and it felt like falling.

Aw, who gives a shit what I was going through? Scott had a shower. We had some great sex and nothing much mattered after that.

The phone rang with all the shrill excitement of a fire alarm. I blinked back the daylight and picked up the receiver. Pig was on the other end singing 'Happy Birthday'. Three days late, but bang on time for him.

I couldn't help laughing. It was so daggy and typical of him, and I was glad to hear his voice. I leaped out of bed and passed the phone out the window and onto the balcony, where I sat with my feet on the wall, smoking a cigarette and roaring with laughter as he gossiped about mutual friends, work and a health retreat he'd been on.

I could feel Scott in the next room.

I could feel the difference in the way we communicated.

I could feel Scott, unseen through the bricks, shrinking from the happy sound of someone (me) who was completely in tune with another person. And I couldn't stop. I couldn't make it less. I couldn't make it better for him because I was so happy to be talking to my friend.

'So what did you get me for my birthday, you pig dog bastard?'

'What you asked for.'

'What did I ask for?'

'I paid off your Visa card.'

The magnitude of what he'd done took a moment to sink in. 'But that's five grand.' He'd effectively wiped my slate clean so I could start again. It was relief. It was gratitude. It was homesickness. I started to cry.

'What are you doing?'

'Nothing.'

'You crying?'

'Maybe.'

'You happy?'

'Maybe. That's a nice present.'

'Oh, Piggy, if I could do this differently you know I would. I tell people what you're doing, and it's like the bravest adventure in the world. Everyone wants to do it, but no one has the courage to just pull up stumps and go. It's fantastic.'

'Hey. D'you hear? They're giving us the money to develop the series.'

'Great! You can pay me back then.'

'No way, buddy, finders keepers.'

We talked more about the project. We talked about our parents. We talked for a month about all the things that had happened since we last spoke.

He'd been on a retreat called punjakama – an indulgent week of meditation and massage, including one where they bathe you in eleven litres of heated sesame oil. I'd done the same retreat after a recurring nightmare where I was being pursued through an underground car park – a true landscape of horror.

In that dream I went into the stairwell (bad move) and ran downstairs (worse). My pursuer used stealth rather than speed to corner me. As they crept up on me, I summoned all my courage to pounce. I jumped, and in mid-air saw my assailant was a street woman – an abyss of rage fuelled by despair. I understood if I added my fear to hers we'd both die in a ball of violence, so I dropped my arms in supplication and she melted into me. I did well to embrace my dark side, but then I was living with a lunatic inside me, someone who could expose us both to murderous violence at any time. (I think you've met her on this trip.)

There was a sequel to this nightmare during punjakama. The crazy lady came to visit again, this time washed and serene, wearing a loose white robe. While I congratulated her on how well she was doing, she turned into a laughing brown dog, sprouted angel's wings and flew away. Isn't that the most fantastic affirmation of love and healing for a dyslexic agnostic? God as a laughing dog – the ultimate angel of mirth and mercy.

We spoke for about forty-five minutes. When I hung up and went back into the room, Scott had gone to the shower. *Fair enough.* I lay down on our messy bed giving thanks for everyone's generosity and marvelling at the sense of relief and freedom having money brings.

Scott came back with a towel wrapped around his improbably handsome body. 'Was that your husband on the phone, then?' he asked.

'Sure. He was ringing to say happy birthday.'

He nodded, and nonchalantly filled the basin so that he could shave. There's a reassuring intimacy in a man's shaving ritual. I love the rhythm, the meditation, the quietude. Scott had the charmingly old fashioned habit of using a brush and soap. Pig cleaned his razor by tapping it on the side of the basin, like a Buddhist's bell rung three times. Scott swilled his in water, which was also evocative of renewal. *In the washing of the water …*

'You two get on well …'

'Yeah.' I watched him stir the bowl of soap with his shaving brush, his face flickering with unasked questions. 'He's paid off my Visa card as a birthday present.'

Scott nodded. The silver blade slipped over his soft skin. It was like before, when there was a wall between us and I couldn't make him feel better. I didn't want him to feel bad, but I didn't know what to do or say to reassure him. I wasn't even sure it would be honest to reassure him.

Pig said 'I love you' as he hung up the phone. From some men that might be ambiguous. It might mean, 'I want you to come home' or 'I want to be with you' or 'I want to take our breakup back'. But from him it meant nothing more or less than he loved me. That he was still my friend – a man who left me not because he didn't care, but because he wanted something hazy and dangerous that wasn't inside 'us'.

Scott's concern was understandable. This woman for whom he had just given up his job and income was plainly still attached to another man. He finished shaving and wiped his face clean with the towel that had been wrapped around his waist. 'Do you wish he was here instead of me?'

I pulled him towards me. 'But he's not here, and he doesn't want to be. You are, and it's scary.' It's not the answer he wanted. It's not the answer I wanted to give. Scott may have found it reassuring that he was compelling to me, and while we didn't have the emotional history to know how to be easy with each other, it was exciting to walk on prickly hot coals with him.

'I'm glad you're here,' I said, 'but it might take a bit of getting used to.'

Before he arrived, I bought Scott a black mini-Maglite torch and attached a copy of Betty's key to it. I wrapped it and made a moment of giving it to him – the key to his own adventure. I wasn't on a mission to torture the poor man. I could see he was in a cruel, hard place travelling with me. I didn't know what he was doing there, but I was glad he'd come.

Sure, it was also practical to give him his own key. Betty was more than capable of locking us both out if we left her unattended for too long, but that was a secondary consideration. Honest.

With the ceremonial duties out of the way, it was time to face up to buying a tent. There was no way, not even with my fresh five grand, we could afford to spend every night in a motel.

We went to a camping store in Georgetown which had a comprehensive display of pre-assembled tents for you to crawl around in like it was a massive Tracey Emin installation. Scott was standing next to a tidy blue one that cost four hundred dollars. 'We can't afford that,' I said. 'We may as well stay in Motel Sixes.'

I climbed into the cheapest one. 'If Tracey Emin married Marshall Mathers, would she become Tracey Emin-Eminem?'

'You don't want to sleep in that.'

I bristled. *Don't tell me what I do or don't want.* 'What? Not stylish enough for you?'

'No. It's a one-man tent. We won't fit.'

'It says it's a two-man tent.'

'Well, they must have been very little men.' Scott was standing back watching me. My tent wasn't nice, and it was a bit cramped. 'Look at this one,' he said pleasantly.

I didn't want to look at *this* one. It looked expensive. 'How much is it?'

'Don't be like that. Just come and look at why it's a good tent.'

Don't be like that. It was already starting, the not-so-subtle emotional jujitsu couples practise on each other.

'Please?' He sounded so reasonable, and I was feeling so

unreasonable. It was my money – why was he dictating the choice of tent? Apart from the fact that he had an opinion, and had actually been camping before.

'Here are the things I like about this tent,' he said when I finally stuck my head out. 'Firstly, it has a double skin, which means that the dew will settle on the outside and not soak through onto us if we roll up against the walls, which we are likely to do. Secondly, look at how nicely designed it is …'

Ha. I knew it. It's a style thing.

'… these windows open on the inside to let air in when it's raining. There's room for your shoes outside the door. It's fully contained, which means it lets in less sand and dirt than normal. The windows have insect nets you can zip up, or not. There's netting on the roof to let air circulate when it's raining and, if the night is fine, you can take off the outer skin and look at the stars. But this is the best bit. Look at these.' He flicked the sticks in his hand and they became solid, like a magician's wand. 'Flexible tent poles. You feed them through these loops and they support the tent automatically.'

He was right, of course. It was an elegant tent. It looked easy and comfortable. It looked like it was worth more than the $400 (plus tax).

'Yeah, alright, it's pretty. But what's wrong with mine, apart from the *colour*?'

'It's canvas, which is nice because it breathes, but unpleasant because it retains moisture and is hard to dry and therefore prone to getting mouldy. Heavy rain tends to seep through the roof and walls. It requires stakes and cleats, which are difficult to assemble in the dark, so we'll always need to be at our campsite before nightfall. We'll need a ground sheet and a coverall, or you'll get cold and wet. You have no protection from insects, which can be particularly distressing if you pitch it near an ant colony. I don't know you well yet, but I suspect you'll be uncomfortable in that tent, and your hectoring me over it will probably be the death of us.'

My eyes narrowed to slits. *Hectoring, huh?* Was it his pleasant Welsh manner that got my dander up? Or was it his tone of unassailable reasonableness? Either way, you'd have to be a stubborn boof not to see he was right. I can be nothing if not ungracious in defeat. 'Oh, have it your way. We'll buy the fancy designer special. But you have to put it up since you love it so much.'

Funny little monkey. He was absolutely delighted that we were going to buy the nice tent. Not crowing victoriously that he got his way, just genuinely pleased to be pitching this really very pretty tent.

Of course, forking out nearly ten per cent of my available money broke the seal on my frugality. Mind you, those who know me are probably laughing at the idea of 'me' and 'frugal' in one sentence. But here's the scary thing – Scott outclassed me as a spendthrift. We ended up buying the tent, two space mats to keep the ground chill out, sleeping bags that could be zipped together and doubled as bottom sheets, pillows, a battery-operated hurricane lantern and a billy for the campfire.

Scott also bought himself some shirts, shorts and running shoes. And what every tent away from home needs – a set of speakers. This man's capacity to spend was terrifying. In comparison, my relatively pathetic purchases were some new underpants and a cute dress that shrank in the first wash and became baby-doll too cute.

Buying undies with Scott was fun though. His taste was like nothing I'd known or read about. He liked the sporty look. How lucky could a girl be? He thought plain, simple, comfortable underwear was sexy. He took the Calvin Klein brand personally, and I liked it a lot. It felt womanly. Real womanly, not magazine womanly. It was like Scott had discovered women by being in love with them, rather than through porn. This turned out to be true, and Scott was baffled by the idea that it might be any other way.

I wore my fancy new undies that night to dinner with Tony and Sarah. They lived in an elegant two-storeyed house in the mid-alphabet near the White House. Sliding into their world was lush. Since he was Australian and she was English, they pretty much mirrored Scott and me in some looking-glass world where everything turned out perfectly.

'Hey, look at me. Upright,' said Sarah, who'd been sick since I arrived. Although we'd spoken a few times on the phone, this was indeed our first opportunity to meet properly. What I discovered was a smart, blonde woman in her mid-twenties, who had an infectious curiosity about everything – how Scott and I met, why we were driving around America, what happened to my marriage, how we were finding the accommodation.

When the shoes and feet were swapped, I learned that Sarah had studied at Kings College, part of the same University of London where Scott and Michele were studying philosophy. When she graduated, she'd worked as an art reviewer before throwing it all in and moving to Paris. 'I woke up one morning knowing exactly where I'd be in twenty years, who I'd marry, where my 2.4 children would go to school. I wanted more from life than certainty, so I chose something fierce and unpredictable.'

'That'd be me, then,' said Tony, arriving home from an editing session.

'How did it go?' she asked as he greeted her with a kiss.

'A puff piece, but good for that.' He'd just finished a story on a statue of Crazy Horse in South Dakota.

'Is this "Hoka Hey" Crazy Horse? The Indian chief?' I asked.

Scott had grown increasingly quiet as Sarah and I waded deep into each other's lives. Now he looked plainly baffled.

'That was his war cry,' I explained. 'Hoka hey, a fine day to die.' I turned to Tony, 'What was his war paint? Something fabulous.'

'Lightning and hail.'

'Isn't that great?' I said trying to include Scott, 'the King of the Plains decorated himself with dots and zigzags.'

'Quite the fashion statement,' he said uncertainly.

'And a small white stone behind his ear,' added Sarah.

'Ooh. Matching earrings.' That was me.

Hearing Tony's voice, Matt came down for dinner. Now was as good a time as any for me to introduce Scott to the concept of a travel companion. Yeah, not my finest humanitarian moment.

'So, this is Matt,' I said. 'He's driving with us to New Orleans tomorrow.'

Matt deployed his dazzling movie-star smile and shook Scott's hand, 'I'm pretty pumped about Betty. Your girlfriend's nice, but mine's *so* much sexier.'

Scott blinked like a vole in the headlights.

'It was Matt who introduced me to Curtis Mayfield,' I said, thinking maybe they could connect over music.

Matt had an actor's talent for the anecdote, the sort of stories that are made in the telling. They often revolved around a friend of his called Sam. They were good icebreakers, and meeting Scott was the perfect snowy Tundra to set one loose.

Connecting it to our driving adventure, Matt told the story of Sam being pulled over by the highway patrol for speeding. Sam convinced the patrol officers that he wasn't speeding, but driving extra fast to try to catch another vehicle that appeared to have a loose wheel. Alerted to a potential emergency, the police thanked him and sped away, sirens wailing, without issuing a ticket.

Matt told it well and we were all laughing – Scott somewhat nervously.

'Well,' Scott said, blushing, 'I look forward to the anecdote of our holiday.'

↔

After dinner, Scott and I ambled back to the hotel. He hadn't said much all night and was now even more taciturn, finally reduced to a bunch of flinching, twitching, hand-on-hip gestures rather than actual words.

I expected that he was cross about another man travelling with us, but he hadn't said anything so I couldn't tackle it head on. When we got back to our room, I couldn't take it anymore. The tension which had been throbbing since the airport needed relief. 'What is it?' I asked, in my not particularly nurturing way. 'What's the matter with you?'

'Oh, I'm just stupid, and I'm cross with myself.'

Well, I wasn't expecting that. 'I don't understand.'

'"The anecdote of our drive"?'

'I thought that was pretty good.'

'It wasn't meant to be *good*.' He scuffed his heels unhappily. 'We go to dinner with these fascinating, dynamic people and I have nothing to contribute. You light up like a Christmas tree and I wonder why you're with me.'

He kicked a cane chair in frustration, and it flew blithely across the room. I think he expected it to be solid like the rest of the furniture, because he sheepishly retrieved it. 'Well, don't you have anything to say?' he demanded, righting the chair and looking asthmatic.

'Um, no. You're plainly cross.' To tell you the truth, it was the most animated he'd been, and quite entertaining for that. It was also true. He *didn't* say much when others were around, or when they weren't, for that matter.

His opening line to me in this relationship was that I made him stupid. I thought it was romantic at first, that I took his breath away, but I'd come to accept that some part of it might be true. I was trying to be as natural as possible, to give him space to express himself, but you and I have been on the road together long enough to know the space I gave him was frequently booby trapped. So I did nothing. I sat in the chair and let him vent his inner cyclone.

'I'm considered quite outgoing in certain circles. My friends think I'm amusing. I have two and a half degrees in art and philosophy. I'm designing a revolutionary cartography program. But I meet your friends and they've lived in war zones, or been artists in Paris, or gone to acting classes to learn how to tell amusing anecdotes, and I have nothing to contribute.'

He went on like this for about fifteen minutes until he'd exhausted himself. 'Aren't you going to say anything, well?'

'Wanna go play pool?' I asked cheerily. He frowned at me, presumably trying to read subtext on my forehead, so I gathered up my purse and door key. 'You're clearly not going to sleep. Why don't we go out for a beer and a game of pool? We can play for kisses.'

Unlike the skanky dives at home, America has a culture of female-friendly pool halls with plenty of tables, all lit from above – good music, young waiters, food if you want it.

Scott racked up the balls and broke like a champion. He won a lot of kisses that night.

TWO MEN AND A CAR

I don't know where Scott found the courage to give up his job and travel halfway around the world to be with me. All I know is that I couldn't have started this leg of the trip without someone else to absorb some of the friction. So I opened the car door and sucked Matt into our maelstrom.

Matt sheepishly heaved one of his four enormous bags onto the back seat.

'What have you got in there, man?' I asked. He had the luggage of a starlet on tour.

'Well, you know, I'm going for a couple of weeks.'

'But it's not going to fit. The boot and back seat just aren't that big.'

Matt laughed his self-deprecating handsome-man's laugh. 'Scott, can you hold this?' He needed someone to press the front seat forward so he could get extra purchase to push his second bag through.

Packing the two door coupe was first theoretical, then practical. Matt finally got it all in by filling a third of the boot and the entire back seat. Sarah and I stood on the pavement, teas in hand, watching him stuff it up.

Culturally, Matt and I knew each other well. So well that any mystery or romance was unlikely. He was the fair-haired youngest child, the charming larrikin who could manipulate the affection of aunts. I was the little sister of brothers, the pesky dark-haired girl who could swim fifty metres under water on a single breath, and fry ants with a magnifying glass. I was the lippy bitch who had witnessed the secret rituals of boyhood and, while I wasn't about to tell, I wasn't about to shut up either.

I didn't know what Matt's personal agenda was for this trip but I wasn't on it. That Matt was contributing to the petrol and expenses mattered to me. That he would act as a buffer between Scott and me was essential – but his baggage was not coming. Not all of it, anyway. 'Mate, there are three people and four seats in this car, and your luggage is taking up two of them.'

Finally he relented by unpacking his stuff onto the pavement and then ejecting his hair dryer, moisturisers, sound system, books and winter clothes (including two overcoats and several pairs of boots).

It was early afternoon when we waved off Tony and Sarah, me at the wheel and Scott in the front. Matt was in the back with his knees around his neck in a lover's knot. I promised him we'd rotate the seating, but first I wanted him to feel the full pain his luggage was going to inflict on us all.

By the time we finally drove over the Potomac, my vision was pulsating with anxiety. *What was I thinking?* A four-week-long date with a man I barely knew and a chaperone who had just revealed himself to be a secret princess.

Having spilled his guts on the pavement, Matt was also feeling vulnerable. The mood in the car was awkward, like a lull in a dinner party conversation. Our discomfort was intensified by the bumper to bumper traffic through the suburbs, along a freeway lined with walls built to maintain an illusion that whatever went on behind them was either discreet or desirable.

Scott turned on the radio. He fiddled with the settings until he found a station playing American spiritual music. 'This should get things going,' he said as the slow *a cappella* choir invoked the Lord's name in a moment of crisis.

'Imagine going west in a wagon train,' said Matt, finally breaking his silence. 'All that pain and loss.'

'Or in a pickup truck during the depression,' I added, 'with granny dying for want of grapes.'

'Or in a big red Chevy, chasing the blues.' Scott grinned at us.

'Are you laughing at us?'

'I most certainly am,' he said, putting his hand on my knee.

We'd agreed to travel the musical ley lines from Washington to New Orleans via Memphis and Nashville. Both boys observed that Route 66 went west into the Appalachian Mountains, and wanted to start there – maybe camping out in the Shenandoah National Park.

'So do you know about the American Spiritual?' asked Scott, apropos the radio. 'It's a great story. When the early settlers first came here, they bought their hymns with them. With their bibles in hand, they sang back their fear, and incorporated the landscape into their songs. Slaves working the plantations did the same against the darkness of oppression, sometimes changing the words to include clues to escape routes and the names of people who'd help them on their way.'

Matt perked up in the back. He leaned forward, a muscular arm on each of our headrests. 'That's amazing, dude. And that started here?'

'Oh Shenandoah' came on the radio and Scott turned it up. 'Certainly did. Listen to this one. Mournful like a Welsh Colliery Choir.'

> *Oh Shenandoah,*
> *I love your daughter,*
> *Away, you rolling river.*

'Is this about Pocahontas?' I asked. 'Her father, Powhatan, was chief around here – if you believe everything Walt Disney tells you.'

'I'm talking much earlier than that.'

'Can't be much earlier, Pocahontas lived at the same time as the first Queen Elizabeth. They kidnapped her and took her to medieval England, where she died of tuberculosis. Bloody Brits.'

Scott smiled, like another part of the puzzle had been placed down for him.

> *For her I'd cross your roaming waters,*
> *Away, I'm bound away across the wide Missouri.*

We turned off Route 66 onto the 55, following signs to the Skyline Drive in Shenandoah National Park. As we rose into the liquid green, the air thinned, cooled and finally blew away the heat of Washington. We opened our windows and let the adventure in.

We'd agreed to rotate the driving so that no one person was stuck in the back the whole time. I'd asserted my right as owner to go first, but was proving to be a slow driver. That didn't matter when we were bumper to bumper on the freeway, but once we were wiggling up into the sky, my passengers were begging me to open up.

I had a go at driving faster, but slowed again when I heard a strange hissing noise coming from the rear wheels. *Oh Christ, what now?* I pumped the brakes to see if they were the problem. Sure enough, the harder I pressed, the louder the hiss, especially on the corners. *Perhaps they were about to give way.* I pumped them again. The steeper the bend, the harder I broke, the louder the noise in the rear.

'Why are you doing that?' asked Scott as we rounded a hairpin bend.

'Can you hear that hissing sound? What do you think it is?'

'I think it's Matt.'

Sure enough, every time I broke into a corner, Matt inhaled air through his clenched teeth – his tottering pile of luggage about to fall and crush him.

We pulled into the park commissary and asked for suggestions where to camp. The woman behind the food counter was motherly warm and welcomed us with dimples. She told us some of the history of the park (carved from failing farmland during the Great Depression) and recommended a pleasant campsite at Loft Mountain. 'It's glorious, and the amenities for RVs are better in other places, so there's never many folks up there.' She sold us our permits and gave us the run of her kitchen to fill our thermos and make a perfect cup of tea.

'You'll be wanting to get your tents up soon though,' she said in that soft southern drawl. 'This rain looks like settling in for the duration.'

From the car park, all I could see were rows of numbered allotments vanishing into the trees. The boys ran down to choose one, while I stood there with a childish sinking feeling that it was all a whole lot tamer than I'd hoped.

I picked my way down the stepped campsites, grumbling aloud that 'I was expecting a little bit of wilderness'.

'This vista's pretty wild,' said Scott, causing me to look up from my path.

In the gloaming, the view opened and closed onto the vast rolling green of an arboreal ocean, dark clouds above us and mist forming on the river below. Here and there, God used an elegant finger to spotlight a lime green tree or clearing. The distant mountains were pale blue like the range behind Sydney.

'What makes the mountains blue? I thought it was eucalyptus. They're not eucalypts, are they?'

'You may as well ask why the sky is blue,' replied Scott. 'It's light bouncing off the atmosphere.'

'No. Then all mountains would be blue.'

'A lot are. Smell that?'

I breathed it in. The clouds were settling for the night and the last of the sun washed them in soft light. It was transcendent – an American spiritual sung in gold and smelling of pine.

'It's the oils a pine tree gives off. Lemon trees do something similar, maybe eucalypts too. Oil vapours affect the way light passes through the air, refracting it through the blue spectrum.'

Matt ran down and chose two campsites on a cliff overlooking a valley. 'No way we can be built-out here,' he said. He was right. The massive drop to the valley floor more or less guaranteed that.

He got out the twine, canvas and ground sheet he'd bought in Washington, and made a determined show of being a bushie. He fashioned his lean-to into a welcoming tent just in time for the threatening skies to open with such torrents that we were all forced to shelter with him.

Figuring that the rain might ease, we broke open the foodstuff and ate an early dinner. I handed around the teacups – Sue's bright yellow one for Scott, the dainty Royal Stuart with spring flowers for Matt and the crazy little Phoenix for me. And there we were, three urban types out in the wild, sipping Matt's Jim Beam from dainty china cups and slurping pot noodles off Mamie Eisenhower's bangs. It was pure happiness seeing those great big man hands holding those itty bitty porcelain handles.

'So where do you go camping in Wales?' Matt asked Scott.

'I haven't done much. I come from a caravanning family, but we did spend one holiday on canal boats. It was brilliant fun, steering the boat, opening the locks and watching them fill with water.'

'I've always wanted to do that, live on a river boat.'

'They're surprisingly cosy, but cold with all that water around them.'

'You?' said Matt, looking at me. 'Where d'you go camping?'

'I don't. I've always wanted to – that's why we're here.'

That much was true. I'd always wanted to go camping, but Pig didn't like it. He offered to show me how bad it was, like that was a tantalising prospect. So I arranged for us to walk to the Annapurna Base Camp in Nepal, with the help of Sherpas to carry our equipment, set it up and prepare the food. So, yes, I had been camping once. In tents. In the Himalayan mountains. In the winter. With a whole other love.

Avalanches eventually blocked our way and threw us off the mountain, but not before we had three astonishing weeks walking through rhododendron and daphne forests, sleeping in snowbound tents and trekking under the brilliant light of a full moon.

I remember walking with Pavarotti singing 'Nessun Dorma' in my ears. He hit that exquisite final high note – 'All'alba vincerò! Vincerò! Vincerò!'– as I rounded a corner high in the sky, and there was the Annapurna range, laid out with Machapuchare set like the patriarch at the head of his table. It was so poignant, so moving that tears sprang to my eyes. I ran back along the track and gave my headphones to the man carrying my load so he could enjoy the revelation himself.

> My secret is hidden within me,
> (sang Pavarotti in Italian)
> No one will know his name,
> Fade away, stars!
> At dawn, I will win! I will win! I will win!

I would have told Scott and Matt that story but there was no way to introduce it without revealing how much Pig was a part of my life. When people split, who gets custody of the stories? What happens to all that life when love dies?

I changed the subject instead.

I'd clocked some tall poles on the path to our campsite. Matt said they were bear poles, for hanging picnic baskets to keep them out of the way of the bears. 'They're really smart, bears,' he said. 'They can work out how to get into cars and everything. They'd think nothing of coming into your tent if they smelled food in there.'

'Do you think we should have eaten in here?'

We all looked around Matt's little lean-to. 'I guess we can shake out the crumbs.' He didn't sound convinced. 'Besides, you can always tell when a bear's around, they smell incredibly strong. I've only smelled it once. It was almost human – like BO and bad farts. Horrible, musky. Extremely intense.'

By the time we'd finished dinner and made a passable dent in the bourbon it was dark, and the rain hadn't eased. It was going to be a lot colder than we expected, and particularly bleak for Matt, who had been forced to offload two bags and now had nothing warm to wear. He accepted the offer of my cashmere Dolce & Gabbana overcoat. It wouldn't fit him, but with its deep green shot-silk lining, it might make a nice throw rug.

I was sticking to my original plan of having nothing to do with the erection of our tent. I wouldn't even hold an umbrella while Scott unpacked it. I left him fiddling around with his torch in his mouth while I went to work out how to get our food up a pole.

Walking through the nearly empty campsite gave me time to reflect on my only other hands-on camping experience – with my brother. We'd gone on a surfing weekend with some friends even though none of us could surf. Turned out none of us could camp either. We were all teenagers. After struggling first with the fire and then the tent, everyone retired to their cars to sleep. We had driven down in our parents' Volkswagen, so it was a night of memorable discomfort.

This was pretty well what I expected as I stumbled down the dark path towards our campsite. Instead, I found (glowing pale blue with Scott's Maglite torch inside) our tent sitting up like it had in the shop. Three hearty cheers for Scott and his profligate wisdom. And while we're at it, let's salute Kelty tents. They're so fine you can put them up on a cliff, in the dark, in a rainstorm, when drunk.

Inside, we were soft on our thermal mats and warm under our double sleeping bag. I was so happy that Scott had made this perfect cubbyhole for us. For the first time, someone understood what I wanted from my wild picnic adventure and leaned into it with love.

We snuggled together and did our Waltons routine for the first (but not last) time. 'Goodnight, John-Boy; Goodnight, Matt.'

Scott and I lay listening to the rain beating on the outside of the tent. The wind in the trees sounded like the ocean – it was so evocative and romantic that we made our second mnemonic recording. When I listen to that memory the synaesthesia is complete. I feel Scott's chest rising and falling under my ear. I taste the sweet smell of his skin and I am golden with certainty.

The next morning came in grey steel. The rain was momentarily distracted, and there was mist in the valley below. Our thermal mats stopped us from being stiff, but Matt's ground sheet hadn't afforded him the same comfort.

We threw down cups of lukewarm thermos tea and moved on

as quickly as we could decamp. Our plan was to have a thawing hot shower in the nearest amenities block before driving out to find a hearty breakfast.

Neither of the menfolk made any secret of their desire to control Betty. Scott was first up and Matt would take over in the afternoon. I chose to take the back seat, leaving Matt and Scott to fish around for conversation. They hit on music immediately. Whenever things got tense or torpid, they'd revisit this happy hunting ground.

'Talk Talk?'

'*Colour of Spring* or *Spirit of Eden*?'

'Does it matter?'

'*Spirit of Eden*,' they said together, and then laughed.

We found an amenities block and caused a stir by having the wrong male to female ratio. Happy campers seemed confused as to whether we were a ménage à trois, a gay couple and friend, or family. Scott and Matt looked enough alike to seem like brothers, but was I with Matt? Was Scott our son? Americans are curious critters.

Back in the car with Scott behind the wheel, we began plotting our route to Nashville. Matt had a dog-eared guidebook and was reading from the chapter on Virginia. 'Here's one,' he said, '*Originally home to the Native American Monacan tribe and later the Powhatans.* Didn't you say Pocahontas was Powhatan?'

I nodded. 'That's her father in the Disney cartoon.'

'Quotes her sources,' said Scott, 'I like that.'

Matt kept reading: '*The Natural Bridge of Virginia is the oldest tourist destination in North America. The area was surveyed in 1750 by a young George Washington whose initials can still be seen carved on the wall of the bridge …*'

'He was a vandal!' Scott said with mock shock.

'George Washington, the Father of American Graffiti?' I said. 'I bet he *did* chop that tree down.'

'He said he did, didn't he?' replied Scott. 'Wasn't that the point?'

Matt carried on: '*Thomas Jefferson purchased the Natural Bridge from King George III of England, calling it the most sublime of nature's works.* Look, here's a painting of it.'

He held up the book to show us an etching of a man lecturing a woman in a hooped skirt under a natural arch that curved high above them like a viaduct.

'Shouldn't there be a river there somewhere?' I asked.

Matt looked at the picture. 'Whaddya think, Scott? Water or wind erosion?' He held the book so Scott could see it while he drove.

'Both,' he said at a glance.

'*While president, Jefferson personally surveyed the area –*'

'Because one president land-surveyor is never enough.' That was me interjecting again. Get used to it.

'*Herman Melville alluded to the bridge in describing Moby-Dick –*'

'Oh, you're making that up.' I put my hand out and Matt passed me the book. He wasn't kidding. I continued reading where he'd left off. '*Along with Niagara Falls it has been described as one of the two most remarkable features of North America ...* Oh my God! You didn't say there'd be a wax museum.' I handed the book back so he could see a photo of Cher in wax.

'She's had so much surgery,' he said. 'How can you tell it's a waxwork?'

'Let's do it,' I concluded. 'I love me some kitsch.'

'I don't get you,' said Matt. 'One minute you're all hoity-toity about art, next you're running off after shitty waxworks.'

'Those shitty waxworks *are* art. They're pure Dada – they're anti-art. They're the perfect antidote to the capitalist war machine.'

'Well shoot me, but kitsch isn't an art movement.'

'*Bang bang.* Kitsch is the pornography of real emotions. The commandeering of art for propaganda. The better the art, the more ironic the subliminal message, the better, funnier, and *kitschier* it is.'

We paid our $15 each and pushed through the turnstiles of the Natural Bridge Park.

'Which way to the wax museum?'

'It's shut.' The cashier checked me up and down like a seasoned evaluator of the human condition. 'We're going for a classier theme.'

'Doesn't that just stick a blade of grass up your nose,' I said as we walked down the path past the old wax museum. I stopped for a moment to salivate through the closed windows at the fading display art. 'Who do you think that is?' I said, pointing to a photo of a particularly androgynous waxwork.

'Michael Jackson?'

'Hilary Swank?'

'It's Whitney Huston.' I covered the name on the next poster. 'Scotty, you should be able to guess this one.' Another waxwork of indeterminate sex with bouffant hair.

'Margaret Thatcher?'

'It's Kenny G!'

The Natural Bridge itself was impressive … as long as you'd never seen a freeway overpass before. 'I'm sorry, Matt,' said Little Miss Disappointed, 'I think we're going to have to revoke your privilege concerning the right to choose detours.'

'What about your whole Dada-kitsch-art thing?'

On the way out, we passed a penny press machine. For a dollar it was possible to buy a penny with an image of the Natural Bridge badly impressed on it. I paid my money and handed the elongated coin to Matt. 'It's all yours until someone comes up with a worse detour.'

This was the way our morning ran away from us. To make up for lost time, we abandoned the green dots that indicated pretty scenery on our map for the bold blue line of the interstate freeway.

It was past lunchtime already and I was hungry. With Matt at the wheel, I suggested we drive to Radford to get something to eat. 'That way you can flirt with all the college girls.'

Turned out Radford was now firmly co-ed, and had been for a million years. More pertinently though, it was summer holidays and the town was pretty well deserted. We had a burger and Matt gave me my penny back.

Our waitress approached asking if we wanted dessert and Scott lit up his smile. 'I've always wanted to try something as American as apple pie.'

'Sorry, hon, we don't have pie. Got ice cream, carrot cake, cheesecake.'

'But don't apples come from here?'

'They do, so most people have had their fill. Why not try the cheesecake?'

'But I've set my heart on apple pie.'

She thought for a moment. 'Y'all headed to Nashville?'

'How do you know?' asked Matt.

'You're not gonna get much huntin' done in that big ol' town car.' She then gave us complicated directions to a place off the highway near a town called Marion. 'It's small, called the Apple Pie. Don't look much but Mrs Douglass makes them herself. There's the best apple pie you'll find in all Virginia.'

'They were quite some instructions,' Scott said as Matt slid in behind the wheel. 'Are we prepared to travel two hundred odd miles for a slice of pie?'

'Hell, yeah.'

Rural Virginia in mid summer was all green with white dots. It was filled with weatherboard homes that had swings on their porches. It was pick-up trucks and men in blue overalls. As a life glimpsed at high speed, it looked hard-working and God-fearing.

Just as the waitress described, we found a small weatherboard cottage in the middle of nowhere. Outside, a hand-written sign welcomed us saying, *Apple Pie.*

Inside was dark and sugar-scented. Someone had converted their front room into a cafe, with pale blue walls and small wooden tables. Red and white checked gingham cloth gave the impression of a child's doll house. On a wooden table was an array of homemade pies that sets my mouth watering just remembering them.

The blueberry and cherry pies had cross-hatched tops so that you could see the fruit below. The pecan pie was open, but decorated with a ring of nuts indicating where to cut. The apple pies were old-school deep pan 'coffins' with shiny brown sugar pastry crusts on top.

We ordered one of each. 'How do you want your apple pie?'

'Hot?'

'À la mode, cheese or with cream?'

'My mother uses *à la mode* to mean naked,' I said.

'Here it means vanilla ice cream.'

The local style was to serve apple pie with a slice of crumbly cheddar cheese, not that I could make up my mind. 'Can I have it all? Cream, ice cream, slice of cheese?'

She smiled indulgently. 'I'll bring extra on the side, so you can play with your food.'

The berry pies were tart and sweet in a way that swirled together in your mouth as perfection. The pecan pie was a nut bar on a crumbling biscuit base – delicious with the cream, which liberated it from being too sticky. But it was the apple pie that won us all. The caramelised apples were packed tight like in a tarte tartin – not too moist, and with a perfect shortcrust pastry. And the combination with the cold ice cream and crisp cheese? It was as sophisticated as it was simple, and it was simply delicious.

'Why do you suppose it's as American as apple pie,' I asked my companions, 'when it's mentioned in Chaucer?'

'It was the Swedes, wasn't it?' suggested Scott. 'The ones who settled here.'

'Johnny Appleseed?'

An older woman came out from the kitchen, wiping her hands on her apron. 'It was the bees,' she said.

Turned out she was the chef, landowner and mother of the waitress. Mrs Douglass didn't run the shop all year round. Summer was her busy season, with all the campers coming down the road to the nearby Hungry Mother campsite.

'There weren't no bees in America before the pilgrims. No bees. No native fruit. What they did have were these sour little crabapples. So they caramelised them in the fire and added cinnamon, mace, whatever they had to make them sweeter. Then wrapped them in pastry to keep fresh. Imagine coming to a country with no fruit? Those crabapple pies must have been quite the delicacy.'

The first settlers brought plenty of seeds with them, but had to wait for the new trees to reach fruit-bearing age, and then had to pollinate them by hand. Successive immigrants brought bees, which the Indians called 'white flies'.

Johnny Appleseed (his real name was Chapman) was late to the party. He was an eccentric religious mystic who lived around the turn of the 1800s.

'Seems God told him to plant as many fruit trees as possible,' said our hostess. 'People think he just scattered them seeds, but he didn't. He owned thousands of orchards. Bought cheap land and shared his profits with the farmers who tended them. Turned out he was a good businessman: planted thousands of acres with fruit trees to feed a hungry nation.'

'So you're carrying on an American tradition? Growing apples to feed the weary travellers.' Mrs Douglass smiled at Scott, who was winning two nil in the 'charming southern women' stakes.

Matt was teasing Scott about it as we left the restaurant when an enormous butterfly flew out of the bushes and startled Scott. He screamed like a Hammer Horror actress, and I laughed all the way to sundown.

Matt was still at the wheel when we pulled into the Hungry Mother campsite that Mrs Douglass had recommended.

'No wonder they called it Hungry Mother,' said Matt. 'Check out the tits on those hills.'

The campsite was nestled in between two pudding bowl mountains, as Mr Cartography described them, the twin cores of an extinct volcano. Unlike the previous night's campsite, which had some semblance of the great outdoors, this was a family picnic spot filled to capacity with squealing children, barbecues and strumming banjos.

Actual banjos.

Our allocated site had a wooden picnic table with two benches, and a grate in which we lit a fire and boiled some water. The weather had cleared as we drove south from the Blue Ridge Mountains. We ate under a deepening red sky – salad, olives, humus and bread I'd picked up in Radford.

Scott plugged in his new speakers, and the night filled with soft talk, insects, and Sheila Chandra singing *Weaving My Ancestors' Voices*. The evening was so perfect we recorded another mnemonic, this one filled with the smell of barbecue and the squeals of children chasing fireflies.

We were finally settling into each other's company, easing out of the first phase of friendship (*Where are you from? What do you like?*

Who do we know in common?) and into phase two (*What do you think? How do you feel? Who do you belong to?*). These were stories told in the oldest tradition of campfire yarns.

Unable to tell stories from my marriage, stories of my adult life, I reverted to ones from my childhood. Particularly about my father. One story was meant to be funny, about how he fell from the cabin of a friend's truck while drunk, then told everyone he'd been in a 'traffic accident'. But the story exposed my dad as an alcoholic, and led Matt to reveal similar dark stories.

When it was Scott's turn, he told one about coming home drunk from a party when he was fourteen. He commandeered his parents' dinner guests with witty banter, as you do when you're a pissed teenager, but instead of words, a stream of vomit exited his mouth. He reported looking at the mess and saying, 'Oh, I seem to have vomited,' which everyone else took as a cue to leave.

He told this story with such simple candour that Matt and I were laughing at our own Adrian Mole. He was so enlivened by our response, he told a second, more convoluted anecdote about his twenty-first birthday, the punchline being that he dropped a slippery oyster mushroom into his soup and it splashed his shirt. I can't embellish this story, because nothing will do justice to how remarkably unremarkably funny it was. While Matt and I laughed at the absurdity of it, Scott was looking at us like a dog taking a shit – certain we were laughing at him, but not so certain it was fair. And it wasn't fair. He had a blessed childhood. Loving parents gave him the self-confidence to tell a story as delightful as that of The Slippery Mushroom.

Later that night, our laughing at his story led to a silly argument in our tent – or at least I thought it was silly. I wanted to make love but Scott didn't, arguing that I only wanted him for his body. I thought he was joking and played along.

'We don't have enough in common,' he said.

'That may be true, but why throw out the one very good thing we do have in common?' I asked, invoking my best sexy kisses.

When I think of the mnemonic for Hungry Mother, it's not of the music and barbecue we recorded, but the two of us having a fight in super-hushed whispers so Matt wouldn't hear.

'You only want me for my body,' Scott hissed.

'But it's a really nice body.'

GRACELAND

The morning was mint crisp like a new hundred dollar bill. Scott announced he'd been his school's 1500 metres running champion and suggested we go for a jog. I said, 'Yes, please,' because the novelty of travelling with humans was doing wonders for my manners, and the romance of being with someone energetic and sexy put a real bounce in my step.

We discussed where we'd stop for breakfast while I stretched and warmed up. Matt, for his part, limbered up with a cigarette, smoked in urbane detachment. He wasn't coming on the run with us.

In his enthusiasm to get going, Scott began executing martial arts kicks in the air. 'Do you think we'll find eggs and hash browns?' he asked. 'I could really go for some protein this morning.' Being a devout vegetarian was proving tricky for Scott in rural America. More than once he'd had to reject a salad because it had been laced with bacon – and if another person asked him if he ate fish …

While daydreaming about the food he'd like to eat for breakfast, Scott punctuated each syllable with an air punch: 'Muesli, fruit salad, yoghurt, egg on toast, jam, peanut butter and jelly. Whatever that is.' He wanted to finish the list with a flourish and performed a spectacular flying air kick (kung-fu, I think) which landed him flat on his back.

'Well, knock yourself out, kid,' said Matt.

For want of something clean to run in, I lent Scott my crew t-shirt from the film *The Adventures of Priscilla, Queen of the Desert*. It declared, *Drag is the Drug* on the back. I chose not to tell him about the gay motif printed behind him, wondering what sort of response it would get in rural Virginia.

My cultural anachronism and I ran out into the fields, past the other campers, down the linden tree-lined lanes. We jogged past cows and horses into a world that smelled of hay and river reeds. It was delightful. As expected, Scott caused quite a stir in his gay t-shirt. There was a lot of pointing. One guy in a campervan tooted. Scott waved at him. An old man on his porch gave the thumbs up. The woman in the shop smirked at him and said, 'Right on.'

Who knew? 'Drag' in rural America is a two-car hot rod race.

Twiddling the car radio dial as we drove out unleashed the iconic steel guitar of NPR's *Car Talk* program, hosted by 'Click and Clack the Tappet Brothers' (otherwise known as Tom and Ray Magliozzi). I turned up the sound and Betty filled with love talk about diffs, donks and drive shafts.

The first caller identified himself as Charles from Exton in Pennsylvania. 'It's near Intercourse,' he said.

'And you never want to be far from there, do you?' said Click or Clack.

Car Talk was one of the funniest shows on local radio, and one of the most informative. The caller that morning had stuck a stick in a damaged muffler to stop the rattle and wanted to know if it was safe.

'What kind of stick?'

'A wooden one.'

'But what type of wood?' They were interested in the flashpoint because exhausts can heat to temperatures which might set fire to wood and burn everything around it.

It was like being in a poster for American Values. Betty purring in the sun, a warm breeze through the windows, a smiling couple out for a Sunday drive in the country. We pressed *record* and made a mnemonic of our lungs filling with happiness.

A few miles down the road, near Seven Mile Ford, we found a natty wooden diner with a view into the valley. There were seats outside and hash browns on the menu. Three happy campers stopped to plot their route.

A group of weekend bikers pulled up at the same time, which started a discussion between Scott and Matt about Robert M. Pirsig's *Zen and the Art of Motorcycle Maintenance.*

The book had been given to me when I was about fifteen by a friend of my mother's who was having either a midlife crisis or an inappropriate crush – or both. I hated the book. Hated the sentimentality of what the author thought was a 'good' life. Although maybe I just hated the man who gave it to me.

Or maybe not. Both my travel companions loathed it. Matt from the perspective of someone approaching forty, and Scott as a student of philosophy. 'His reasoning is sloppy. It's like he can peer into the canyon of deep thought, but doesn't have the intellect to build a bridge over it.'

'I found it smug,' said Matt. 'Like life is about maintaining your own motorcycle. What if you're a shit mechanic? What if your smarts are subtle and poetic? The book is just a lame excuse for a midlife crisis.'

As they talked, they stabbed their food and pronged the air with their eggs. If they needed anything beyond music to bond over, this was it. I was free to leave now, my work here was done.

I turned the map around and showed them the route I was thinking for the day. 'It's about five hours west to Nashville, and then another two or three to Memphis.'

'What are the chances we might find a revival church?' asked Matt. 'We're deep in Baptist country.'

'Are they the ones that don't sing?' asked Scott.

'The ones that don't dance,' I said. A friend was the daughter of a Baptist minister. 'Something about Salome's seven veils and the whole John the Baptist head-on-a-platter thing.'

'So it's not because people might think they're fucking standing up?' offered Matt.

The boys checked the map and agreed to try getting to Memphis in a single shot. 'But,' I said with the wisdom of the road, 'doing it means we can't take any lame detours.'

'Hey,' said Matt, his hands in the air, 'I think you'll find you're still holding the Crap Penny.'

Leaving Seven Mile Ford, we drove out of Virginia and into Tennessee. An oversized guitar by the roadside announced our arrival into the musical state. Although the artistic welcome was somewhat undermined by the state motto: *Agriculture and Commerce.*

Driving through the crown territory of the media evangelist, every two-bit preacher was having Sunday airtime. All sorts of hellfire rained down on us as we flicked from station to station.

'When God comes visiting,' howled the radio, 'do you serve him refreshments on cracked china? No, sir. You do not. You take down your best plates, your best cups and saucers, and you show your respect.'

'Well, fancy that,' said Scott. 'Mr Beaton's etiquette guide for when God comes to visit.'

'Don't worry, Scott, we're crockery-compatible.'

Scott was driving this leg. We didn't have a conversation about it, but we both made a mnemonic of the radio preacher. In it we're happy, and I am so wholly in love with Scott in this moment that it's the clearest of all my recordings.

We drove west through Tennessee, now deep into the chirruping summer of the American South. From time to time a soldier would appear on a plinth. War memorials in other states were from the Vietnam, Korean, and one or two World Wars. Here it was the memory of the Civil War that still cut the deepest.

We'd only travelled an hour when we came to the small town of Abingdon. Its main street, lush with magnolia trees in the full bloom of lemon scent, was a wide, slow tide of children with fairy floss, couples in their Sunday best, and men wearing Turkish hats and carrying tubas.

'What's happening?' asked Matt from the back seat.

'I don't know. I think a Masonic band is forming somewhere.'

The musicians led us to a field packed with blue and white striped tents under a heat haze of barbecuing meat. Like being given the keys to the city, we were welcomed by the Abingdon Arts & Crafts Fair. I wanted to wheedle my way into the knick-knacks, but since I was currently holding the Crap Penny I didn't have the power to choose.

'Wow!' I said. 'Is that a bluegrass band?'

Sure enough, among the beehives and honeycomb, four old men were sitting in a circle of guitars and steel banjos. The boys suggested we stop and take a quick look.

'To speed things up a bit,' I offered, my plan taking shape, 'why don't we go separate ways? I'll see if I can find some food.'

There were plenty of elegant handmade homewares, and I began wondering what treasure I might find for my crockery quilt, when I chanced upon a woman selling the cotton variety – hand-sewn depression-era bedding made from flour sacks. Surprising as it sounds, they were sublime. The woman selling them told me that during the Great Depression, the flour mills discovered women were cutting up their cotton flour bags and sewing them into children's clothing. In response, the mills started to print the calico fabric with joyful designs – bright yellow daisies, pink Cécile Brünner roses, shapes and motifs in mauves, greens, browns and vivid blues. When the clothes wore out, the leftover fabric was then transformed into quilts.

I went back to find Scott, to see what he thought of buying some bedding. (Ah, young love, when they'll still browse the crap stalls with you.) I took him to the quilts and we discussed the artistic merits of one with a large dark blue patch where a unique blue bag had created a postmodern negative space. Or, at least, that's how the double-degree designer described it.

'We need something warm for the tent,' I said. And we did. It was a lot colder at night than we'd expected. 'God knows how Matt's coping on his lonesome.'

But the price tag! Scott showed it to me and I blanched. 'That's as much as the tent.' The asking price for the old flour sack special was three hundred dollars!

'It'd be a perfect memento of our trip,' he suggested.

'You could take a photo, and I'll keep that as a memento instead.'

'We could go halves.'

'You don't have any cash. Can we just think about this for a moment?'

We went for a walk, a cooling off period, when we ran into Matt poised over a table that sold *sticks*, walking sticks fashioned out of branches. Some had their rough spots sanded off, but otherwise they were still just sticks. The able-bodied Matt was contemplating who made them and whether he should buy one. We convinced him to think about it over a cob of barbecued corn, and in the process he snapped out of whatever hypnotic trance he'd been placed under.

Scott and I weren't so easily released, and our love-tent was now replete with an expensive hand-sewn antique quilt.

A civil calm descended on the car as we left. Scott and Matt were in the front. Scott had found a copy of Jack Kerouac's *On the Road* and was reading aloud while Matt drove. Scott seemed happy to cast himself as Sal Paradise, and Matt as Dean Moriarty. I guess that made me their travel agent. It was nice though. My plan to baffle any tension between us was working.

Another 250 miles and nearly five hours later, we stopped at a diner near Smithville. We were still an hour or so out of Nashville and everyone was getting punchdrunk from the bum-numbing road.

'I don't think we're going to make it to Nashville tonight,' I said, breaking the bad news to the fellas, 'much less Memphis.'

'Well, it's not like we're on a schedule,' offered Scott.

'Where does the time go?' asked Matt, stretching over the wooden chair, trying to get his vertebrae to line up.

'It's weird. The same thing happened when I was by myself. I figured I was being stolen by aliens. Oh my God. Are you guys the aliens?'

Matt liked this thought. He put his hand under his shirt and started hamming up an alien bursting through his chest. 'What is it, Scott? Get away from him, you bitch. *Yaaaaaagh.*' He shot his hand out and over Scott's face.

Our laughter was a bit raucous. Other diners turned to see what the fuss was about.

'Not so scary, Matt,' I said. 'Mork from Orc. We got stolen by *Mork and Mindy*.'

'*Shazbot*,' he switched to a passable impression of Robin Williams, 'I've been studying the humans at close quarters. The female is a supernova of kitsch-lit blazing fury. Like a dragon holding a Donald Duck teacup.' He mimed roaring fire breath over a tiny cup, his pinky finger crooked. 'Capable of boiling water with her rage. She does, however, make a fine cup of tea, but I have yet to find the mute button.'

The other diners were fluffing up their interest. Whole tables were craning to enjoy his performance as he turned his crazy light onto Scott. 'The male of the species is the Balm of Calm, possibly made from asbestos, as he can withstand the female fires of hell and still manage to erect a tent. I have concluded that the sex must be hot because the language is explosive.'

'Oh God, you can hear us?'

'Hear you? Sometimes the mountains tremble.'

Our laughter had the attention of everyone in the room. Finally the waitress pinpointed their interest when she came over to Matt. 'Some people want to know – are you that actor?'

Matt beamed his affable best. 'Yes, ma'am, I am,' he said, making no attempt to hide his Australian accent, 'but probably not the one you think.' The entire diner groaned and went back to their dull lives without Matt Damon.

We huddled around the road atlas to choose a camp site, finally settling on one called the Cedars of Lebanon. It was just outside Nashville, about fifty miles from where we were. 'We can check out the city in daylight and make plenty of time for Graceland and Memphis,' suggested Matt.

I couldn't believe my luck to be travelling with men willing to bow down before the King of Kitsch. My friend Amanda visited Graceland a decade earlier and returned with a delightful Swarovski wristwatch in the shape of a police badge. In its centre was a crystal-encrusted White Elvis with mutton chop sideburns. I could only imagine what treasures waited for me inside his actual home.

Back in the arms of Betty, Matt curled up in the back seat (there was still no room for his legs) and went to sleep. It was getting dark, so Scott took my turn to drive.

Matt's breathing became regular in the way of a sleeping man as Scott and I sat in companionable silence, the windows down, the night air rushing around us. At one point the sound of Betty's engine roared up as an echo against a highway retaining wall. It combined with the night sounds of frogs and crickets to become our sixth mnemonic.

It's perfect because it's exactly the sort of memory you wouldn't photograph. I'm in the passenger seat, Scott is driving, and a dim glow from the dashboard lights his face. It was so starkly *not* the sort of picture you take on holidays that I took one, and I know exactly what it sounded like.

The Cedars of Lebanon campsite was nearly full when we checked in. A lot of the families were already asleep, so we turned off our headlights in an attempt to be discreet about our late arrival.

We found a spot near the river and set up quietly. We were doing really well until Betty did her famous self-locking door trick with the doors wide open. When I shut them, her alarm went off waking everyone, dogs and babies included. I fumbled to find my key, which was now locked inside the car. Scott found his and clicked the alarm off with a loud *pipping* sound.

'Sorry,' I called out into the grumbling night. 'Sorry, it was an accident. I'm sorry.'

A loan male voice shouted, 'Shut up.'

I think it was Matt.

The night was fair so we took the outer layer off the tent and looked up into the starry sky ringed by swaying treetops. It was blissful under our brand new quilt.

Scott put on an album, Van Morrison's *Poetic Champions Compose.* The saxophone started up on the first song and it was like listening to a memory unfold. I had to ask him the artist's name again, and he was surprised I'd never heard of him.

'He's been around forever. The tunes of our fathers,' he said.

One song, 'In the Garden', was so beautiful it made me homesick for a world I had only imagined – one filled with infant acrobats rolling in lush grass, and generations of deep visceral love wrapping them well into their futures. I found myself unable to control sentimental tears.

'Oh, this is stupid,' I said. 'His voice is so nostalgic, and I've never even heard him before.'

'The Welsh have a word for that,' said Scott. '*Hiraeth.* It means homesick for something that never existed.'

'Then maybe I'm Welsh. I used to get so homesick as a child, even when I was at home!' That irony wasn't lost on me. 'I always thought it was because my parents went to a strange place when they were drinking.' Scott held me close and let my tears puddle into his chest hair.

'Have you ever had that?'

'Sort of. I once went somewhere that was so beautiful it made me cry.'

The mnemonic we made has Van Morrison's rasping Irish voice muddling in with the mating frogs of the Mississippi – it's a conversation in hushed tones about the icy blue-green light inside Switzerland's Grindelwald glacier, as Scott softly recounts a magical road trip when he was sixteen. Underscoring it all is the palpable, humid sensuality of the moment. How could anyone make high school geography sound so damned romantic?

↔

Scott and Matt were now inextricably bound by music. Nashville was ten minutes down the freeway, and even though neither were country nor western fans, like pilgrims from another faith they wanted to show their respects at the Temple of Twang.

Officially known as the Ryman Building, the Grand Ol' Opry was built as a revival hall for Christian evangelists. It was a formal two-tiered proscenium arch hall that until 1974 served as the studio for the country and western radio show of the same name.

A wild cross-section of artists had performed there: Enrico Caruso, John Philip Sousa, Sergei Rachmaninoff, Johnny Cash, Sheryl Crow. (Plainly we paid the price and took the tour.) I even bought a replica poster that says *Elvis was here,* but this is Tennessee so Elvis was everywhere.

After a dose of stardust we drove up Charlotte Avenue to see the Downtown Presbyterian Church (*the best Egyptian revival architecture in America*) and the Tennessee State Capitol Building (*Greek revival, used to be a Catholic cathedral, one of only twelve state capitols not to have a dome*). We crossed Music Row where the record companies were. We careened onto Broadway and Ninth for a bit of Victorian Gothic with the Batman Building. Right and left onto Charlotte Avenue to see a full-scale replica of the Parthenon.

'Wow, two thousand years of architecture in one morning,' said Scott.

'The founding fathers sure were keen to get some culture in our guts,' added his new best friend.

'Doesn't this appeal to either of you?' It certainly appealed to me. While working on an arts program for the ABC, I developed a theory about the connection between architecture and revolution which seemed to be playing out here. I thought it might interest Scott (the student of design) or Matt (the master of arcane music), but no. Both boys were grinning like loons. Sal and Dean had had enough red brick and white marble, they wanted some get-down dirty blues. So we kept driving towards Memphis.

The three and a half hour journey on the Interstate 40 – a monotonous corridor of trees – created the perfect setting for me to explain my theories to a captive audience. 'Every political revolution – the Greeks, Romans, even Adolf Hitler – all planted their flags on Corinthian columns.'

'But the antebellum houses here in the south …' said Scott.

'Antebellum?' asked Matt.

'Before the war,' I said, 'like *Gone with the Wind*.'

'I'm confused, what war are we talking about?'

'The American Revolution,' said Scott.

'Is that after the War of Independence, or before the Civil War?' asked Matt.

It was like talking to a bucket of puppies. 'The War of Independence *is* the American Revolution. After it, Thomas Jefferson built Capitol Hill. He was the architect of it and his home, Monticello, was the original antebellum manor house.'

'Okay, revolution ends in marble columns,' said Matt. 'Got it.'

'Ionic, Doric or Corinthian?' asked Scott.

'Do you s'pose Graceland will have columns?' asked Matt.

'I do hope so,' replied Scott, 'then Sheridan can develop a theory about rock and roll as a revolution.'

'But it *was* a post-war revolution,' I said, before I realised he was teasing me.

↔

Memphis lies on the river at an apex between rich farming land to the north-west and the humid wetlands of Mississippi and Louisiana in the south. During the Civil War, thousands of freed cotton workers came here and met thousands of Irish escaping the potato famine. This blend of hope and frustration created the blues and later its red-necked sibling, rock and roll.

We were nearing our destination when we had our first brief glimpse of Mrs Zippi, her arcing bends and sand bars racing us while we drove south by her side. This was the mighty river I paddled in before Chicago. I wondered if any of my atoms had passed by here yet.

We chose the Meeman-Shelby Forest campsite from the map. It was a short drive into town and seemed to be right on the river, but when we pulled up the boomgates were closed.

We got out and walked around. It was a simple matter to lift the gate by hand. 'Do you think there's a safety issue? Mosquitos, maybe?' I asked Scott and Matt. 'Ross River fever?'

'Maybe there are snipers,' replied Matt.

'Or flash floods,' said Scott.

They were making fun of me, but it didn't answer the question. 'Do you think they're closed for the summer?'

'No. I think the ranger's office has closed for the night.'

I pulled Matt's travel guide from the back seat and was checking for other nearby campsites. I was about to suggest a hotel when some campers leaving the park told us to take a ticket and pay in the morning. It's all so simple when you know how.

The good fortune of the closed ticket office was that we weren't the only ones who were put off. Not only did we find a charming campsite right on the Mississippi River, but the place was almost deserted at the height of summer.

We set up our tents within earshot of the bubbling water, and unpacked all the bedding so we'd have something nice to come 'home' to after dinner. We then drove five miles into Memphis.

It was that time of day favoured by music video makers, when the light in the sky is a rich blue and neons go *ping*. It was perfect for sightseeing, and the sight the boys wanted to see was Graceland

'Maybe we can pick up tickets for the morning,' suggested Matt.

'Is it that busy?' I was still under the delusion that we were visiting the King of Kitsch. I had no idea that for Scott and Matt, this was a sentimental journey into the music of their fathers. They were excited to get a sense of the optimism of an earlier generation, and glimpse the young men they'd been born to.

As such, the drive-by didn't go well. Graceland (wanting to make it plural won't make it so) was no longer in the best part of town. Elvis Boulevard was now lined with strip joints and sad looking shops with busted neon signs. There were broken cars and clapped out people. The boys were gutted that their gentle childhood dream had dissipated.

'Oh dear, White Elvis,' I quipped, alluding to the late-era Elvis who'd gone to seed. My silly joke didn't liven the sombre mood in the car.

Since Graceland was closed, we cruised on into Memphis proper. I tried to lift the vibe by offering a grab bag of facts from Matt's guide book. '*Memphis is the Pork Barbecue Capital of the World. It has the busiest cement terminal in the country. The lion who roared at the beginning of MGM movies lived here – his name was Volney.* Here's a good one: *Memphis is the only five-time winner of the nation's Cleanest City award.*'

'You can laugh all you want,' said Matt. 'Kathy Bates, Morgan Freeman and Aretha Franklin come from Memphis. It's home to B.B. King, and you see that guy there?' He pointed to a statue of a black man holding a trumpet. 'That's W.C. Handy, he recorded "St Louis Blues" and gave the music its name.'

'I keep forgetting, it's not music for you – it's religion.'

We parked the car and walked down Beale Street, passing a place jam-packed with a blues-jazz fusion blowing out the front door. The music was amazing. A rhythm and sound that cut the brain and went straight to the body. It made you want to dance. People had gathered at the shopfront and were craning to get a look inside.

'Who's playing?' Matt asked the doorman.

'The boss,' he said, indicating a neon sign flashing overhead that read *B.B. King's Blues Club.*

We pressed our noses to the window but could only see bodies bopping as one. On a steamy Memphis Sunday night, the joint was jumping.

We wanted to go in, but there was no way another body could fit. When the song finished, we walked away, and Matt picked up his theme. 'Muddy Waters, Furry Lewis, Albert King, Alberta Hunter, Bobby Bland, Minnie McCoy. Do you know who any of these people are? Okay, what is B.B. King's real name?'

'Bruce Barry?' I replied

'Oh, man.' Matt was getting sick of me, but Scott was enjoying himself. He knew them all and even had a Bobby 'Blue' Bland CD with him.

'Brandon Block?' I said, this time taking a stab I knew was stupid.

'It's Riley, you fool. B.B. is for Blues Boy. He's Riley 'Blues Boy' King.'

'Well hang on, Matt, I can't know everything.' He wasn't the first man to accuse me of not liking music because I didn't have an autistic talent for detail. 'How do you fit it all in and then make space for Curtis Mayfield or Santana, Danny Elfman, Talking Heads, Prince, Bach or Mozart? I like music. It takes a part of my brain and fills it with feelings instead of thoughts, but the names don't stick.

The feelings stick, but there are no tags to connect them. It doesn't mean I don't like music.'

What spooked me were the names which poured from my mouth. The first few came from the primal bog of adolescent crushes. Santana belonged to John, my first true love. I could have thrown in Frank Zappa, John Martyn and just about anybody good with a guitar. Pig collected vinyl. He had a taste for weird electronica (theremins, moogs, and music made by quasars.) He introduced me to Peter Gabriel, Talking Heads and world music, for which I'm eternally grateful. Scott was shaping up to be the same sort of autodidact if Talk Talk, Tortoise and Boards of Canada were anything to go by.

'Maybe I don't have the language of bands and genre,' I continued, 'because I have the language of feelings. Wouldn't that be a revelation? What if I just discovered that men who love music can't talk about their feelings? What they play is what they want to say.'

My neoclassic architecture lecture may have been a dud, but this one hit home. Scott smiled, put his arm around me and said, 'Let's find something we can all understand.'

We strolled like that for a few blocks until the sound of a 70s funk band reached out and dragged us in. The place was heaving. A local college band was playing, and what they lacked in tightness, they made up for in looseness.

Matt was in his element, hopping from table to table, introducing himself to Mephistoes (or whatever they call themselves in Memphis). I was happy to sit back and let the music talk for me. The band began performing a jazz-funk standard that my first love, John, used to play. It had a swing in its hips that's fun for fucking and useless for fighting. If it was a single image, it'd be that 60s illustration by cartoonist Robert Crumb of the loose-limbed dude stepping out under the words, *Keep On Truckin'*.

Scott and I looked at each other and pressed record on the mnemonic tape. It's a great moment. I'm in it, and in all the moments where this song has played. 'Pick up the Pieces.' That's its name. It's what I'm doing here. In this room. In this country. In this moment. With this man. It's wooden tables, in wooden bars, on sunny days, at jazz festivals, on boats and beaches with no schedule and no destination. It's my life in the arms of the great living now.

The next morning we zipped our tent, paid our rent at the ranger's office and piled into Betty. Matt slipped some vintage Rolling Stones into the player and we cruised out onto Highway 51 like a trio of dudes on a mission to rock *and* roll.

Although still early, queues had already formed at Graceland. Summer is peak season, and hundreds of thousands of people visit here annually so they allot times for the tours to avoid overcrowding in the house. After forking over $30 each, we had an hour to wait for our turn.

Graceland is divided in two by Elvis Presley Boulevard. On one side is the home, on the other is Graceland Plaza with the modern ticket office, museum, parking lot, souvenir shop and bus terminal. We each bought a nerve-steadying cup of tea and muffin at the Rockabilly Diner, then took it all outside where we could sit under the cement awning and watch tourists being shuttled across the road to Graceland proper.

The day was already hot and humid. It was still early, so it was going to be a stinker. From the comfort of our plastic chairs we contemplated the sweeping lawn, gates and façade of the comfy ol' Presley home. And, yes, the revolutionary King of rock and roll had columns outside his front door.

'But Corinthian tops on the Doric columns,' observed Scott,

scandalised. 'And those ones,' he pointed to a free-standing sign, 'they're not even structural.'

It was a supportive joke, and I kissed him.

'So how'd you two meet?' asked Matt.

'She was visiting a mutual friend–' he said, pointing at me.

'We met at the Philosopher's Ball–' I said at the same time.

'Oh, that's a bit grand,' rebuked Scott.

'Alright, the Philosopher's Summer Solstice Party,' I said, raising an eyebrow as a challenge.

Matt cocked his head and frowned at me. 'Jeez, I didn't think it was going to be controversial.'

We both looked at him. 'A mutual friend introduced us,' I said.

'At a Philosophy Society drinks party,' Scott added.

'Aw, cute, they can get on when they try real hard.'

Maybe it was the Elvis magic, or sense that Graceland was a sacred site, but the conversation sort of unravelled from there. Like pulling a loose thread of knitting it all came out: why I was driving across America, my relationship with Pig and how the perfect relationship came to an end.

'Well, obviously it wasn't perfect or you wouldn't be sitting here squabbling with Scott, would you?'

Hmm. That ol' chestnut. If my marriage had been so good, why did he leave? 'You can kill healthy things, you know, with a car, or a gun, or a blunt instrument.'

I'd mentioned infertility and IVF to Scott early on, and there's no missing the enormous scar across my bikini line, but we hadn't talked about it since.

'There are lots of routine dull things in life that erode love. Alright, maybe not love, but the enthusiasm for being together. It mightn't have been the only cause, but we'd been doing IVF for seven years and I think that rubbed a lot of fun out of our marriage.'

Matt lost his usual sophisticated air. He looked crushed. I've seen that look before. I've seen it on Pig. I've seen it in the mirror. 'Why did you have to do IVF?' he asked.

'I had a couple of ectopic pregnancies. The first one in high school was the worst because I didn't know I was pregnant and it got to about three months before it – burst, really.' I was talking to Matt, not ignoring Scott, but talking to Matt because it seemed to mean something to him. 'And then two with my ex, which were just miserable in comparison. After the second one, they saved the tube by putting it back together, but the third pregnancy got stuck where they joined it and that was the end of that.'

Normally at this point I give my laymen's explanation of fertility – about the exquisite filigree of the human body. How the fallopian tubes arc up and out to caress the ovaries. How they release an egg once a month. How the egg travels down the tubes where, should they meet an oncoming sperm, they fertilise in the low-alkali environment to make babies – and how without tubes it's necessary for a squadron of doctors to coordinate the release of the eggs in order to intercept them before they float off into my abdomen. They fertilise them in vitro (which means in glass) and then return them.

Everyone wants to know about the 'spunk in the jar' bit. They're fascinated by the man's perspective – the salacious wanking in hospital cupboards with back issues of porn magazines. You can usually derail the conversation at that point and turn it into an amusing sideshow. Better that than tapping into the female perspective, which is long, complicated and uncomfortable. Daily injections of hormones, blood tests, ultrasounds with a sonic dildo, anaesthetic, bloating, discomfort and emotional unbalance.

But Matt knew this already. 'Katie had an ectopic pregnancy. It was terrifying.' Katie was his girlfriend, he had shown us a picture of her. One of the reasons he was travelling was because now that she'd recovered, they were fighting about how to proceed. He was trying to resolve what he wanted from life. He loved the idea of having kids and wanted to settle down, but she wasn't ready for that.

'It's awful for you both, really awful. The only thing I can say is that I mightn't have had the third ectopic if I hadn't been so impatient to have a baby after the second. Waiting for certainty is okay.'

The ectopic pregnancies, as a group, were the single worst catastrophe in my life. They had not only been life threatening, they had snuffed out the miracle of conception and handed any possible parenthood into the hands of science. They were expensive, time consuming, and wrote infertility across all my love.

I could sympathise with his girlfriend about not wanting to go there again in a hurry. I could sympathise with Pig for not wanting to go there. I could sympathise with Matt that his life had been turned upside down. He'd followed his love to death and it had taken something precious away from him.

Scott didn't say much, but it was a rare moment in which the three of us showed who we were without our armour. Three humans on the Plain of No Judgment. It doesn't happen often in a friendship, and it's hard to reverse once you've been there with someone. Matt became my friend in that moment. And it all took just long enough for us to finish our tea, and for the bus to arrive to take us to Graceland. The mood was set for a deep and meaningful exploration of the shrine to American possibilities.

Graceland was everything I ever imagined, only more. More ordinary, more kitsch, more indulgent, more gauche, more adolescent, madder. I only wish one of my girlfriends had been there to share it with me. Instead, my travel companions went into reverential introspection, and I had no one with whom to share my glee.

My buddy in kitsch and crockery had already told me about the Hawaiian den with the large leather batwing chairs and matching cane walls and bamboo-patterned curtains. It was so much better than I imagined: the engraved Polynesian dark wood furniture, the leopard-skin printed couch, palms, ferns. *Sigh.* It was the perfect panel-van dreaming. The sort of lurid fantasy you might see airbrushed onto the side of a shaggin' wagon. Everything I loved in one King-of the-Jungle-themed snapshot.

I looked to Scott to share the joke, only to find him misty eyed. He was moved. When I poked him he shrugged it off as nothing, but it wasn't. The same was true in the fabulous Moroccan pool room. It was decked out like a Bedouin tent. Genius. Where was Sue? She'd love this. She'd loved the television room in deep chocolate and cream, with a mirrored ceiling and a bank of tellies reflected upside down in the roof.

The TV was a motif. Every room had at least one. I thought maybe the racquetball court had been spared, but no, there was a mini set outside the glass wall. Graceland is a 70s time capsule, and God bless it for that. It may be the decade that style forgot, but America is the cultural amnesiac.

While queuing to view the family graves (a ritual that concluded the comprehensive tour) I looked at the fake flowers strewn around the memorial garden. 'How often do you think you have to change fake flowers?' I whispered to Scott, who didn't respond.

I overheard a man nearby tell his companion that we were all 'pushing the frontier of ignorance'. I turned to smirk in agreement, but when I caught his eye, it was me he was talking about. As such, there was no one to share my astonishment with when I saw a copyright symbol on Vernon Presley's grave. Instead I just pointed at it and said, 'Because that's some smoking-hot poetry right there.'

Scott shrugged.

'Seriously though, why would you copyright a grave? Isn't the point that you want everyone to remember?'

I looked at Scott. His eyes were filled with tears. Actual. Tears.

I looked for Matt, but he had shuffled away and was wiping his face as well.

Oh God, spare me.

Elvis Presley is selling more records dead than he ever did alive. He toured America as a hologram, becoming the first performer ever to headline a live concert tour while no longer living. It wasn't small either: his tour included Radio City Music Hall in New York, the Las Vegas Hilton and a debut European concert at London's Wembley Arena – twenty years after he shuffled off his mortal fat suit. I like to think that the Londoners might have got the joke, but I'm not sure anymore.

The boys were gutted. I was glutted. We'd seen police badges, sunglasses, motorcycles, cars, buckles, belts, necklaces, the back yard, front yard and the eternal flame to his dead twin brother, Jessie Garon Presley. Everything except the royal throne rooms, which were all off-limits. It's just not a done thing to think of the King taking a dump, much less choking back a handful of pills and gagging on his own excess.

There's only so much bonding and togetherness a trio of strangers can take. It had been a great day at Graceland, although I think my lack of reverence may have rubbed Matt up the wrong way. We decided to split for a few hours and meet again later for dinner.

Scott and I drove around until we passed a blues band playing on the pavement outside a bar, like an ad for American groove. The night was hot, the music was cool, we stopped for a beer in the gloaming.

It's strange to realise that we didn't make a mnemonic at Graceland. Maybe because of the dissonance in our experience. I would have recorded the wallpaper in the TV room – it was that loud. Scott would have kept the fountains tinkling in the memorial garden with piped music playing 'You'll Never Walk Alone'. But if we'd recorded that, it would have been underscored by my inane twittering, so we did neither.

However, no sooner did we arrive at the bar and see the buskers than we started recording the whole set. I think Elvis would have approved: these musicians were the real deal, blues written on the Mississippi. We recorded their music, the people talking, the tram bell as it passed by, the deep blue in the sky and the orange of the mercury vapour lights.

The musicians appeared to be a family. Mom was on keyboards in a big floppy hat, father and son on guitars. (The son was good, the father was great.) There was also an uncle – a methodical middle-aged man more at home behind his drum kit on a street corner than any man I've ever seen doing what they're good at.

The son worked the crowd with gormless ease. He asked for requests and a young man called out 'What a Difference a Day Makes'. The woman with him smiled softly. Lovingly.

The singer took his microphone over to the man and asked if he wanted to dedicate it to his wife. 'No,' he said, 'it's for our son, Luke.'

The singer blanched. 'Is he over at St Jude's?'

The woman looked like she was going to cry. Now it seemed obvious they were both exhausted. 'Yes, he has leukaemia.'

The singer's face softened into an expression of total compassion. 'Well, y'all know he's in the best place in the world. My uncle and I, we painted that place inside and out, didn't we?' He turned to the drummer, who waved. 'There isn't an inch of that building that wasn't made with love, and the staff there are the best in the world.'

He turned to include the rest of us. 'Didn't they tell us all that when they gave Dr Doherty that Nobel prize for being so good?'

'It's true,' replied the father with the confidence Americans have talking in public, 'and Luke's doing real well. We're real proud of him.'

'Well, you two just take a moment to relax and we'll all pray that the next twenty-four hours make your son better, and then you'll be able to say, '*Oh what a difference a day makes …*''

He sang it slow. He sang it as the blues. I found myself praying for a boy called Luke who I've never met, and wondering how people survive parenthood.

In the morning we were tidying our camp and getting ready to leave when Matt found some baby snakes under his ground sheet, where they had snuggled in for warmth. He was terrified, dancing around and batting them away with his towel.

I stepped in with all the authority of a former children's TV host. 'The most poisonous snakes in the world are in Queensland, you crazy wahini. Except for the rattler, none of the top ten are even in America.' I got a stick and shuffled the little fellas out of the way. 'Either way, rattlesnakes live in deserts – these are probably tree snakes, or baby pythons.'

Matt was not convinced. 'You grow up with tiger snakes, you learn respect, even for the baby ones.' He continued warily packing up his kit as though he was defusing a bomb booby-trapped with tripwires.

I was still teasing him about his 'itty bitty baby snakes' while we ordered breakfast. 'You watch out for those little suckers,' said our waitress, 'ground rattlers have a bad attitude.'

Matt went white. 'Ground rattlers?'

'Small snakes that'll kill a horse quick as looking at them.'

Who knew? *Sistrurus miliarius* is a venomous pit viper, a tiny member of the desert snake family with a heat-seeking sensor that helps them find humans and other mammals for warmth.

Oh. How. We. Laughed.

This revelation spurred Matt on. He was keen to reach New Orleans where a bed was waiting for him. A safe, warm, inside bed.

Scott was happy to set his beacon for 400 miles due south. 'We should be able to do that in a day. It's what, six hours on the freeway? Three more for mucking around and getting stole by aliens.'

His words went through me on a spike of fear. By the end of the day Matt would be gone and it would just be Scott and me. What would we talk about? How would we get on without our filter, our chaperone?

You're safe, I reminded myself, *it's only change.*

The waitress also told us there was a storm warning on the radio. A hurricane was forming in the Bahamas and heavy rain was already falling outside. 'You might want to get on your way,' she advised. 'You won't be able to make speed in this weather.'

She wasn't wrong. In the rain, Betty the LA road car turned into Betty the Bitch, the Tonya Harding of the highway. Every breeze and puddle sent her skating all over the shop trying to kill us. She was terrifying in the wet. I wasn't strong enough to hold her, and driving in and out of skids was nerve wracking. The boys took over, racing south while I sat in the back trying (unsuccessfully) not to fret about it.

Matt was a good driver but Scott was better. Both were in a whole other league to Pig, who generally drove so inattentively it was impossible to relax. We couldn't drive at full speed, so the five hours reserved for getting to New Orleans only got us halfway through Mississippi before we pulled over for a break.

In some sort of inverse logic, the Matt Damon sightings became more frequent the farther we got from civilisation. Now each time we stopped someone had a hissy fit over him. Travelling with an impostor became pretty entertaining. Every time we'd enter a diner Matt would put off saying anything for as long as possible. Like in Jackson, where we stopped at a service plaza and sauntered in for lunch.

I'd slip his name in, just to get the wind up. Like, 'Whaddya think, Matt? You going to support the vegetarian, or will we go the full dead animal today?' He'd chuckle, and the waitress would be curious to learn more.

'So where you folks from?'

'I'm Australian,' I'd say.

'I'm Welsh,' Scott would say, which usually confused them, so he'd add, 'that's like England, but next door.'

Then they'd put their full beam onto Matt, who'd smile and say something like, 'You got me. I'm Australian too.'

Mostly that was enough to settle the matter, but sometimes, like this day, the waitress wasn't ready to shake the dream tree awake. 'You're that actor, aren't you? Say something else.'

'It's true, I am an actor, but not the one you think.'

'I loved you in *Boogie Nights*.'

'That's Mark Wahlberg! And I'm not him either. I'm Australian. Listen to this accent: "Call 911, someone stole my teddy bear."'

She thought about it for a moment, looking into his face like the truth was encoded there. 'Yes you are. Acting. That's what actors do.'

'You'd do well as a single man around here,' I said to him after she'd gone to fill our orders.

'Matt Damon would, I don't know about me. So how long you been divorced?'

'I'm not,' I tried to say it casually, but didn't succeed. Scott turned his head so fast I thought I heard it snap.

'You're not?'

I shook my head. 'Nope. It's been two years, one of struggle, one of separation. We tried to work it out but …'

Scott's face clouded over. 'Are you thinking of getting back together? Is this a trial separation?'

'Is anything that simple?'

Matt didn't look up. 'Yes.'

'I don't think we're getting back together. But I'm like everyone else – just making it up as I go along.'

Matt mouthed the word 'Sorry' to Scott.

'What are you sorry for, Matt? It's messy. Life is messy. You of all people should know that. Doesn't mean I'm insincere.'

The waitress came back. 'Matt! Your name is Matt.'

Matt put his hands in the air. 'You got me,' he said in a terrible American accent, and then signed his name on a napkin.

The storm warnings became more insistent the further south we went. Hurricane Erin started in the Bahamas, 'jogged' twice across the Florida peninsular and was now moseying along the Gulf of Mexico picking up water and intensity. Her trajectory was for New Orleans, but all of Louisiana, Mississippi and Alabama were on alert. The questions of how far to go and how fast were becoming imperative. In the next couple of hours we'd be stuck wherever we went. At least for a few days.

I wanted to find shelter for Betty. The news was saying that the hurricane hit landfall in Florida with gusts of up to 100 miles per hour. It was miserable on the road, with every expectation that it would get worse. The boys wanted to carry on. I was dubious about driving further south to the Gulf of Mexico, but Matt was adamant about reaching New Orleans.

And bubbling under it all was the tension of what would happen to Scott and me when Matt left. Just the two of us, on the longest date in history. Maybe this is what a honeymoon was like in an arranged marriage – seeking shelter, dodging squalls and hoping that fate would be kind.

Scott pointed out that none of the motels we passed had adequate shelter for the car. 'We could go back to Jackson, but we're halfway there now. It seems best to make it to New Orleans and find a proper cement car park.'

Mr Reasonable struck again. We carried on.

It was past 10pm when we arrived on the outskirts of New Orleans. The rain had eased to a thick drizzle. After twelve hours on the road everyone was tired and fractious. The weather reports had escalated from storm warnings to a full hurricane alert. If Hurricane Erin continued on her path, New Orleans would be underwater some time the next day.

We drove around following hand-written instructions until we found where Matt was staying in the Old Quarter. When we arrived, we were all welcomed in. After such a long drive, it was nice for us all to stop for a moment.

Matt's friend had set up a tent for him in the living room, which looked inviting but was funny after five days of camping. At least it was indoors, with a reduced risk of death by acquaintance who couldn't tell her arse from a ground rattler.

The television in the apartment was tuned to the Weather Channel, monitoring the hurricane's progress. Each update had Erin on target for New Orleans, and included a recap of the devastation of previous storms. The compound effect of imminent threat and past disaster was thrilling.

Scott and I were so in the moment that we made another unintentional mnemonic. In it, the Weather Channel is burbling away like a film score. Hurricane Erin is racing towards us. We have battled the elements as a team, and are now squaring up to round two – Scott and I as a couple. This memory is exciting and daunting. But mostly daunting.

Betty needed to get undercover, so we said our goodbyes to Matt and drove around trying to find a hotel fancy enough to have a parking station. Tricky in the Old Quarter, but we found one. It was expensive but also nice – with a bed and a bathroom.

Scott and I made the most of all the hotel's amenities. We showered, we ordered room service. And after fourteen solid hours of tension, we plugged in our CD player and went to sleep with Anita Baker reassuring us that we brought her joy ...

A ONE-WOMAN HURRICANE

It should have been perfect, but the bitch woke in the morning with a bear in her sore head. I am both bitch and bear in that cockeyed sentence.

Some of it was a backlash against Matt moving on. He'd been a worthy buffer between Scott and me. I'd been forced to keep a civil face on my personal angst. Some of it was the strain of being in Scott's company twenty-four hours a day. God knows it must have been bad for him too, but I felt that my interior monologue had been commandeered. No matter where I went, there he was. The *it*-ness of us was making me crazy with desire to be alone.

The stress of the previous day's drive to New Orleans was one thing, and spending $400 – the equivalent of a new tent – every two days was another, but the most painful source of my disquiet didn't manifest until I woke to find Scott looking at me with the unblinking trust of a man in love. I tensed to his unspoken tribute, thinking, *There he is again.*

We probably could have left it there, but he opened his mouth. 'I love you,' he said with such purity, trust and (damn it) love that I just blew up like a piece of sweaty dynamite.

'Oh, what did you say that for?' This from the woman who'd been moved to say the same thing the first time we slept together.

The open, loving look on his face snapped shut. A flash of pained confusion was chased away by a steely-eyed man's look. He didn't say any more.

'No, really, Scott, what does it mean? What do you want from me? What are you doing here, anyway?'

Scott was out of bed. I don't know where he was going, but he was getting dressed and I was barking and snapping at his heels, hurrying him on his way.

'Well, you asked me,' he replied evenly.

'No, I didn't. I did not invite you. I have no idea why you're here.'

I couldn't stop. He went white like he might fight or faint. He looked like he was dying bit by bit, and I couldn't stop. I just couldn't shut up. I couldn't quietly have a shower and find a moment to think what the hell I was saying, or why.

'Well, I think you did invite me. In the taxi. On the way to the airport.'

'I said if I had the money I'd ask you. I didn't ask you. I don't have the money for this.'

'But I have the money. I have my own money.'

'But you don't have enough. And you don't have an invitation. This is my trip and you're taking it over. I have to consider you all the time.'

In fact he had brought £2000 with him, which turned into nearly US$4000 and was almost the same as me. It wasn't the money. It wasn't the invitation.

'This is stupid,' he said. 'You're not making sense. What's this about?'

He was right. It was the same old thing. The one thing. It was The Thing. 'I miss my husband. I miss my life.' After that I was incoherent.

Being a good man, he didn't leave. He got a clout of vicious mixed messages, but still he found some compassion for his soggy travel companion. 'Well, I suppose that's to be expected, but I can't see why it's my fault.'

'It's your fault because I can't miss him in front of you. I can't talk about him. He's been half of my life for eleven years and now I have to cut him out of my stories so I don't hurt your feelings …'

'But I didn't ask you to do that.'

'You don't have to ask. You just turn up and it's a fight to the death between my old love and my new. I don't want to hurt you. I don't want you to kill my love, *and* I don't want to hurt you.'

'How would you hurt me?'

'Like I'm hurting you now. By leaving you. By putting you in my situation.'

'That's pretty arrogant. Who says I'll get hurt? Who's to say I won't leave you? Why don't you think you're the one who'll get hurt?'

Well, that stopped me. Scott was good in a corner – he gave as good as he got. I stopped snivelling and looked at him.

'I thought I was invited,' he said. 'I certainly came by choice. Unless you want me to leave, I'm also staying by choice, but I think it's time you learned to ask for what you want rather than screaming like a baby every time you're a bit uncomfortable.'

Screaming like a baby.

He'd pulled his shoes and socks on now. 'I'm going for coffee and croissants. Do you want me to bring some back?'

'No. I just want you to hold me for a moment.'

He was agitated, but looked at me like I was a pretty thing that had been trampled. He came and held me. We lay back on the bed and he hit play.

Anita Baker came on again. It was ironic to hear her sing 'You Bring Me Joy', but it was like Scott was saying that, and it made me feel better. It made me feel like I was being forgiven for doing a bad thing.

We lay like that for a while until he finally said, 'Why don't you have a shower, and I'll go hunt and gather something to eat.'

It was a good idea.

After he'd gone, I stood in the shower crying. It's true I missed my ex. It's true I missed my life, but it was also true that nothing was going to change that. The crazy lady had escaped and run havoc, again. I did a terrible thing that morning. I was offered the tender underbelly of love and I punched it. And I punched it hard with a clenched fist. I wouldn't be in a hurry to go back there if I was Scott.

We managed to fill the cracks in our relationship. I was sheepish. He was kind. I felt curiously reassured by him saying that it might be me who would get hurt. Probably not the healthiest option, but at least he was freeing me of responsibility for his happiness when I was having so much trouble with my own.

Also, I'd flushed out the worst truth between us. I'd taken the dead rat of my marriage and laid it at his feet. I still loved my ex. I missed him. If Scott could cope with that, maybe he could cope with the rest of me.

He brought back croissants and coffee. The croissants were good, the coffee was ghastly. Welcome to New Orleans.

I'd booked us into a youth hostel thinking it would be cheaper than a hotel. When I confirmed our reservation, the woman had gushed about a cabin in the garden with a picture window, four-poster bed and mosquito net, so I paid extra for an upgrade.

When we arrived, they appeared to be hosting a Narcotics Anonymous meeting. The 'darling little cabin' was a potting shed that had been cleared of toxic jars, if not of actual toxins. The creaky bed was propped on milk crates and did indeed have a mosquito net, because it needed one. The famous Mississippi Delta had formed a puddle out back and it was a thriving, wriggling nest of mosquito larvae.

I snatched my messages from home and fled to Le Richelieu Hotel, a place my mother recommended from her heyday as an executive in the fashion industry.

As would befit the price (one tent per night) Le Richelieu was simple, elegant and had a balcony opening onto a cobbled street. The concierge informed us that the hurricane was still heading our way and many people had cancelled. When asked if we would be safe there, he added, 'The Old Quarter predates the levees and has survived hundreds of hurricanes. This is probably the safest place in Louisiana. '

I was unconvinced about leaving Betty in their uncovered parking lot. She wasn't insured for hail or flying debris. So we returned her to the original car park and made our way back to Le Richelieu on foot.

The radio and newspapers recommended filling the bath with fresh water and staying inside until we were given the all clear, but the storm was slow in coming our way. There wasn't even a breeze out on the balcony. It was lovely stepping out into the Murder Capital of America.

Matt was only a few doors down the road from us so we rang his bell. He stuck his head over the balcony for a quick chat but didn't come down. My guess is that driving with two prickly newly-mets was more than one man could take. I brought his tea cup and saucer to give him, but ended up carrying the delicate little Royal Stuart back into our lives.

As we were walking away he leaned back over the wrought iron balcony and called out, 'Hey Sheridan, you be nice. And Scott? Not so nice.' It was a benediction. It was the last time we saw him.

The Old Quarter was deserted. The shops and restaurants were boarded up with sticking plaster criss-crossing the glass in the windows. The few bars that were still open were doing a roaring trade in 'Hurricanes', a lethal cocktail made of unnatural colours. My guess was the hoteliers took this opportunity to clean out their liquor displays.

Scott and I were in a quandary about staying in New Orleans. It was expensive, but the car couldn't handle any sort of rain, and the combination with wind could be lethal. In the end we did what was advised: we filled the bath with water, threw in a bottle of French Champagne and spent twenty-four hours in bed under our own quilt.

We woke up to dazzling sunshine and the sound of clopping hooves on the cobbled stones outside our window. It was a sound so foreign and so friendly we made a mnemonic of it.

The storm had 'jogged north' and hit Pensacola, Alabama where it ran out of steam. The cars exiting Louisiana were caught by the tail of the hurricane further north and were flooded off the roads. We did the right thing by coming south and staying put.

Even though New Orleans was untouched on this occasion, there was no point in leaving until the damage further north was cleared. So Scott and I hauled Betty out of her shelter and set out to find some old timers rocking their porches around the Louisiana delta.

On paper, the geography of the Mississippi Delta looked as though the whole place was a submerged shimmering mirage of lakes and islands. From the road it looked more like bogs and marshes but there was still plenty of romance.

We didn't find any old codgers on their porches performing southern magic (no doubt they scooted out of the lowlands) but we did admire the jewelled dragonflies flitting from reed to water. The fish were jumping, and the cotton was high.

I made that up about the cotton. It looked more like brambles and grass.

We went as far south as the road took us, all the way to Boothville-Venice. The fishing boats bobbing on Breton Sound were soothing. The soft pinks and blues lifted off the water as the prawn trawlers puttered out for a night. We had arrived in the landscape of *Forrest Gump* – the bit where he takes to sea in the hurricane. A trawler with 'Captain Scott' painted in large letters on the back was moored in dock.

After the hurricane passed, the Old Quarter in New Orleans revived. The storm shutters came down and windows were flung open. We found ourselves in a world of voodoo shops and shrunken heads. Actual shrunken heads. Scott thought it was exciting – authentic Creole magic. I thought it was creepy – authentic death cult. I'm still bothered by those shrunken heads. *Do they take the bone out? How do they get them to be so small?*

Bourbon Street was warming up. We sat upstairs on a wide wooden verandah and ate dinner overlooking a band in the bar across the road. Their windows and doors were open and it was like they were playing just for us. A fattening moon rose and we pressed *record* on our mnemonics. Now we have our own version of 'Moon Over Bourbon Street'.

After a couple of days' hurricane leave, New Orleans came alive with a vengeance. Dixieland jazz was pouring out the open windows of the Preservation Hall. We found ourselves starring in a Woody Allen film with a trad jazz score accompanying us from bar to bar. The nightclubs got smaller and smaller until we were in one so tiny it was necessary to stoop to enter. We'd found an old smugglers' tavern.

Inside, a TV played silently and a piano played loudly. There was plenty of soft talk between us, which we recorded. It seemed like a precious mnemonic of the calm after the storm. But under it – can you hear the fizzle of my tension?

The hurricane finally jogged into oblivion after spewing a national disaster in its path, but not ours. We could scoot out east along the Interstate 10, and no one would notice.

We retrieved our unopened champagne from the bath (bought for the hurricane that never came) and collected Betty from the car park. Then we went down to the docks to say goodbye to the Mississippi.

A big ol' steamship with a paddle on its back was preparing to leave as well. It let off some steam and, up close, the sound was almost physical. We recorded it as a farewell to arms.

The thing that's not being said here, the thing that wasn't said in New Orleans, down on the Bayou, or late at night in the smugglers' inn, was how much damage I did with my outburst that first morning. It may have been my most vulnerable truth, but I'd delivered it like a bullet. If someone offers you their beating heart, think twice before you shoot it full of hard truth. Some things can't be unsaid.

THE BUTCHER'S TALE

Texas has the biggest sky in the world. I thought Australia had a big sky, but nothing like this. Ours is a formless block of blue – an unblinking eye. In Texas, the sky is populated by towering mountains of billowing clouds and scudding thunderheads so high the rain evaporates before it touches the ground. Those skyscrapers march from horizon to horizon in a dramatic and endless other world.

We crawled into Houston way too late and way too tired to hunt down a campsite. We bought a bottle of whiskey, piled into a Motel 6, turned on the television, ramped up the air conditioning, and downed the whiskey as blessed relief from concentration. It was bliss to let go in our cheap motel room. Some things you don't need to be sober for – Motel 6 is one of them.

Scott was lying on the bed, bare-chested, bugling Jack Daniel's while reading *On The Road*. Our journeys were now running parallel in real time. He read out bits about saying goodbye to Matt and leaning into our next crazy venture. He was drunk on words, on adventure, on whiskey.

The next day we vaulted 150 miles northwest of Houston into the sacred heart of oil country. We were zigzagging across Texas towards Santa Fe in New Mexico, vaguely aiming for Mesa Verde and then the Grand Canyon in Colorado.

We started late and didn't drive fast. By the time the sun was setting we'd only made it as far as Austin. My brother-out-law Marc had gone to uni there, and recommended it as a lively town with good food.

The University of Texas at Austin, as it's formally known, is the richest campus in the world. They found oil there a while back and were still converting it into the one life-giving property money can buy: water. The grass, trees, flower beds – the whole city – looked lush and expensive.

The city had an air of excitement because the annual jazz festival was in town. Sixth Street was adorned with stages and tents. There was a cacophony of bands and a caramel mist from barbecuing meat. Towering over it all was the Sheraton Hotel.

We were looking for a campsite, honest, but Betty pulled us into the Sheraton driveway where a man in uniform (Hussars, I think) opened our door. We fell out in a flurry of crisp wrappers and clanking cans.

'I've never stayed in a hotel with more than two storeys,' said Scott.

'How is that possible?'

'There's no highrise in Cardiff. Not much in London, either.' It was like a challenge – to experience, to profligacy, *to reception!*

The man signing us in looked at my short, short skirt (it shrank in the wash), appraised my travel-weary companion and gave us the junior suite on the seventeenth floor at a standby rate.

Scott had never been so high. I'd never had a suite before. We marvelled at the vertiginous view of the jazz festival – only the tiniest sounds penetrated this high. To the right was the twinkling stream of traffic flowing north on the Interstate 35.

'Do you think they can see us?' asked Scott, both our noses smudging glass.

'In Sydney there's a hotel on the expressway over the Harbour Bridge that's popular with honeymooners because of its view of the Opera House,' I said. 'Sometimes when stuck in peak hour traffic, you see a couple pressed against the window having sex.'

'What, like this?' He pushed up behind me and lifted my skirt. It was sort of scary – such a long drop to the festival below. I put my hand on the window to steady myself.

'Hmm, just like it.'

There was a knock at the door – the maid wanting to turn down the bed. Scott said the bed was fine but took the chocolates.

Down at the jazz festival, people were wandering from stall to stall, a tide of humanity flowing around the stages. People pressed against each other on a hot Texan night. I was very taken by the sight of them.

That's code, right? We made a mnemonic, but it's censored.

By the time we made it downstairs the tide of humanity had ebbed out. A flotsam and jetsam of workers were dismantling everything. The party was over, and I was ravenous. One of the roadies suggested a shopping centre next to the campus that had a twenty-four-hour supermarket.

We never got there. On the way we discovered an all-night bookshop combined with a cafe. Hooray for young people and their irregular lifestyles! It was dreamy floating through this enormous library that smelled of fresh coffee, eating muffins and buying more books than was reasonable for us to spend, carry, or read on the road.

I bought Ray Monk's *Ludwig Wittgenstein: The Duty of Genius*. I wanted to read the biography to understand more about the ideas that excited Scott, but the original work (Wittgenstein's *Tractatus*, for instance) looked way too daunting. I also bought *Off the Road: Twenty Years with Cassady, Kerouac and Gingsberg* by Neal Cassady's wife, Carolyn.

Scott's choices were just as romantic. He bought Immanuel Kant's *Critique of Pure Reason* and *The Economist*, which we took back to our fancy hotel to read in bed.

The bells on the university clock were chiming lunchtime when we strolled through the gates. Entering the grounds was like walking into a Hollywood mansion. There was stardust. Arcing sprinklers made rainbows in the desert. The cool arcades enclosing the gardens were part monastery and part hacienda. We made a mnemonic of the cool smell of wisdom.

Scott said that Austin University had an exceptional library which included a Gutenberg Bible – the original book from the original press. 'There are only a handful in existence,' he said. 'It would be nice to stand next to immortality.'

'Well, when you say it like that.' Frankly, I was pretty pumped about anything that kept me on terra firma and out of the car a little longer.

The Gutenberg press frequently makes it onto the top ten inventions of all time, along with vaccines, electricity and toilet paper. To stand next to its first impression is to be in the presence of something very big and German. The Gutenberg Bible is a weighty tome (70 pounds, or nearly 30 kilograms) with grave Gothic print in case you didn't know the word of God was serious.

The bible is housed in the Harry Ransom Centre, which also has an extensive art collection of 19th century Americana. One painting, *The Cavalry Scrap* by Frederic Remington, depicts an evocative flurry of horses and men cantering all over the place and shooting each other. The dust was flying, the bugle calling. You could smell the horse sweat and adrenaline.

'Oh, can't you just hear that?' I joked.

Scott looked at me and laughed. We recorded the sound of the painting and called it 'Charge of the Paint Pigment'. He then suggested we get back on the road.

The journey may be the journey, but mostly I found it hypnotic. Staying awake in the car was getting harder and harder. Luckily for me, Scott was still excited about driving Betty and encouraged me to sleep while he took the wheel. It was a ruse. As I slept his speed crept over 80 miles an hour, the revving engine giving him away as it started to rattle and hum.

At one point I woke to hear the engine whining above 100 miles an hour and, without opening my eyes, asked how fast we were going. 'Eighty,' Scott said sheepishly, the car slowing dramatically. At which point we cleared a rise on the open road and picked up a state officer with all his lights blazing.

He pulled us over for speeding.

'Can I see your licence please, sir?' asked the kind-looking policeman.

'Yes, officer, but it's in the boot. I'll need to get it out.'

'You keep your licence in your boots?'

'No, the boot,' said Scott, pointing to the back of the car, 'the trunk.'

'Oh. Sure, yeah. Get your licence out of the *boo-oot.*'

Scott handed over his licence, getting sweaty as the policeman scrutinised the strange piece of paper, which looked like nothing but was actually a Welsh driver's licence. 'Do you know how fast you were going?'

'Well, yes. My girlfriend had just asked the same question. I was quite surprised to see I was travelling at 80 miles an hour. It can be hard to tell on these lovely straight roads.'

The officer was looking at him with a bemused smile. The British accent was clearly soothing to his American ears. 'Well, I think that's a bit generous, son. Do you know what the speed limit is?'

'Yes, sir, it's sixty-five unless otherwise marked.'

'We have that speed limit because these lovely straight roads can be deceptive and dangerous. I'd appreciate it if you stayed on the limit.'

Scott took back his driver's licence and they shook hands, 'Thank you, sir.' He got back in the car and put on his seatbelt.

'*Your lovely straight roads?*' I asked.

'I know, I know. I panicked.'

Apart from the fact Scott liked to drive fast, he'd been making up for lost time. We'd only averaged 125 miles a day since New Orleans. We were being done in by late starts and slow afternoons. Today was no different. We figured we may as well just give up and find a place to camp – relax enough to get an early night, and then start tomorrow before the world turned into a shimmering heat haze. So we pulled into a diner to fuel up and find our way.

The diner we found was delightful – full of gingham and Texas hospitality. We hoped the Country Kitchen and Bakery might have something for Scott-the-vegetarian, who was currently living on a diet of omelettes and fries. Not eating meat in carnivorous Texas was messy and complicated, but whatcha gonna do? I found it attractive that Mr Philosophy couldn't explain his irrational eating habits – not to his own satisfaction, anyway. It was the closest thing to faith he had, and I liked that about him.

'So how long have you been a vego?'

'Fourteen, fifteen years …'

'That's weird. There must be things you've never eaten,' I said, ploughing into my chilli con carne.

'What do you mean?'

'Well, you'd have been a kid – kids don't like oysters, lobster's wasted on them. Raw fish, beef carpaccio, squid, caviar ...'

'I suppose you're right.'

'Did you start because you like animals?'

He was pushing fried potatoes around his plate. 'No. I like animals, but it's not that. I worked in a butcher shop when I was at school.'

'Oh, that explains it.'

'No, it doesn't.'

'You didn't get sick of the sight of blood?'

'I did. But blood's not meat any more than eyeballs or bones are. I had to clean up the shop, and I didn't think the guy was particularly hygienic.'

'You got put off because it was dirty?'

Scott smiled thanks to the waitress filling his bottomless cup of coffee. 'No. The thing was ... the guy, the butcher, he didn't like women much.'

'He was gay?'

'A misogynist. I felt sorry for his wife. She seemed nice, but he was always shouting at her, calling her names – all these things in front of me. Sometimes he'd throw things at her, like a cow's eye, which would roll down her apron. *Plop. Plop. Plop.*'

'Couldn't you do anything?'

'I was fifteen. She left him eventually, but she put up with it all the time I was there. And he was seriously into porn.' Scott gesticulated with his fork. 'I think that's what did it.'

'You gave up meat because a butcher you knew was into porn?'

'Yes. He had a whole library of this violent stuff and he was always trying to get me to watch it. Things with animals. I didn't want to look at them, which he interpreted as my being inexperienced or shy, so he'd tease me about it while we were working.'

This was so much more twisted than I imagined.

'He'd be cutting up meat saying,' he imitated the butcher's sing-song Welsh accent, '*So there's this bitch on all fours … Whack.* Off comes a cow's leg.' Scott mimed the butcher chopping. '*And she's naked on the floor … Whack. Whack. Whack.* Slices up a thigh. *And this pig comes in … Whack.* Another leg.'

'He's butchering the meat while describing animal porn?'

Scott put the piece of omelette in his mouth and nodded. 'In graphic detail, and all the while I'm sweeping the bits off the floor. Something had to give – sex, women or meat. I chose meat, but I'm not keen on porn either.'

I leaned forward and kissed him. 'Good choice.'

We ordered apple pie and cream, and unfurled our map. The nearest campsite was called Brownwood. It was on a lake. *A lake.* I hadn't been swimming since Washington, and the idea of running along a wooden wharf and leaping with joy into icy water was enormously attractive. Of course, first I'd have to find said body of water. According to the map, there was a town, airport, river and camping ground. What we found were four streets bundled together and not much else. There weren't even trees. 'Maybe that's why it was called Brownwood. Maybe they died.'

We drove in and out a couple of times before concluding that the water was Brownwood Lake, and the stuff around it must therefore be Brownwood.

We knocked at a house with some tricycles out front. Inside the TV was on and the place was alive with kids shouting and dinner being cooked. A child came to the door.

'Hi, do you know if there's anywhere to camp around here?'

Without opening the door, without taking his eyes off me, he shouted, 'Mom! There's a lady at the door.'

A bunch of other small kids and dogs gathered in the shadows. A youngish woman had to sort of kick her way through. 'Oh dear.' She looked flushed. 'School holidays – they've been under my feet for months. How can I help you?'

She didn't open the flyscreen door, which may have been a natural protection against strangers but was probably a natural protection against flies. For ten dollars, she said, we could camp on the building site across the road. 'There are no amenities or anything – you'll just have to make do with the wild.'

The building site was cement foundations behind a row of shrubs. It had a single shady tree and a view of the water. We ponied up the dough.

'Can we swim in the lake?'

'Sure.'

'Are there any nasties in it?'

She squinted in the way Americans have when they recognise you're not from around these parts. 'A couple of eels and fish, but it's nice for swimming.'

The single shady tree looked like a camphor laurel with its crazed bark and tight, rustling leaves. The sun was settling onto the horizon, so we oriented our tent to be in the shade in the morning.

There weren't any signs of life in the cabins facing the lake. It seemed romantic. Private. We still had the bottle of champagne we bought to celebrate the hurricane which never came. Tonight would be perfect to drink it. We put on our cozzies and set up a picnic on the wharf.

Champagne, candles and slowly arriving stars. Before the night could become claustrophobic with celestial dots, a huge, overripe summer moon rose above the horizon. It was astonishing. Magnified by the heat of the earth, it was bright enough to read by.

The silence by the lake was exquisite – the slight rustle of a breeze, the gentle *plap* of fish, boats lightly tapping each other, tapping the wharf. We made an extended recording.

We ate olives, cherries and nuts. We had bread and that strange stuff that passes for cheese in America. We pulled the champagne from its legally sanctioned travelling space in the trunk of the car. During travel, friction and heat had put a lot of pressure on the poor, demented cork. When we took off the metal outer layer, it flew into the air never to be seen again.

I dived into the water and, rejoicing in how warm it was, took off my costume. Scott followed suit – or followed without suit – and we swam lightly around each other in the dark, warm water.

The honey moon was shining on us. It seemed impossible that anyone could see us, but we moved under the covered boardwalk. In a world as warm as bodies, everything expanded into one loving being.

↔

Lying with the little grey splinters biting my arse, I said, with the full force of the moment, 'I love you.'

Scott looked at me tenderly, and then started to laugh. Not cruelly. Not kindly. Just not going there again in a hurry.

↔

We'd miscalculated the position of the sun and woke up hot in our tent.

I opened the netted windows, lifted the flaps, then flopped back onto the thermal mattress, cursing the northern hemisphere sun which was never where I expected it to be. Scott was stirring under the pressure of my kicking and sighing, before he unexpectedly somersaulted into a high-octane roar as centimetre-long ants piled into our tent and bit our naked bodies. We jigged and danced out of the tent, brushing the little biters off before leaping into the lake.

That stopped 'em. In the cool of the water, everything was calm again.

The morning had dawned warm and still. The freshwater lake was soft like lips. Who could forsake all of this for another day inside a car? We lay down on the boardwalk reading our books while we dried in the sun.

A couple of guys arrived and started messing with their boat. I left Scott talking to the fishermen while I packed up the tent.

I don't know what happens to me. I really don't. It's like I don't know how to be happy. I've thought about this moment a lot since, and I have no excuse for what happened. It's like the crazy lady who sprouted dog wings in the car park of my dreams could still leap out of me. Maybe my dyslexic god was rabid.

I was inside the tent packing away the sleeping mats. It was hot, airless, and the ants were unstoppable. Ants were biting my feet, my thighs. They were nipping their way up north. The sun was beating on the tent. Sweat dripped off my brow. It oiled my nose so my glasses kept slipping. It trickled around my hairline. I pushed my glasses back up my nose. Rivulets of sweat pooled under my breasts. The glasses slipped again. Another ant bit. There was a point somewhere around my groin where the ants and the sweat met, and flipped a switch from annoying to nuclear.

Kaboom.

I threw my glasses out of the tent and followed them with the foulest invective imaginable. To paraphrase: 'Jesus fucking fuck, you fucking little fuckers.'

My tantrum was inexcusable. There was a house full of children across the road. We were in God country. I screamed and rocked the tent so furiously that cleats were flung from the foundations.

Thinking I was being attacked, Scott came running. God knows what the fishermen thought. I exited the tent and sat in the car like the madwoman I was – arms crossed, scowling furiously while Scott dismembered the camp.

We drove off in a plume of foul city smoke – leaving my titanium-framed glasses where I'd flung them under the camphor laurel. What perfect punishment. The glasses cost eight hundred dollars. They were indestructible titanium and came with a lifetime guarantee. When I'd told my mother about the warranty, she'd said, 'Don't be absurd darling, you'll lose them.' How right you were, mother.

To compound my appalling behaviour, I later sent a stamped, self-addressed envelope to Brownwood, asking if the children could be enticed to look for my glasses and maybe post them back to me. Shamefully, I lied and said the glasses belonged to my grandmother and were of sentimental value.

I never saw them again. I hope someone deserving has them. I was so rude, and I apologise unreservedly for both my terrible behaviour and my lying.

But here's my one piece of mitigating evidence: the crazy lady only appears when my true heart is challenged. If I love Scott or Scott loves me then the door is open for her to be hurt again, and out she comes. I said 'I love you' and he laughed. I understood why he laughed, and that's what hurt like a thousand sweating ants.

Sigh. That, and I have a shitful temper sometimes.

THIRTY-ONE
MNEMONICS OF LOVE

Travelling west from Brownwood over iron-flat country, we chased a thunderstorm across Texas for 300 miles, admiring its display of unruly power as it ran ahead of us, spitting lighting and mocking my tantrum. Watching it, I rationalised my dichotomy like this: I could either contain my inner demons to keep the peace, or detonate my soul and let the pieces fly where they may. So far, being true to my inner bitch had cost me $800 and Scott's trust. I didn't want to bend my personality to ease someone else's discomfort, but I did need to get back in touch with my better self.

Texas was good meditation country. There was little in the wide open space to jump out and go *boo!* As the horizons slipped by, my chattering monkeys stilled and then slept. All became peaceful. Betty wrapped us in her loving arms while Scott drove fast and straight throughout the day.

As the sun wound around to the west, we turned the car further north to keep the light out of our eyes. We passed tiny crouching towns that could have been anywhere in rural Australia. Places like Warracknabeal, Coonabarabran, or Ceduna. Only here in Texas they were called Coleman, Sweetwater and Lubbock – towns in the middle of nowhere, to nowhere, from nowhere.

The day was closing when we came upon a collection of weatherboard houses gathered around the intersection of two streets. It was called Littlefield, which was ironic because the only field we could see went all the way to the end of the earth in every direction. Bunting flags snapped their welcome in the evening breeze. A blinking neon advised us that the only cafe in town was open. It was dinner time, so we stopped.

I wanted to record the moment. I wanted to remember that I had found a piece of Australia in the vast emptiness of rural Texas, but Scott was hungry and fractious. He agreed to wait while I pressed record. Stand with me and listen to the dry warm wind curl between us. See the wide street with its hooded shops glowering at us. There is red dust rising, colouring the sunset. Feel all that is familiar to me from Australia and foreign to Scott with his wet Welsh valleys.

We ate dinner. As a pathetic apology for the screwed-up crazy lady who'd helped pack the tent, I made Scott a 'diner dinner' special. Here's the recipe if you want to recreate this astonishing vegetarian cuisine.

Ingredients: refried beans, leafy green salad, salsa and Greek salad.

Directions: Mix in one bowl. Add itty bitty packets of dressing to taste.

There's a Marilyn Monroe quote I like to mangle: 'If you can't love me at my worst, you sure as hell can't love me at my best.' Scott forgave my worst. I'd try to give him a better me to love.

As the afternoon unfurled into evening, we considered camping in the recently harvested fields. You can do that in Texas (it's illegal in most other states) but there was something about the land that looked uninviting, like it might have been recently sprayed or something. You have to wonder, don't you, after the run-in with Matt and the ground rattlers that my biggest concern was Monsanto and weedkiller?

Anyway. We didn't camp in the open because the desiccated lunar landscape looked like it might have been sprayed with chemicals. Instead, we kept driving aimlessly through a gorgeous sunset.

Somewhere between Bula and Needmore the local radio presented an hour-long tribute to Pink Floyd. As we drove under a deepening turquoise sky, Dave Gilmore's wailing guitar rose like mist from the speakers. Jet-black trees slid by as we slowly rumbled along an unpaved back road. Mystery. Passion. Longing. The clarity of being which passes with the moment. The transience which means that living less is not living at all. I am so certain of the drama as it unfolds – and so unsure once it has passed. Fresh love. The thrill of being – two loving souls living on an enormous ball.

On the other side of nowhere we stopped to view the night sky. The moon wouldn't be up for another hour, so we turned off our lights and got out. All the stars were awake in the pitch black. The celestial waltz dancing above us. The stars were utterly foreign to my antipodean eyes, and it amazed me that one planet can have two universes.

'You don't have the Southern Cross up here?'

Now our roles were reversed. As we lay on Betty's warm bonnet, it was Scott who felt at home. He pointed out the highlights from his northern hemisphere childhood. 'That's Cassiopeia,' he said, 'you find her by looking for the 'W' on the horizon. And see the really bright one there? That's Polaris – the North Star. You're never lost when you see him.'

It was, in that most overrated of words, awesome, and we made a recording of the vast silence. Or rather, the vast silence underscored by the rustle of a garbage bin liner that had been attached to an historic marker – the words of which had been bleached off by the sun. This mnemonic of transcendent majesty was thereafter named the Historic Garbage Bin.

↔

We found a motel a few miles down the road and woke up the next morning in Muleshoe, Texas. We pulled on our running shoes and dashed out into nature.

It was difficult running in the recently ploughed fields next to the motel. The dense, dark soil was dotted with deep, slim holes that we skipped around for fear of breaking our ankles. It would have been unpleasant to pitch a tent on.

'What do you suppose those holes are?' I asked Scott.

'I don't know,' he said, dancing around them. 'Some sort of mechanical aeration, maybe?'

Maybe.

'What's a prairie dog?' he asked. 'How big are they?'

'It's a mouse, isn't it? Some sort of rodent, like a squirrel? They're about the size of a hand, though, I think.'

While trying to work out this conundrum a snake slithered from one of the holes. We slowed our trot as the creeping fingers of cold realisation squeezed their meaning into us. We were surrounded by *snakes*. We got the hell out of there.

We travelled the lovely straight roads of Texas into New Mexico and on to Santa Fe, stopping only for Scott to photograph cicada carcasses by the side of the road. Since his first day in Washington, he'd been trying to capture the chunky winged insects and was pixilated to find their shells out in the middle of nowhere.

'Some cicadas live underground for thirteen years,' I told him while he took photos of the cracked earth. 'They have one season above ground to mate, but if it rains when they're coming out, they die without ever knowing what it's like to fly or breathe fresh air.'

'God. Do you collect those stories, or what? You have a library of really depressing parables.'

'But it's tragic, don't you think? Imagine spending your life underground and then just as you're blinking back the daylight – *bam* – you're Icarus.'

'See? Why Icarus? Why can't it be Daedalus?'

'He the father?'

'At least he survived.'

'Well, all the cicadas that don't get washed away, they can be Daedalus. Those nymph shells you're photographing, they're dog-day cicadas. They come up every year then go back down when the weather cools. Suburban cicadas who summer above ground and have central heating and whipper snippers. Is that better?'

Scott was photographing a particularly large shell. I picked it up and pressed it onto his t-shirt. 'Of course, the real magic is discovering you can wear them as brooches.'

His smile revealed the good-natured child Scott would have been: intense, trusting, inquisitive. *What does it say about a man, when you also love the boy he was?*

Friends recommended we visit Santa Fe, the capital of New Mexico. The city sits way up in the Sangre de Cristo foothills. After so much driving flat over Texas, rising into the summer cool of the mountains was heavenly relief.

The city itself was charming. Full of adobe buildings with strange organic shapes and soft, rounded windows. The Spanish first settled here over four hundred years ago, and the locals have preserved the Pueblo architecture using strict building codes. Every house is painted in a sympathetic mud colour – or 'twenty-three shades of government approved beige' as Scott preferred to call it.

Apparently my snark is contagious.

We thought Santa Fe might be a good place to stop for lunch, but when we drove through it was obvious we'd entered an enclave so white and wealthy that Hyundai named a four-wheel drive after it. The effect was quaint, but cloying in its niceness. When we saw a sign to Los Alamos we followed it.

Los Alamos is the city where they first built the atomic bomb. It sits on top of a mesa 7000 feet above the desert floor. The project leader, Robert Oppenheimer, knew the area from his childhood and chose it for building the bomb, hoping the deep canyons would shield surrounding land from the blast or fallout.

'What are you thinking?' Scott asked as we drove up.

'About the Manhattan Project,' (the code name for the atomic bomb). 'I have a soft spot for the scientists who worked here on it, so many European refugees. Imagine working with the best minds of your generation to build a bomb to blow up your homeland. What incredible conflict.'

One they took seriously. Oppenheimer, for instance, understood the ramifications of what they were developing. He wasn't prepared to work on a second (plutonium) bomb, which he saw as an extraneous device that would cause unnecessary suffering, so the government hired someone else to develop it. The bomb that was subsequently dropped on Nagasaki cost eighty thousand lives and immeasurable suffering. Worse, the government then vilified Oppenheimer for his lack of cooperation. He was branded a communist and banned from the postwar nuclear ethics committee.

I'd recently read James Gleick's book *Chaos: Making a New Science*. It was an introduction to the science of chaos theory but also worked as a biography of many of the great scientists of the late 20th century.

'I loved that book,' I told Scott. 'It had all these great sounding concepts, like the Strange Attractor, which explains why my bedroom is always a mess.'

Scott sighed indulgently, 'Well, out with it then.'

'It's to do with "sensitive dependence on initial conditions". Some maths whizz proved that you may know where chaos starts but you never know where it ends.'

'A bit like us.' He flashed me a quick smile, then reached out and put his hand on my leg. I loved his elegant long fingers, seeing them on my thigh while he drove, occasionally letting go to change gears.

During the war, Los Alamos had been an off-limits, super-secret military base. Now it was a modern town with a museum, supermarket and Chinese restaurant. It was still subject to national security, which meant there wasn't a lot for a pair of plain-clothed citizens to do.

We went to the Bradbury Science Museum where holiday crowds were creating a human gridlock, so we only saw the gift shop. There we fussed over a set of Los Alamos shot glasses with a motif of the atom on them before buying some audio lectures by Nobel prize-winning theoretical physicist and all-round wise guy Richard Feynman to play on our drive to Mesa Verde in Colorado.

If that sounds a bit fuggy, don't get me wrong – Feynman's lectures made a deliciously weird jazz riff as we drove out of town. His nasally New York accent discussing electrons and neutrons underscored the mountains that rolled down around the soft green crater in Valles Caldera National Preserve. By the time we were west into the lion-yellow valleys north of Albuquerque he was onto the space-time continuum. Not a shred of meaning penetrated my brain, but some of Feynman's smarts splashed the landscape and coloured our future.

There were three places from my journey east that I wanted to share with Scott: the Grand Canyon, Monument Valley and Mesa Verde National Park. The ancient Pueblo ruins that Laudable recommended were a casual five-hour drive from Los Alamos. As long as we made no more detours, we'd be there before sunset.

The traffic heading into Mesa Verde National Park suggested it was going to be crowded. We mentioned this to the woman on the gate, and she told us to drive to the last campsite first, since most people trawled them from beginning to end. It was a good tip that we took one step further – we went to the last campsite at the end of all the allotments. By pointing our tent away from everyone else's, we got an uninterrupted view of a grassy mountain lea protected by tree-studded hills. The view was all ours.

The campsite came with individual barbecue pits, so we went to the commissary to see what we could buy to cook on it. Not a lot for a vego – frozen hash browns, eggs, fruit, wine, playing cards and marshmallows. They also sold coals soaked in lighter fluid which you could throw, unopened bag and all, onto the barbie with a lit match. *Woomph.* The whole lot went up in one go – a bit like my marriage, really.

That night, as we sat around our campfire, I told Scott the story of my love life. The whole story. Back in London, I told him that I'd only had one relationship – by which I meant I'd only had one relationship of any enduring love and emotional commitment. I didn't mean to infer I'd only slept with one person in all my life, although I could see in retrospect how it may have seemed that way.

The structure of my youthful relationships had been a search for the perfect man: one who embodied wit, intelligence, honesty and good looks. I didn't know then (although I tell every teenager who's interested) you don't normally find your ideal partner until you're free to make your own choices and live life the way you want. The boys you meet in high school are all there by coincidence, not choice, so finding someone in high school is a lottery of chance, not shared interests.

Not knowing that, I'd developed a pick'n'mix approach, choosing one boy for his sense of humour, another for looks, a third for wild adventure. (I'm certain only a woman would've conceived of Frankenstein, as surely as only a man could imagine penis envy.) In attempting to create one perfect lover, I sometimes dated two or three different boys at the same time.

Here's a joke to help you understand: What's the difference between a slut and a bitch? A slut sleeps with everyone, a bitch sleeps with everyone but you.

It wasn't until my early twenties that I decided to try a year of celibacy to see if I could date in a more emotionally steady fashion. That's when I met Pig. My first and only monogamous relationship – so far.

Scott was pretty quiet while I detailed the roll call of my fickle heart. Most advice columns tell you not to do this, and that's probably good advice, but there was more to telling him than plain honesty. I told him everything because I didn't want anyone to have secret knowledge that could come between us. I didn't want someone to have known me intimately, and for Scott to be outside that knowledge. Some people find the secret world of shared intimacies exciting, but I find it disingenuous. I had forgiven my youthful self for her lapses in self-esteem. I now asked my lover to do the same.

'So how many men are we talking about?'

'I don't know. It was a long time ago.'

'Well, you could use a ballpark. Ten? Fifteen?'

I mumbled my reply.

'It's no good mumbling.'

'It's very good mumbling. You looking all cross like that, I don't feel in the least bit like answering you.'

'So, what? Twenty?' I winced. Twenty didn't sound quite right. 'What, more? Fifty? A hundred?'

'Yeah, well, a hundred's probably closer than the others. But I don't know. It could just seem like that in hindsight. It was a long time ago.'

'A hundred …'

He was really miffed. At least I had him trapped on a mesa in the middle of a desert in the middle of America. It wasn't like he could run far. I waded into the bog and did the maths. 'Okay, I didn't start till I was seventeen. I started dating my ex when I was twenty-three. So that's what, six years? No, you see. It couldn't possibly be a hundred. It's probably closer to fifty or sixty.'

'But that's like a different guy every five or six weeks.'

'Hmm, what would thirty or forty be?'

'You're just going to have to give me a little time to let this settle in.'

'I don't see what difference it makes. That was another person. Someone who did a lot of work sorting herself out.' I raised my eyebrows and smiled in what I hoped was a reassuring way. 'At least I'm not curious anymore.'

He sulked for about forty-five minutes, which wasn't too bad in the scheme of things. After that, I figure he must have forgiven me. He never mentioned it again, and once the pall of expectation was lifted, he reverted to treating me like I was a good person.

I believe in karma. I believe in instant karma. When I do something bad and something bad happens back, I give thanks for the short, sharp slap. I also give thanks when something nice happens. I didn't give Scott my sexual résumé to hurt him. It was a gift of vulnerability and intimacy which Scott accepted graciously. Our reward was one of the best showers of our entire lives.

I'm not by nature a shower queen. I like a nice bathroom (what's not to like) but I view the ritual of washing every day to be part chore. Camping definitely hones your appreciation of the warm wet stuff. The amenities in most of the campsites were okay, but there were plenty of shitty showers as well. The one at Mesa Verde was coin operated, and it was also broken. It was broken on. It was broken on hot. It was broken on full force.

For Scott coming from London where water pressure was a subject for dinner conversation, the amenities block in the Mesa Verde was an enclave of deep hedonism. For an Australian subject to frequent water restrictions, the sheer profligacy was overwhelming. It was silly fun showering with Scott and trying to keep quiet while litres, gallons, waterfalls of hot water cascaded over our born-again nakedness.

We steamed up the generously proportioned cement cubicle and had so much fun we had to make a memory of it. It was the best twenty-five cents I've ever spent. In my whole life. Ever. By the time we'd finished, we were so clean you really could eat off us.

And that wasn't our only reward. When we booked our tickets to see the Cliff Palace, Scott bought a delicious espresso coffee – his first since Washington.

Hooray for good karma.

We ordered takeaway and drove around until we found a peaceful place on a clifftop under some pinion pines to eat our picnic breakfast. Scott photographed the world from our sandwich – there's a bit of crust at the bottom of frame, our legs sticking out, the thermos is to one side and the valley below us. It was so serene we made a mnemonic of the ocean in the trees.

Across the valley, we could see the Cliff Palace at Mesa Verde. As Laudable had promised, it was an ingenious ancient city built into the cliff face. Front-on like that it looked like a medieval New York carved out of a sandstone escarpment.

Our tickets came with a brochure, which Scott read aloud while I ate.

'*The Cliff Palace was discovered in 1888 by two ranchers looking for stray cattle. It is the largest of six hundred cliff dwellings in Mesa Verde National Park to be built by Ancestral Puebloans, also known as Anasazi or The Ancient Ones. They lived in this particular valley between 1000 and 1300 CE. The Cliff Palace contains 150 rooms, access to which was via a system of pathways and retractable ladders.*'

'Sneaky.'

'*The Palace also contains twenty-three kivas – sunken round rooms considered to be churches and used for ceremonial or religious purposes.*' He stopped and looked up. 'Or meeting rooms. Why does everyone get mystical just because it was ye olden days? The Egyptians were big on accounting. The Romans loved bureaucracy. Why couldn't Puebloans want to do a little business in private?'

'Okay,' I conceded, 'or maybe they were like 70s sunken lounges with surround sound and mood lighting.'

'Exactly,' he said. '*The kivas* – or rather, the nookie nooks – *were completely sealed. They had an air vent, central stone and bench seating around the outside wall.*' He looked up. 'You're right, kivas aren't churches, they're passion pits.'

The brochure concluded: '*It's not known why the original inhabitants chose to live in such a complicated dwelling, nor why they suddenly vanished in the end of the 13th century.*'

'Isn't that amazing?'

'No,' said Scott, who wasn't buying the whole Indian mystique thing. 'Why wouldn't you want to live here?' he asked. 'It's gorgeous.' He flicked through the pages of the brochure and read aloud again: '*They analysed tree rings and concluded there had been catastrophic droughts. So hey, mystery solved.*'

'I think if it was that simple, they wouldn't be making such a point of it.'

'What mystery? Unless you mean why didn't the Puebloans leave a note saying, *Gone in search of food.*'

'But there was no sign of war or disease. They left nothing behind.'

'Maybe they had a meeting in one of their twenty-three kivas and voted to go, then got the removalists in and tidied up to get their bond back.'

'Fair enough,' I said, 'what do you reckon the rent would be on a place like this?' It was time for our tour to start.

Inside the Cliff Palace, it was easy to see why you might think this was a great cathedral. It was built five storeys deep into the escarpment. The overhanging cornice of sandstone provided a shield from the elements and protection from prying eyes. The medieval masonry and extraordinary construction gave it a feeling that I expected Santa Fe was going for: organic and appealing.

Our tour guide, who introduced himself as Lance, said that the palace may have been an administrative centre, and Scott elbowed me. 'See, twenty-three meeting rooms.' The guide caught his eye and smiled, before finishing up the same way as the brochure.

'The Anasazi – also called the Ancient Ones or the Pueblo Indians – lived here over six hundred years ago. They decamped and vanished into thin air,' he said. We all applauded and dispersed to allow the next tour through.

'You don't believe that hokum, do you?' asked Scott. 'About vibrating in a different dimension?'

'Maybe it's like Heisenberg's uncertainty principle: "If you know how fast a particle is travelling, you don't know where it is."' *Hey!* Maybe some of the Feynman lectures leaked in after all. 'If the scientists are right and chaos is the natural order,' I continued, 'and the world is made of a neverending series of never repeating similarities that swirl and collapse and unfurl like ferns, then why can't there be rock pools of human existence that are different to ours?'

'Because there are no humans vibrating at a different frequency. You do know that, don't you?'

Did I know that? Here I was on a completely romantic journey with a completely unfamiliar man. Was it possible that my old life was happening somewhere without me – or with me making different choices?

Scott was right to give me the squint of reason. 'Alright,' he conceded wearily, 'but you're going to have to go back to the bit about "chaos is the natural order".'

Lance, the Hopi Indian guide who'd led us through the Cliff Palace, overheard us and interrupted. 'I hear a lot of discussion about the Anasazi, but I thought I was the only one who ascribed their disappearance to chaos.'

What. Are. The. Chances?

Actually – absolutely nil. It turned out he was studying economics, and his thesis was on *Social Symbiosis: Anarchy & Chaos in Marxist Economics*. His approach was pragmatic and realistic and had nothing to do with the nuclear whirling dervishes I was conjuring, but I was so delighted by the coincidence that I danced around clapping my hands as though I'd been proven right.

'You see, Scott, chaos is only the constant in the push and pull of destiny and determinism.'

Lance sounded like he agreed. 'My sympathetic response is that the Anasazi were probably Hopi. Look at the rituals, and the way they interpreted the world through architecture and work.' He pointed to the Cliff Palace. 'It has twenty-three kivas. The classical interpretation is that they are twenty-three churches, but if the Pueblo people were Hopi, then they might also be twenty-three clocks.'

'Scott thinks they were meeting rooms.'

'That too,' said Lance. His theory was that the Cliff Palace was a giant almanac, built to track the seasons and prepare for planting and harvest. 'It makes sense in a world where you only have 120 possible farming days a year, and need 110 to grow your crops. You would want to know exactly what day it was, and how long before the heat or snow comes,' he said. 'In that sort of climate and civilisation you end up with no separation of church and state. Which is the basis of my thesis about Marxist economics and the theory of chaos.'

Meeting Lance was fun, but the only point where our argument really met was this: if you take the long view of life, then time is your church and change is the governing principle.

Monument Valley was only two hours down the freeway from Mesa Verde. We entered the start of it as the sun was lazing around the horizon, hemming and hawing about staying or setting. A storm was brewing to the east behind the majestically front-lit El Capitan, the butte that stands guard over the valley. The wide plain opened behind it, and the ribbon of road vanished into a point in the future. Faure's 'Requiem' was playing on Betty's stereo. The moment was physical, and it felt like love.

Mexican Hat to the north of the valley provided a good campsite above the San Juan River. We set up the tent on the border between Utah and Arizona, then drove into Bluff and halfway to Blanding looking for food.

There weren't a lot of choices to start with, but then everything closed at 8pm. We ended up getting a sandwich in a tourist centre. The woman inside was cleaning out the fridge and gave us her leftovers. We were grateful raccoons.

Back at our campsite, gnawing on the sandwiches clutched in our tiny paws, we could dimly hear the roar of water coming from deep below us. There seemed to be other campers, perhaps with a small bonfire or large lantern. We stretched to hear their voices – maybe they were there, maybe it was the babble of water and stones. It was unknowable, but we listened long and pressed record.

The night was moonless, and as the Milky Way wound around the horizon we made love under the stars. The rough-smooth texture of bodies and stones, the Jack Daniel's, the fear of snakes, the reality of scorpions and the unknowableness of strangers gave everything a clawing urgency – and shooting stars.

Lots of them.

A meteor shower bloomed across the sky, leaving a trail of light. 'Did you see that?' I squealed, just in time for Scott to look up and see a shooting star.

It was like a cowboy cartoon. Another long-tailed meteor dragged its pin across the night's smoky glass. 'They're Perseids,' said Scott, enjoying me enjoying the sky. 'The Perseid meteor shower happens every year as we rotate through an asteroid belt.' Another shooting star. 'You see that group of stars just under Cassiopeia? That's Perseus. The Greek warrior.'

The night was alive.

I've stood patiently on crisp winter's nights when the Australian sky was claustrophobic with stars, and never seen one fall before. And yet here, in the arms of love, stars rained down on us.

I woke in the stiff predawn under a duvet of dew and fine dust. The rocky ground was poking through the thermal mat and into my kidneys saying, *Get up, lazy bones.*

I crawled clumsily over Scott and out of the tent into the vast emptiness of the Arizona desert. The sun was below the horizon, but already it was chasing the chill from the air. I leaned back into the tent to wake Scott.

'Come on, let's go.'

A tousled groan came from inside the quilt.

'Or at least pass me the keys.' They were in a nifty little compartment in the tent above his head.

'Hang on. Where are you going?'

'Out.'

'Out where?'

We were in the middle of nowhere. 'Out out. Out into the dawn. Out into the woo woo.'

'Well, can I come too?' He'd woken with a lungful of desert and was wheezing as he took out his Ventolin.

'Hurry up if you're coming.' I was pulling on my shoes.

He let out his Ventolin breath. 'I am hurrying.'

'I want to see the dawn at least once in America.'

'Well, that's not entirely fair.' Now he was hopping into his shorts, which was proving difficult since he'd already put his shoes on. 'What do you want to do with the tent?'

'Nothing. Zip it. Leave it. Come on – let's go.'

He was still tying his shoes in the passenger seat as I got behind the wheel and roared out of Mexican Hat.

Every time we lapsed into silence, I lapsed into remorse for my tone. 'Sometimes I want to do things without explanation.'

'And am I supposed to wait in the tent, wondering how long you'll be and where you've gone?'

'I just want to see the dawn … peacefully.'

'Fine.'

'Fine.'

If my tone was ugly, the valley was beautiful. Soft morning light was painting the valley crimson. The sharp rays etched the sides of the buttes and gave them an even more monumental air.

It was perfect

We came to a scenic viewing area where I pulled over and ran into the desert. I didn't want to be mean. I didn't want to cut him out. I didn't want to leave him worried or wondering. I just wanted space. You couldn't get any more space than in Arizona. If I couldn't be happy with this lot, we were doomed.

I was happy with this lot.

I turned and waved and ran away. Scott followed.

Away from the road even the silence of the desert was complete. We stood together and made a recording of the valley. Here's a weird thing about this particular mnemonic: there's a buzzing on it. I thought at first it was a fly, but it's not. It was so quiet that there's the slightest hum of tinnitus in this memory.

Did I feel shitty about my tone? *Yes.* Was I glad I saw dawn in Monument Valley? *Absolutely.* Did I know how much space was enough space for me to be happy? *Not a fucking clue.*

Highway 163 stretches the length of Monument Valley. It took about an hour to drive, and at the south end we ate breakfast in Kayenta with some early-rising Navajo families. Well, next to them anyway, like you do when you share a table at the Amigo Cafe.

For a man who'd been surviving on a steady diet of omelettes and chips, Scott's huevos rancheros breakfast was divine reward. It consisted of chili beans on a tortilla with great gobs of tomato, onions and guacamole, capped with a fried egg sunnyside up. That put a smile on Scott's face.

Kayenta is a small town at the crossroads of Highways 160 and 163. We asked what there was to do locally, and the waitress recommended an exhibit housed in the local Burger King about the code talkers from World War II.

I told Scott the story about Bernard's grandfather from Tuba City, and about the Marines using the Navajo language as an unbreakable code in the Pacific.

'But no code is unbreakable,' he said with philosophical pedantry.

'Noam Chomsky proved that in his 1973 essay on linguistics.' Apparently Scott had attended a lecture by Chomsky when the great linguist visited London University. Like many other students, he knew the great professor as a formidable social critic, and was shocked to have to sit through three hours of minutiae about language.

'Well, someone made a code out of the Navajo language and no one worked it out.'

So we went to see the small but fierce exhibit curated from the family collection of King Paul Mike. It was a son's pride in his father's life, dedicated to all the Navajo servicemen who acted as radio operators in the Pacific. It was a powerful reminder of the gift of service these men gave, and not only to Americans. Australia fought in the Pacific. My uncle was assigned to the engineers in Borneo, and no doubt his safe return was in part due to code talkers.

I wasn't keen to sleep on stones again. We returned to our campsite and wrapped everything up, then drove north into the Valley of the Gods, seeking somewhere soft to lay ourselves.

The Colorado Plateau on which Monument Valley rests is the most stable landmass in North America. It was first laid down 500 million years ago, when the Rockies were anthills. It was then carved by the Colorado River and polished by the wind. How reassuring to find something that was bedrock-stable while I ping-ponged from Nutsville to Love and back several times a day.

Scott slipped Van Morrison into the speakers, and we started driving up the treacherously steep gravel road to get an aerial view from Elk Ridge. By 'we', I mean Scott. I was driving to start with, but a couple of hundred metres up the gravelly U-bends and it was clear we'd never make it with me behind the wheel. Each of Betty's tiny skates on the loose dirt road was accompanied by vivid imaginings of us flying, Thelma and Louise-style, off the edge and down thousands of feet to the valley floor.

Nope. Nope. Nope.

We swapped seats and I could barely watch as Scott roared up the mountain like he was on the fairground rails of a Mighty Mouse. Bastard Y chromosomes. He thought it was fun.

The single most terrifying road of my life resulted in a view that was heroic – truly the Valley of the Gods. We'd been traversing Monument Valley at eye height, viewing everything from the lowlands where the buttes and mesas towered over us. Now our heads were in the clouds. Our dusty road scratched out on the plain below.

'Do you think we'll ever see our life like this?' I asked Scott. 'Laid out with all pain carved away so that only the resolution remains.'

He smiled, and then kissed me. His kiss was made of love. Like the view, we were only a small part of it. We could try to catch it, slow it, hold it, remember it, but it all moved on. We pulled apart and then drove away, hand in hand.

We took the long way back over the gently sloping Elk Ridge, where whirlwinds of tumbleweeds rose up to dance in front of us. In Texas we'd seen hundreds of tumbleweeds corralled into a paddock, their sad little arms poking through the wire fence, pleading for clemency. I even killed one by running over it in the car. It made a pathetic, bone-crunching sound as it passed under Betty's wheels.

But these dancing tumbleweeds are something else. They're suspended in my mind as time stops and hundreds of them spiral upward – pale brown dust and branches against burnt yellow grass. Oblivious, foolish and sensual in their entanglement, they are perfectly adapted to being free.

What is it about them that stays so vividly? That tumbleweeds can fly? Their sheer elan? Their madness?

A tumbleweed isn't a dead 'other' plant. It's a living thing that gathers food and water as it rolls over the world. It has relinquished the constraint and expectation of roots and embraced the exhilaration of uncertainty. The fence was cruel, because tumbleweeds are free.

We checked into the Mexican Hat Lodge, about 100 metres from where we'd camped the night before. Inside the foyer was a shrine to John Wayne. The receptionist was excited to tell us that the big man had stayed there in 1956 when he was making a film called *The Conqueror*, in which he played Genghis Khan. Imagine, American cowboy John Wayne as the great Mongolian warrior. What were they thinking?

While they were making the film, a nuclear bomb was detonated in nearby Los Alamos. The wind changed and radioactive fallout spread over the entire film crew, most of whom (including Wayne) subsequently died of cancer. To make matters worse, the production shipped tons of dirt back to Hollywood for the studio interiors. I wonder what the half-life of that is? I wonder what the half-life is for the sand we'd been camping on and breathing in the night before?

Our room wasn't going to take any prizes for luxury. It was dark green, wooden and serviceable. All that mattered was it had a television, air conditioning and a shower.

I turned the water on, tested the temperature and stood under it with a sigh. I was washing my hair when the temperature shot up and scalded my face. I lunged forward and turned the tap – the wrong way. The water became boiling. Shrinking away from the nozzle I lost my footing. I reached out and grabbed the shower curtain which came adrift – *plink, plink, plink*, just like in *Psycho*. I slid into the bath, cushioned only by invective, and in one slick move, my little toe rammed up the tap and snapped.

Scott leaped into the bathroom Kato-style (from the *Pink Panther* movies). He kicked the door in with a single karate move, his arms raised ready to do battle with whatever foe had me in their death-hold – only to find me lying in the bath, still being scalded, still screaming like a banshee, with my toe rammed up the faucet.

He calmly turned off the water and walked out chuckling. 'What are you like?' Maybe you level-headed types don't appreciate the majesty of that action. He doused the crazy lady with adult cool and then left me to gather my shredded dignity and put myself back together in private.

I loved him even more for that. I loved his calm resolve. I loved him for not beating the flames of my temper. I even loved that he left me naked in the bath with my toe stuck in a tap. Seriously. Sometimes life gives you what you deserve, and you don't need anyone putting cherries on it.

THE CRUX OF THE MATTER

The next morning I hobbled out to see the eponymous Mexican Hat. It looked like something from a Road Runner cartoon – a large, flat rock, balanced on an enormous boulder. Freaky.

The rest of the day was a bum-numbing rumble along corrugated dirt roads to Vermillion Cliffs, where I saw Al Gore in my underwear.

That's quite a sentence, huh?

We wanted to swim in the Colorado River, and on the north side of the Grand Canyon it's possible to drive to the water without needing to hike down. Not a whole lot was going on when we arrived. We found an empty parking lot with a boat ramp into the river. The day was hot and the water was cold, so we stripped, dipped, and then stretched out to dry.

Scott and I were talking idly in our undies when we became aware of a shuffling in the underbrush. This was no metaphor – it was the sort of noise which made me grab for my clothes. Scott put on his machismo and shorts, and went to investigate. He came back saying there were a lot of Tarago vans with black windows in the parking lot. 'There are men in suits crawling under Betty.'

I stood up to get a better look and was confronted by a very well dressed Peeping Tom. 'What are you doing?' I asked in an imperious voice, which I must remember to return to my mother.

'Standard security,' said the man who emerged from the nearby bush.

'That's pretty thorough,' I replied, making little allowance for the fact I was standing in my double-D bra and matching white panties. 'Have you found anything insecure?'

He blushed, said, 'Have a nice day, ma'am,' and left.

Scott followed him, 'Is someone important coming?'

There was no need for a reply, because Al and Tippy Gore appeared out of one of the Tarago vans, along with some young adults and extra agents looking stiff in their official white water rafting gear.

What an absolute shriek.

I waved. There was a moment's hesitation while the former Vice President of the United States of America weighed up the protocol of waving to a near-naked woman, before raising his hand in a casual salute. They all then got on a raft and drifted away down the river.

We got in our car and drifted towards the south side of the Grand Canyon.

I'd only been able to book one night's accommodation and it turned out to be quite a step down from the glamorous Bright Angel Lodge. I tried to hide my disappointment but did a lousy job. I hated the room, which seemed suburban and dreary. Isn't that the problem with expectations? They're too easily crushed.

Fortunately, the kettle in our room was sturdier. It allowed us to make a life-restoring cup of tea. Scott bought fresh chocolate chip 'cookies', and we dipped them into it. In a dull moment, those biscuits became a magical aphrodisiac. If you want to recreate the pleasure, make a hot beverage to your satisfaction, take a fist-sized, freshly-baked chocolate chip biscuit (American-style, buttery). Dip. Eat. Repeat.

Close your eyes.

Become the biscuit.

I wanted to get going early the next morning so we could hike to the bottom of the canyon and back in one day, but come the dawn I was unable to wake the urbane Welshman. Another long, hot day was unfurling, and I started getting shitty long before it was necessary. 'I am not going to be the timekeeper in this relationship,' I said, and left.

To my horror, weeks of sitting in the car and my new addiction to nicotine rendered me useless for hiking. I could barely make 100 metres without stopping to catch my breath. It didn't take Scott long to catch up.

Four hours walking downhill and we had barely made it *halfway* to where I stopped last time. We ate our sandwiches then hid in a mule shed while a squall poured rain on our heads.

We swapped backpacks because I was certain mine was heavier. It wasn't, so we swapped back. I wore two hats because Scott wouldn't wear the one I bought him. We argued about it while taking a selfie on the edge of the canyon, the magnificent cliff rising on the other side, unobserved.

We made it two-thirds of the way to Indian Gardens, where it became clear there was no way I could make it to the bottom – I simply wasn't fit enough. So we started the long, slow trudge back to the top.

The sun was setting when we reached the rim. We bought ice creams to celebrate and sat on the edge of the canyon eating them as the universe did a lurid lightshow just for us.

For the second time, I admired how little could detract from my shitty self-absorption – not even the timeless majesty of nature. 'I'm sorry,' I said to Scott, 'I think I killed that with anticipation. How about we go to Las Vegas? What are the chances that it's exactly what we expect it to be?'

↔

Las Vegas is only a 124 miles west of the Grand Canyon. Arriving around midnight was like arriving on a movie set of Las Vegas. The city was totally awake – a grown-up theme park burning wattage, burning money, burning lives.

Cruising the main drag we were greeted by a pirate battle going on in the street next to the strobing pink feathers of a Flamingo. There were dancing fountains and colonnades at Caesars Palace; a replica of Paris complete with Eiffel Tower and Arc de Triomphe; one replica of New York and another of the Pyramid of Cheops. More altered realities than Burning Man. More lurid colours that a child's fever dream. We ended up staying at the new MGM Hotel, which, weirdly for Las Vegas, looked exactly like a hotel.

We showered. We made love in our glamorous bathroom. We drank Jack Daniel's in bed and watched cable television. We could see the world going on outside our hotel window, and at about two in the morning we went out to join it.

Man, what a crazy scene. Craps, cards, jingle jangle. We made a recording of the cacophony of poker machines. It was a heaving, luminous pit of greed in high-heels and sequins.

Given how late we got to bed, it was even later when we got up the next day. We ordered room service and packed, ready to leave. Scott seemed flat. He was disappointed not to have played roulette. 'You come to Las Vegas …'

'Well, that's not right, is it?' I said pinning him down on the bed. 'Scotty comes to Las Vegas, Scotty plays roulette. How much are you prepared to lose?'

So far we'd got out of Vegas cheaply – a couple of ten-cent pokies and some expensive cigarettes. The rest had been underpriced to make us feel rich.

'I won't necessarily lose,' he said truculently.

'No. But this place is predicated on you not winning.'

We were still strapped for cash. Winning a million dollars and finishing the trip in style would be great, but losing all our money was more likely.

'Sixty dollars?' he offered gingerly.

'Then that's what we take with us.'

The cheapest tables we could find had a twenty-dollar bet minimum. Scott announced to the croupier that he was a spinning wheel virgin and asked for instructions. Doing what she said, he placed one twenty-dollar chip on a square that indicated half the numbers on the table – and lost.

Still following her instructions, he placed his second chip over four numbers, one of which came up. He turned to me with a gentle 'this is fun' smile, and I rubbed his back in congratulations – while the croupier swept away all his chips.

'I say,' he said politely, 'I think I won then.'

She looked at him, slit-eyed tired. 'You have to place it on a winning number to win.'

'I did. I placed it at the intersection of those four numbers.'

'He did,' I chirruped helpfully.

'I told you, you have to place it clearly. Yours was between those two.'

'I placed it as you explained – there, like that,' he said, putting his last chip on the table, 'at the intersection of four numbers.'

'You wanna speak to management?'

No doubt an American novice would have punched the air and kissed the girls, or vice versa. Scott's understated English victory was not convincing to the American croupier.

'Well, what good would that do?' he asked. 'You explained the rules and I followed them. I would like my winnings, please.'

The other gamblers shifted uncomfortably. They wanted to get on with the game. There was even a sense that Scott was an ungracious loser – that he was trying to cheat.

'Well, you could always complain,' she said, every ounce of compassion having been leached from her.

'There's no fun in that,' he said, picking up his remaining chip. He squared her up, 'I clearly placed that chip over the four numbers and *you* didn't look.' And that was that. We rode away together on his high horse.

'They probably have cameras on the tables if you want to complain,' I said. 'There must be some sort of line-call dispute capacity.'

'I can't be arsed,' he replied. 'She'd probably lose her job and I don't want to be responsible for that. Let's go. This place is creepy and desperate.'

His real victory was in not having someone sacked over money he was prepared to lose. He lost his money and won this girl. We cashed in his chip and went to Caesar's Palace to eat the proceeds.

Inside Caesar's was designed like a Roman piazza, complete with a sky that morphed from day to night and back again every hour. The curved roof with its painted clouds shifted in tone as the lights dimmed and the colours warmed or cooled. Morning, noon, evening, night. It was remarkably soothing. At Bertolini's, one of the restaurants facing onto the fountain, they served real Italian food made with real stinky garlic and teary onions, a rare treat in scent-conscious America. It felt good to be hypnotised into thinking that we were somewhere old.

'You know, that might be the best $40 you ever spent,' I said, sucking down a delicious spag bol. 'Gambling's a mug's game.'

And the vegetarian pasta was delicious, too.

↔

We stepped out into the desert heat and mystery evaporated like conjurer's smoke. In the broad light of day, Las Vegas was as glitzy and tawdry as a hooker's parlour.

We were loosely aiming for San Francisco, and after a brief discussion set course for Death Valley. Days were now drifting under a cotton ball-studded summer sky. Onto the radio came a documentary about film choreographer Busby Berkeley – famous for his synchronised swimming routines in the 1930s. It was so surreal to imagine him in the Nevada Desert that we made a mnemonic of the dusty landscape with watery dancers making kaleidoscopic patterns in the swimming pool sky.

We saw Joshua trees.

We chased a roadrunner.

The landscape started to rise and bend into the Rockies.

No, it didn't. No sooner had we gone up than we went down again. 'Are you sure the Rockies come down this far?' asked Scott. 'I think this is the Mojave Desert.'

'No, that's south of Las Vegas.'

'But we're travelling south and this is awfully flat for a mountain range,' said Scott. 'Would you at least look at the map, please? Someone went to a lot of trouble to make it.'

He had a point. It was damn flat, but then Death Valley is the lowest point in the States so it makes sense that it would be flat. I pulled out the map but couldn't find any landmarks to anchor onto. 'Corn Creek, Amargossa, Indian Springs? You seen any of those towns?'

We stopped in Baker to get our bearings and learned we were driving at high speed in completely the wrong direction. 'I don't know who's navigating,' said the station attendant, smirking at me, 'but you've gone the long way around.'

A brilliant 127 mile detour south instead of northwest. I'd been so keen to get going I hadn't even checked whether there might be *two* highways to San Francisco – going in completely different directions.

I was disappointed with myself. I felt stupid and wrong. I was *sore* at myself, as they say here. I was also physically sore from the hike, pocket-sore from Las Vegas and saddle-sore from the car.

The sensible thing to do would be to either get something to eat or get back on the road. Did I do that? No I did not. There was a self-service carwash out back of the petrol station and I decided that 8pm, after a long day driving, was the perfect time to clean the car.

It wasn't. It was a perfect storm for the worst fight yet.

Having argued about Elvis, chaos theory and sleep, it won't surprise you to learn that this particular crisis of passion was over the correct way to wash a car. And we're not talking tiff here. We're not talking hissy fit. We're talking homicidal maniac with a sponge – a shrieking banshee with a power hose of rage and a two-dollar soap gun.

Logically it couldn't possibly matter. Quite possibly, Scott had a better idea than me of how it should be done. But what shat me to the depths of my Australian vernacular was that even in this simple matter, I had no autonomy.

'Frankly, I'd rather do it alone than discuss the logistics of washing a car.'

'Aren't I allowed to have an opinion?' asked Scott with infuriating reasonableness.

'It's not your car,' I said crankily. 'I'm busting a gut here to include you and you're keeping me at arm's length. Everything gets translated into the minutiae of domestic detail while we skate around the real thing.'

'What's the real thing?'

'New Orleans. Me saying that you weren't invited. Me not getting the "I love you" response right.'

Well, that shut him up. We'd just done the bulk of a 3000-mile journey and here I was raising the spectre of a fight he thought had been resolved. He shook his head.

'I've been trying to make it up. I'm sorry I said some of the things I said, but are you going to let me back in, or are we going to keep dicking around with petty crap so you can ignore what's really going on? I'm doing everything I can to say I love you, and you're doing everything you can to avoid it.'

Technically this was only our third date and already we'd broken up twice. Here we were breaking up again – under the plastic sheeting and strip lighting of the DIY carwash – this time about whether to rinse the car before soaping.

He was right of course. You should rinse the car before adding soap or risk scratching the duco, but you know what? No one argues about that stuff. They argue about the foundations that underpin it. They argue about subtext more often than text.

'Come on, babe,' he leaned over and gave me a kiss. 'Let's find a place for the night, before I have to kill you.'

Daybreak in Death Valley was sunny. It always is. It's a desert.

We'd found the Stove Pipe Motel in the dark and now discovered that we were surrounded by watered lawns and palm trees, with an aquamarine swimming pool and a battalion of soft white chaise longues. There was also a laundry. Rather than argue ever again, I told Scott I loved him and flaked out by the pool. He could wash our clothes any way he wanted. I didn't even care if he separated the whites and colours.

When all that was wet was dry, we drove out into the desert in our clean clothes and shiny car. At 282 feet below sea level, Death Valley is the lowest part of America. It's easy to imagine the early pioneers stumbling around in the hallucinating heat and dying with buzzards circling above them, but no one died here. The Sierra Nevada mountains to the northwest were the big killers, particularly in the winter. They called it Death Valley because it looked so barren.

We stocked up on water and followed signs to Scotty's Castle, where we took pictures of him standing outside a Tex Mex folly built by either a successful gold prospector or a hustler, depending on which story you prefer.

We became entranced by an arcing rainbow that stretched from one side of the valley to the other. It seemed to float in front of us as we drove. Eventually it started to grow larger, until it was more like a curtain of light than a rainbow. When it was finally overhead and out of view, we were amused to discover there was no rain.

We drove back along the road to see it again in the distance. Sure enough, there was the rainbow again. The radiant heat of the land was evaporating the rain before it touched the ground.

We pulled over to look at it. 'Do you suppose that's what the aurora borealis looks like?' I asked, pulling out Scott's camera to take a photo.

'The northern lights?'

'Have you seen them? Do they look like that?' I was photographing the back of Scott's head with the rainbow around him. I loved the way he was leaning on the car, cradling his head in one hand. His strong apricot neck and head of fine blond hair.

'I love you,' he said, softly, his back to me.

'What?' I called out. I'd heard, but not heard.

'You heard me,' he said, turning around and looking cheeky, 'and I won't tell you twice.'

'What was that you said?' I asked, my hands loosely on his hips.

'You heard.'

I lightly applied pressure to a couple of fingers. Not all of them, you understand, just enough to give the impression that a tickling would be in order.

'Nooo.' Scott said few words with a Welsh lilt, but 'no' was one of them. I loved the way he said 'no'. He could say 'no' or 'I love you' all day – they both sounded the same to me.

I was tickling him, when, with a flick of his foot, he unweighted me and lightly flipped me onto his hip in a karate roll. 'Anyway, it's your turn,' he said, holding me in one arm, while using his free hand to tickle me back. 'Say it, or the girl gets it.'

He started pressing his fingers under my ribs, tickling me.

'I love you. Stop. I love you. Please stop tickling me.'

In the beginning, before I didn't invite Scott to America but when I probably fell in love with him, he advised against chasing time, and we hadn't. Since then a damper had been put rather magically on the pendulum – but now time was straining to be free.

Maps and books were cluttering the luncheon table while we wrote postcards. We had a view of the Lone Pine Mountains, which looked like an old-fashioned Disney animation cell. 'They give prizes to the tourists who can find the copyright symbol,' I joked.

Scott didn't laugh. He was doing maths on the back of a serviette. I thought he was working out the tip. 'How long will it take us to reach San Francisco?' he asked.

'I don't know. A couple of days maybe. I was hoping to spend some time in Yosemite National Park. Then go to Monterey for the jazz festival.'

'We're near Yosemite?' he asked. 'I thought it was further north.' I turned the map and pointed it out to him. I was hoping to do the Yogi Bear thing, or Yosemite Sam, or some other cartoon character. Smokey the Bear, even.

'Ansell Adams,' muttered Scott, almost salivating.

'Of course, Ansell Adams.' The photographer of those famous black and white landscapes. 'How silly of me.'

'My plane leaves in three days,' he added.

That grinding, snapping sound was time finally breaking loose and flicking around inside my brain. 'Three days. I thought you were staying for a month.'

'I have. Today is four weeks, in three days it's a month.'

I wanted to inhale him, kiss back his words and squeeze him inside of me so I could carry him around forever. 'Three days,' I moaned, 'I'm not ready.'

We seemed to be in an orbit of objects with a larger gravitational pull than either of us. Scott had taken a loan to make this trip. He needed to return to his income. The conditions of his ticket were such that he would have to pay for changes. He simply couldn't afford to stay any longer.

We drove north to Yosemite. Regardless of the outcome, we'd be staying there overnight. It was just a question of how fine we'd cut it getting to the airport in San Francisco.

'Baby, can't you find a couple of extra days?' I asked. 'Say, until Sunday. Who goes back to work on a Thursday anyway?'

I convinced him to ring the airline and see what they'd say.

We stopped a couple of times but couldn't find an international pay phone. When we did, it was attached to a tree in the middle of the park – utterly nowhere. Scott made a singularly bizarre sight, using his tree phone. A sight that became even more peculiar when a queue formed behind him.

He returned to the car beaming. 'Done. I leave on Saturday evening.' Time was unfettered.

Yosemite was magnificent – a glacially carved wilderness. Powerful forms of granite rising out of dense forests. An astonishing national park. A treasure. A monument. The grandeur of Ansell Adams' photography is only a percentage of the freshness of the landscape when seen by living eyeballs.

The clock was ticking. I was trying to squeeze everything in.

We found a private campsite to pitch our tent and then took a long, slow drive into town to buy provisions for a meal of spinach cannelloni – not easy to cook on a campfire. I really earned my Girl Guide Italian Cooking badge later that night.

Afterwards we sat around smoking, talking, drinking red wine and necking. It was close and romantic. We recorded the crackle of the campfire. It was perfectly quiet, no insect noises – no cicadas, no crickets, no frogs. Instead there were smells – of Scott, woodsmoke and … and … and a truly dreadful waft of musk and sweat and farts.

I started to laugh. 'Scott!'

'What?' Looking injured.

'What, what? You farted.'

The humour of farts came late to me, but once they arrived, I was transformed into a true believer. Farts are proof that God has a sense of humour. His gift to children. Something that can only be shared with affection.

'Why do farts smell?' I asked dancing away from him. 'For the benefit of the deaf.' This was truly the worst fart ever. Even Scott stood up and moved away from it. Then, with dawning recognition, we remembered Matt's warning that bears smell incredibly foul – that they smell like farts, which is why most people don't encounter bears, *because they smell them coming.*

Scott and I scrambled to clean up the food, trying not to leave any scraps while sealing everything in plastic and getting it all into the boot of the car. Windows up, shades down, our selves washed before anything came any closer.

We never did see the bear, although the next morning we found some fresh poo in a nearby clearing. I took that as proof – not only does a bear shit in the woods, it must have come close to our campsite in the night. I can also confirm that nothing is quite as stinky as a big ol' stinky bear.

↔

I woke in a pre-dawn blue space filled with love. A young woman was smiling into my soul. I stared into her face, rejoicing in her gaze while trying to remember who she was. In the grappling distraction of knowing but not knowing, she disappeared, and I realised I was peering into the infinite blue of our tent.

We went for the short exploratory walk which revealed the bear poo, and then tried our Ansell Adams best to capture the grandeur of Yosemite. Our images were sillier and more intimate – me running towards Scott, Scott and Betty, Scott and me kissing in a magenta glow, our faces sealed, oblivious to the camera even though we're holding it.

Something wonderful happened in Yosemite. The seeds that were planted in London and struck by lightning in New Orleans finally sprouted green, sweet love.

Most love grows in the fertile soil of its heartland. Occasionally the season is barren, or conditions aren't right and then life clings to the rocks and pavements of unlikely nurture. We photographed a perfect pinion pine growing on the sheer granite face in Yosemite. It was an irresistible metaphor for what was growing between Scott and me. Perfect love growing in a strange place.

↔

Oh – hear that? Time's behind us. She's riding a horse and using a whip.

↔

We were a day's drive from San Francisco, a journey that took us through the rolling hills of northwestern California, a landscape that looked like western New South Wales, with dry fields full of cattle and sheep and the occasional farms under plough or harvest.

We made a fire for breakfast and then packed the car. The thought that we had spent our last night in the love tent was a little death. Lots of organisms feel compelled to replicate when threatened. We were no different. We put the fire out with water. Smoke and steam billowed up, looking for all the world like an enormous bushfire. As we waited for it to settle we got to talking, and talking got to kissing, and kissing got to rooting. There's always more than one way to put a fire out.

Burn, baby, burn.

The realisation that Scott was leaving focused my mind. I'd only known him for five weeks, less than one percent of my life with Pig, and yet in that first crush I had an almost chiropractic feeling of being myself. I had bent my character so far out of shape trying to relieve Pig's unhappiness that in the end I barely recognised myself. With Scott I had no need for emotional gymnastics. I liked who I was with him.

For all my genuine confusion at his arrival in Washington, I loved him for the positivity of his action. I loved how it made me feel – that he'd wanted me and seized me. Soon Scott and I would be living in different hemispheres, with ten years, two cultures, three oceans and all the continents between us, no matter which way we travelled. This was the end.

A GENUINE HAIGHT-ASHBURY LOVE-IN

San Francisco at dusk glows with hope and youthfulness. There are few sights in the modern world as exhilarating as driving over the Bay Bridge at magic hour. The awe and majesty of buildings that appear to grow as you near them, swelling until the whole world is made of glass and steel and lit from within.

David Bowie's 'Wild is the Wind' came on the radio. It had been our song – Pig's and mine. It always made me laugh because of the line about being touched by mandolins. I don't know, it's a funny instrument. I debated whether to mention this to Scott (when is enough enough?) but did anyway.

After a moment's silence for the dead, he asked, 'So what's our song going to be, then?'

'Hmm. Song? Anita Baker, 'You Bring Me Joy'. But the album is *Poetic Champions Compose*.'

'What about *Leftism*?'

'Oh God. You're right. And the one with the guy who sounds like he's singing in his sleep?'

'Mark Hollis?'

'I love him.'

They were our tent songs. The albums that underscored this trip.

What would I do when he took his music away?

We drove around until we found somewhere to stop. Our budget was well and truly blown, so we chose the romantic Hotel Vintage Court. I don't know whose life I was living, but they were fiscally irresponsible.

No, that's not fair.

I'd grown up with my mother clinging to debt, working hard all her life to barely make ends meet. She'd always made choices that protected us – our education and our home always came first. Sometimes they'd cut off the electricity, sometimes we ate the same thing for a week, but we were safe and we were fed.

I was the only girl at my posh school who knew where the bursar's office was, because I went there on Mondays to deliver the fees. I once complained to Mum that it was embarrassing and she said, 'Look after the luxuries, because necessities look after themselves.' That's advice to live by. I wouldn't be in America if the decision was based on money. Now was not the time to stop trusting the universe.

We woke to the fairy tinkling of cable-car bells and the smell of salt on the breeze. We both grew up by the sea and it was magical being back in a harbourside city. We had come home. We pressed record on a moment of ultimate peace, just as the recycling team started breaking bottles under our window – lots of them. A happy clattering that sounded a lot like the holy recycling bins of Primrose Hill.

We could have stayed in the hotel room forever and it would have made no difference, so we ventured out for food and light. Along the way we found Chinatown, Haight-Ashbury and Fisherman's Wharf, where we parked Betty, figuring we'd get something to eat.

We went bowling.

We vouched for an under-aged kid buying beer.

We drove to Berkeley and ate Cambodian food.

We went mad in a music shop and bought everything we'd enjoyed together on the road. I got Van Morrison's back catalogue, not knowing how I'd missed him the first time around. Scott bought Peter Gabriel's *So*.

We ate at Thank God It's Friday, which meant something to Scott.

We got ripped off by a homeless guy who sold us used cable car tickets.

And when we weren't doing all of that, we drank wine in bed and watched telly. We read our books and made the hotel staff bring us room service. I lay on the bed and watched Scott shave, like it was the most sacred thing in the world.

Happiness only exists in the present. When we drove across the Bay Bridge talking about 'our song', we left my marriage behind. All that remained was Scott and me. I was happy.

My period came in a rush that surprised me. I know, I know, it's gross. How can I tell you this? How can I not?

We had driven to Sausalito, a friendly harbourside village with the laidback ease of a 60s hippie. We'd bought coffee and strolled along the water talking about our future. We talked about my age and IVF, and how I still wanted children. We talked about Scott's age and his needs, and he embraced it all. He looked at me in Sausalito with love, and said he couldn't imagine anything that would make him happier than growing someone with me.

A lot of men would have run screaming. One had.

I loved Scott just for saying maybe.

I loved him even more for understanding that they may never come.

We went to lunch, and a dizzy feeling washed over me. A wave of soft panic and tingling unreality. 'You alright?' he asked. 'You've gone awfully pale.'

'Hmm. No. I don't know. Where's the bathroom?'

Man, what a mess. You'd think after twenty-something years I would have worked this shit out. But I hadn't. It came when it came. Sometimes big. Sometimes slow. This was big. This was remarkable. This was carnage.

I had to throw my undies out, rinse my dress and throw myself on Scott's mercy. 'Can I have your undies?'

'Eh?'

'Your underpants. I need your underpants.'

He was looking at me with a smile of confusion. 'A memento?'

'No. Period. I've ruined mine and I don't think I'm going to get far without another pair.'

'Didn't you know it was due?'

'In principle.'

'And you don't have anything?'

'No. And if we stand here talking like this ...'

'Alright, alright. '

He went to the bathroom, and returned with a warm pair of Calvin Kleins. 'Thanks, love,' I said and dashed back to the bathroom. God knows what the other patrons thought – that we were coke heads probably.

'Okay,' I said, returning to the table, 'I reckon I've got about fifteen minutes to find a chemist.'

Scott had already paid the bill. 'You're not going to ruin my pants are you?'

'Scott, they're undies.'

'They cost twenty pounds each.'

'Jeez. That much?'

'Other women seem to be a little more prepared than this.'

'I'm sure you're right.'

'It's not much of a mystery, you know. Doesn't it come every month?'

'Yes. It's just – it's never been regular. Thirty-five to thirty-seven days, and then five- to ten-day periods. It's hard to keep up with.'

'Well, what about panty liners?'

'Excuse me?'

'Panty liners. Those things you put in your pants – oh, for goodness' sake.'

Scott went into the chemist and bought a selection of tampons and panty liners for me. I can't tell you what a revelation this was. Well, I am telling you. It was a revelation. They're great. But how weird is it when your new boyfriend is a better woman than you are?

In one of our getting-to-know-you conversations, Scott revealed that if he'd been a girl his mother would have named him Helen. It would have suited him. There was a very Helen quality to Scott. Practical. Serene. Womanly. Especially when it came to feminine hygiene products.

Maybe this was what a honeymoon was supposed to be. Babies, blood and love. I didn't want it to end there. I couldn't drive him to the airport if I thought I'd never see him again – I had no vision for our future. The only thing I knew was I wanted to see him again. I made him promise that if he got back to London and changed his mind about me, and if I got back to Sydney and realised that it couldn't work, that we would at least end it face to face. I made him promise that he would see me at least one more time after he left San Francisco.

Hoka Hey. It's a good day to die.

Saturday came too quickly in a flurry of music swapping. Scott wanted it all. I made him give me his Anita Baker and Tindersticks. He took my Curtis Mayfield and Peter Gabriel and I made him take a copy of Ennio Morricone's soundtrack to *The Mission*. He didn't want it, but it's brilliant.

I got the tent and the quilt.

Scott kept the camera – well, it was his.

I held onto the books, because we'd finished them and he didn't want their weight in his luggage.

I offered him the dainty yellow teacup I'd bought for Sue. He looked at it for a moment like it was a fledgling bird. 'No,' he finally said handing it back, 'you hold onto it. I'll come and collect it from you.'

The rest we pretty well sorted according to who owned what in the first place. Our relationship was barely a month old and we were already splitting up stuff like an old, soon-to-be-divorced couple.

It was horrible watching him pack. It was overwhelmingly tempting to take things out of his bag until he missed the plane.

We got to the airport with plenty of time. Scott and I sat in a bar having a Scotch while we wrote out our mnemonic tape on the back of his boarding pass. The tape is absolutely precious to me, and the dub (the written copy) is the key to the mental box that it's kept in. Like the rest of my knowledge about sound and music, I'm hazy on names and places, but when I invoke them from the list, it all comes back with a clarity that no film or recording could ever conjure.

I would never have made the tape without Scott. I wouldn't have known to. I wouldn't have pressed all those sounds, smells and textures into my brain, any more than I would have heard all that music, or learned about Wittgenstein, Gutenberg and Brownwood. I probably wouldn't have camped. I wouldn't know about the northern stars. I wouldn't have felt like the world was a positive place. I wouldn't have learned what the rewards for action were. Or that money is an energy source and not a reason in itself. Or panty liners.

We stood at the departure gate holding each other, too numb to cry. *How much of the language of travel is a euphemism for death?* Terminal. Departed. Goodbye.

I wrapped him in light. Perfect. Whole. Every colour white light. We kissed. We parted.

'I love you,' I whispered under my breath, 'and I forgive you for everything. May you be blessed in every possible way. I release you into the highest possible good. Whatever is perfect for us, in a perfect and balanced way, let it happen now, with thanks.'

He turned as he walked through the magnetic machine and raised one hand in a salute. 'I love you,' he mouthed.

I kissed my hand and showed it to him. 'Fly, little birdie, fly.'

WISH YOU WERE HERE

Driving south out of San Francisco listening to a selection of rare jazz recordings on NPR was an exercise in appreciating the moment. The moment had just passed, and I appreciated that. For the second time in a short time, I was split from someone I loved.

I was once again weighing up my choices: do I stay, or do I go? Do I return to Australia or travel to Britain? Could I turn my back on someone who was willing to give up everything to be with me? Someone good. Was this finally the end of another relationship?

How do you ever know what you're supposed to do? How long do you wait? What do you wait for? Wisdom? Chastity? Patience? Which of the seven deadly virtues would be mine?

Or do you look at what you're doing and say, '*This* is my choice'?

It was my choice to be driving a shiny red car back to its home in LA. What I'd do after that – I'd find out when I got there.

The Monterey Jazz festival clogged the highways and motels south of San Francisco. Driving the Big Sur was no better. By a quarter to the witching hour I was experiencing rising panic that I would be seeing dawn in LA, if I hadn't crashed the car before then. Every town and cabin was full. There wasn't a hovel to be found.

At last, in the middle of nowhere, a Rasta white guy showed mercy and let me sleep in the car park of his pub, as long as I set the tent up close to the car and was gone by morning, because it's illegal to camp on the roadside in California. Finally, just off the Cabrillo Highway, here was the independent adventure I dreamed of, and I was grateful to Scott for choosing such a clever tent.

↔

I packed the tent dewy wet and left at first light. I wasn't more than half an hour on the road when I passed what looked like a drunken manx cat.

I pulled over to see if it was alright and found two other drivers had done the same. Pete was a family man with said family hanging out his car windows. DJ was a biker rugged up in sub-zero thermals.

The cat, a bobcat kitten, had slunk under Pete's car from where it stared desolately out at a world that seemed to have hit it at high speed. I lay down to take a photo, which I now gather might be pussy talk for 'attack', because that's what the cat did. Pete and I hid behind DJ as the kitten latched onto his thermal leathers.

Thinking of rabies, DJ pulled a bowie knife and threatened the furball with it – to be fair, up close a young bobcat looks a whole lot more like a lion than a kitty. He shook it off and the cat hid under Betty. As a group we decided it would be best for me to drive away, exposing the cat, which Pete would then catch.

I got in the car and gingerly pulled out onto the road. The cat followed by sort of wandering at the same pace under the car. I could see the two men in my rear vision mirror shouting, 'Go for it. Go faster.' So I did, and at about five miles per hour I ran over the cat.

What sort of horrible omen was this? *Does this mean Scott and I as a couple will die like so much roadkill on life's highway?* My heart thumped with fear. *Did I just kill the wild thing?*

I ran back to see the cat sitting in the road, looking at me like I was a complete fuckwit. '*What did you do that for?*'

The highway up Big Sur is famous for deep, winding curves. Each corner is a blind one, so I ran to the bend, shouting for the traffic to stop. I then took off my Dolce & Gabbana coat and threw it over the kitten like a blanket. It seemed to like the warm darkness and lay down.

The others came running. DJ was the most suitably dressed to touch the soft bundle of seething carnivore, but the big biker was afraid of cats. Pete, the more domesticated male, removed his jeans and padded his hands with them. Standing in the middle of the road in cartoon-patterned boxer shorts, he leaned over and stroked my cashmere and silk coat. The cat, while not purring, was at least mollified.

More cars and more bikes stopped. The black puddle of coat in the highway made it look like a young child was dead on the road, so at least the mood of the traffic was sombre while we discussed what to do with Bob the Cat.

I felt totally responsible, but I wasn't driving anywhere with a wild cat in the car, so our family-man-hero removed his shirt and bundled it into his car.

'See kids,' he said, as I retrieved my coat, 'Disneyland *and* wildlife. Ain't California great?'

'What some men will do for a little pussy,' DJ replied wryly.

I got into Betty, lit up a fag and drove like a stunned mullet down some of the most beautiful coastline in the world.

Scott would have loved it. He would have loved the sweeping road. He would have loved Big Sur, the bikers and the bobcat. Ocean on one side, winding curls of bitumen on the other. But me? I'd had enough of the road. By the time I got to LA, Scott was already in London downing beers with his mates.

While I was away, Marc and Stacy moved in together, into a proper home in Glendale with a garden and everything. They gave me my own special room, a glassed-in balcony with a comforting view of rolling hills and a pale blue sky. I put the quilt on the bed where it became the memento Scott intended. When I curled underneath it, I felt him with me.

The next morning I took Betty to make sure she was roadworthy for sale in California. I'd put 8974 miles on the odometer – nearly 15,000 kilometres – over which she'd kept me safe and found like-minded friends for me to play with. I really wanted to find a way to save her for myself, but I needed to pay Sue back so, reluctantly, I phoned in an ad: *Utterly loved, six-cylinder red coupe, fully loaded, extra security, no accidents, $6000.*

Back in my cubbyhole I was in a holding pattern, neither home nor away. I was using the sale of the car as an excuse to stay longer, because Sydney seemed like a feral pack of sirens trying to lure me onto the rocks. Mum planned to throw me a welcome home party and was unhappy when I told her I wouldn't make it.

When I didn't get any response to the ad, Marc told me about a place on Sawtelle Boulevard where you could take your car and sell it privately on a common lot. I'm not sure my heart was in it. As long as I didn't sell Betty, I could cling to my life there. And yet I spent the long weekend sitting with the car, wearing my spotty red dress and reading Ray Monk's biography of Wittgenstein.

The first guy to show interest was Mexican. He didn't look like he had enough money, but he did have a bucket of oranges which he shared with me.

He sat behind the wheel. We talked about LA and how hard it was to get ahead there, and how there were plenty of opportunities if you were willing to work hard. I liked him. He wasn't letting this flat, grey city wear him down. He asked if he could come again to visit. I said of course, 'But if I sell the car and I'm not here anymore, you mustn't take it personally.'

He smiled and walked away, hesitated and came back. Shyly, he asked, 'You know I sell oranges on the freeway for a living?'

'Yes,' I said with my best smile.

'And I can come and visit tomorrow?'

'Come and visit tomorrow.'

The next potential buyer was a young woman who came with her four brothers. They all fell in love with Betty. I lowered my expectations to $5000 but it was still more than she could afford. She wanted to pay $3500, but she might be able to get it up to $4000 if I'd take a cheque. I liked her and we swapped numbers, but I needed as much money as possible to repay everyone at home.

Then a kid came down with his mother. He was about fifteen or sixteen and was learning to drive. He wanted Betty. He wanted her bad. His mother was a cliché desperate housewife – pretty, mid-forties, in tight pedal pusher pants and bleach-blonde hair. She was willing to pay me $5000 in cash, on the spot.

Cool.

We piled into the car while junior took Betty for a spin. Junior needed a pillow to see over the dash. He clashed her gears. He broke in the middle of corners. He accelerated at the wrong times.

I asked the mother if she'd wait while I phoned Alicia because she'd made the first offer. Truth was, I couldn't do it to Betty. She'd loved me well. If I sold her to Junior, he'd kill himself. He'd make Betty a murderess and I'd be an accessory to bad parenting.

I rang Alicia and asked if she could scrape together $3600 in cash. That's what I borrowed from Sue. It would be hers if she could get me the money.

Like the bankers say, *You're safe, it's only change.*

When I went to Alicia's home to pick up the money, I found out she was a nurse. She'd just come out of a bad relationship and Betty was the best thing that had happened to her in ages. It was a good transaction. There was nothing left to keep me in LA. I had to go home.

HOMECOMING

'Surprise!'

You betcha.

I might have wanted to tiptoe back into Sydney, but Mum threw an afternoon tea party to welcome me home. My sister strung a banner across the door, and Mum laid out her full contingent of Royal Worcester Bacchanal – fluted white china with a border of intertwined grapes and vine leaves.

'It's for you, darling,' she said, giving me one of her teacups and a saucer, 'to help you rise from your crockery carnage.'

I was touched. She bought her china service a lifetime ago as part of her wedding trousseau, building it piece by piece from her weekly pay cheques. It reflected the choice of a young woman wanting more from life than the dull suburban offerings of Australia in the 1950s.

'I can't believe it, Ma – are you throwing me a divorce shower?'

She was. Family and friends had been invited to bring a teacup or plate to kickstart my new harlequin service. Aunty Pat gave me two large white Wedgwood breakfast cups in the Strawberry & Vine pattern. These larger than normal English breakfast cups instantly became my favourite for my morning cuppa.

Satty gave me one of her Villeroy & Boch Petite Fleur so we

could continue to celebrate all the years of boys, jobs and jokes we'd swilled in those cups.

Rebel from work gave me the most delicate baby bath disguised as a white Rosenthal Sanssouci breakfast cup.

'Teasmade' Amanda delivered a cake tray (complete with cakes) and a vase emblazoned with the face of the last emperor of China. He now guards my kitchen with a spiky head of hair made from the cooking utensils I keep in him. In return, she became custodian of Ike and Mamie Eisenhower. Some friendships are fired in a potter's kiln.

Sue, who's known in certain quarters as Our Lady of the Garages for her most excellent garage sales, gave me six 19th century Imari trios made by Kensington Fine Art Pottery. Finally I understood why my grandmother baulked at using 'the good stuff'.

Mum had one more surprise waiting for me. Scott had posted a brooch to replace the earrings he'd bought for my birthday. (The poor, lovesick fool must have carried those bloody pearl things all the way across America.) The new brooch was a nutty jewelled dragonfly like the ones we saw in Louisiana, only this one was made of garnets and turquoise.

My sister looked at it and said, 'He knows you well.'

He does now.

When you fall in love with someone who lives on the other side of the planet, it creates a schism that almost nothing can repair. The immigrant heart belongs in two places, and no place at all. Soon after arriving home I asked Scott if he wanted to come to Australia. He only had a year left to be eligible for a student visa, and needed to come sooner rather than later.

'What's the worst thing that can happen?' I asked. 'You have an adventure and go home again.'

He came. He finished his philosophy degree and eventually became both an Australian and the geek philosopher we always knew he'd be.

Years later, Scott honoured his promise to do IVF with me, but we were yet again vexed by its failure. The old evil forces were at play in my life – the hormones, the disappointment, the lack of direction – and infertility began to undermine my heartland all over again. I was feeling particularly low after another failed attempt when I ran into Pig at a party. We'd long ago made our peace, and it was nice to have someone to commiserate with.

He was sympathetic to the loss of another baby, but his impression of me on hormones was worthy of a Perrier Award for stand-up comedy. Once he'd stopped making me laugh, he asked how Scott was coping, and compassion went through me with a mild wash of shame.

There are plenty of disappointments in life, but loving someone should never be one of them. The thing that defines life is that it ends – that's what makes every moment precious. Don't waste energy regretting things you can't control. If you open yourself to the love that's in front of you, it's everywhere.

Love is like the sun – up close it's hot, but far away it's still another star in the night sky. The love doesn't change, only how close you are to it.

Scott and I never got to make the babies we wanted, but I'm blessed with nieces and nephews who let me stamp them with red lipstick. I'm blessed to have family and friends (frequently interchangeable) who rise to the challenge of adventure, and sometimes crawl into the dark place where I'm hiding to keep me safe. But mostly I'm blessed to be loved by my beautiful husband, a man who said yes to the crazy lady, who loves me at my worst, and who can love me forever at my best.

Life is messy.

Love is irrational.

Gratitude is good.

Scott and I eventually got married in a hot air balloon over Alice Springs. Technically, we got married over the Owen Springs Maximum Security penitentiary, but that was a trick of the wind.

AFTERWORD

Having spent time as a journalist, I'm aware of the importance of 'facts', 'accuracy' and 'sources'. (Yes, in inverted commas.) Having spent time as a screenwriter, I'm also aware of the difference between Truth and Fact. (Yes, the platonic ideals.) I am therefore qualified to tell you that this is a true story, but not always an accurate one.

For starters, it lies by omission. So many girlfriends contributed to the healing of my life, but aren't represented here. Some because their stories were not mine to tell. Some because it wasn't the most direct route to romance. Some because they arrived after this story ended, but I thank you all for the love, kindness and raw laughs you've given me over the years. Your love is truly a force of nature.

To the handful of friends who do make the cut ... I am so sorry that I have mangled your image into this cartoon. I've put words in your mouths and paraphrased your meaning. A few of you have even been squashed together so that neither one nor other are the person you might think you are. Here your golem returns clumsily formed from plasticine, barely recognisable, but carrying a golden bowl of love. Thank you for being so important to my heartland that I couldn't cut you out. Wouldn't want to. Didn't know how.

I've changed lots of names, but not all, and I won't say which ones. Why not just pretend I changed them all? Unless you love the portrait – then it's you, baby.

THANKS

Who knew it took so many people to write a book? Thank you to my early readers: Zoë Coyle, Ceri Radford, Sue Burrows, Kim Jackson, Stephan Elliott, Bronwyn Grantham and Cathy Chua. To Mike Hanley for introducing me to Tara Wynne at Curtis Brown – the best agent ever! Thank you Fiona Henderson for being the smartest, kindest and most resolute spare brain a writer could ever hope for. Thank you to Christa Moffitt for capturing the whimsy in a book cover. Thank you, in fact, to the whole team at Affirm Press who have scooped me up and made me a published author. I am living proof of your magical powers to make dreams come true. Special thanks to my family, and particularly mother, Joy Jobbins, who has always rejoiced in the telling of a good story.

ENDURING GRATITUDE

I wrote this book as an anniversary gift to my beautiful husband. I love you like cool loves a pair of shades. You have always been the mature one in our relationship, if not the elder. You make me lucky.

ABOUT THE AUTHOR

 Born in Melbourne, Sheridan Jobbins is a third generation Australian film maker. She kickstarted her career at nine as one of the original celebrity chefs on *Cooking with Sheri*, earning a Guinness World Record as the youngest host of her own show. She went on to present numerous TV programs, including *Simon Townsend's Wonder World!* and *Good Morning Australia*.

She was a director of Latent Image Productions, the film company which produced the award-winning film *The Adventures of Priscilla, Queen of the Desert*. Since 2000 she has co-written screenplays with director Stephan Elliott for Disney, Warner Bros, Working Title and Hopscotch, including the adaptation of the Noel Coward's *Easy Virtue* for Ealing Studios. She has published numerous short stories and articles, and mentors other screenwriters on her website www.scriptwhisperer.com. *Wish You Were Here* is her first book. Her body's in Switzerland, her heart's in Australia – fortunately they get together quite regularly.